Early reactions to Leaving World War II Behind:

"This is a book of wide synthesis and trenchant commentary. Keep it near to hand for those all-too-frequent moments when you hear someone using World War II to justify yet another horrific military adventure." — Nicholson Baker, author of *Human Smoke: The Beginnings of World War II, The End of Civilization*

"A mythic history surrounds 'the Good War,' but the truth is far more complicated than that told by Hollywood and in high school history books. Swanson demolishes the myths by amassing a huge number of facts, all carefully documented, and leaves us the true, if unpalatable but liberating, history of World War II." —Kent D. Shifferd, Ph.D., author of *From War To Peace: A Guide To The Next Hundred Years*

"If you, like me, thought that WWII was the exceptional 'good war,' think again. In *Leaving World War II Behind*, David Swanson brilliantly cuts through the myths surrounding WWII, and in the process cuts through the fog of all wars. Reading this book, I started to dream. What if Swanson was a regular commentator on CNN, destroying the arguments of every Pentagon pundit, Raytheon lobbyist and warhawk politician? What if Swanson was hired by Hollywood to review all war films for their accuracy? What if he could oversee the history books taught in U.S. schools? We would have what the military-industrial complex most fears: a well-informed public. As we build the platform that Swanson and anti-war academics/activists deserve—and the world so needs—we can start by reading this superb book and encouraging everyone we know to read it." —Medea Benjamin, author/cofounder CODEPINK for Peace

"In his latest book, David Swanson passionately debunks many of the common arguments used to justify the horrific violence of World War Two. By revealing the less-than-humanitarian decision-making leading up to the United States' involvement with the fight against the Nazi government, he demonstrates the inherent tensions behind the myth of a 'good war.' No one hates war more than Swanson and no one alive has devoted themselves more fully to its abolition. This book is an expression of his deep moral commitment to peace." —Scott J. Shapiro, Professor of Law and Philosophy at Yale Law School, Director of Yale's Center for Law and Philosophy, coauthor of *The Internationalists: How a Radical Plan to Outlaw War Remade the World*

"The proximate goal of David Swanson's new book is to challenge the moral arguments for World War II, the war that supposedly justifies war. Its ultimate goal is to make the case for ending war once and for all. This is a brave, passionate, brilliant book, which should be read by anyone who gives a damn about humanity's future." —John Horgan, science journalist and author, *The End of War.*

"David Swanson's *Leaving World War II Behind*, could have been easily entitled leaving revisionist history behind because he shatters all the self-congratulatory distortions that justified U.S. participation in the 'good war' of WWII. In systematically dismantling the moral and political reasoning of U.S. policy-makers leading up to, during, and after the great war, Swanson reveals how little has changed with the arguments and technics elites use to mask their real intentions and win over ordinary working class people, who fight the elites' wars, to an agenda that does not have anything to do with them. In a rational society, Swanson's latest would be incorporated into the school curriculum from middle-school on. But this is not a rational or a moral society. And this is why the existence of a David Swanson is such a wonder." —Ajamu Baraka, contributing columnist for the *Black Agenda Report* and writer for *Counterpunch.*

"Brick by brick, David Swanson demolishes the wall of mythological history behind which we cower in manufactured ignorance and fear. As the wall comes down, we step out into a world where all is possible and nobody's children need ever again be sacrificed on the blood-drenched altar of war." —Nicolas Davies, author of *Blood on Our Hands: The American Invasion and Destruction of Iraq*

"David Swanson achieves two worthy goals. One, he proves that nearly everything we are told about World War II is false. The United States played a role in creating Nazi ideology and American businesses like IBM and Ford literally helped build Hitler's war machine. Two, the lies about WWII persist and have been used to justify every act of aggression committed by this country since that time. *Leaving World War II Behind* is a must read for everyone who works for peace and against the indoctrination that invariably leads to endless state violence and human suffering." —Margaret Kimberley, author of *Prejudential: Black America and the Presidents*

"David Swanson argues persuasively against justifications for World War II as 'the good war.' What if there were alternatives? And who did WWII really help? *Leaving World War II Behind* amply refutes war marketers' assurances that the U.S. only goes to war as a last resort because there are no alternatives. Swanson insists we must reckon with relentlessly racist beliefs and practices which actually fuel wars, trample human rights, and enable repressive elites to control resources. The book offers a momentous rallying cry to activists seeking equitable relations in a sustainable world. Use this book to generate a massive shift in public opinion, demanding we abolish war." —Kathy Kelly, Co-Coordinator of Voices for Creative Nonviolence

"If war is ever to be abolished through rational argument, this is the book that will do it. Leaving behind World War II is essential to abolishing war and *Leaving World War II Behind*, the book, explains how. It is an inspiring

and profound service in the ongoing effort to a safer and saner world." —
Mike Ferner, author of *Inside the Red Zone: A Veteran For Peace Reports from Iraq*

"When it comes to revealing the wretched corruption of war, David Swanson is in a league by himself. His uncompromising power of conviction is the sledgehammer needed to obliterate the myths and lies inherent in America's murder machine. In fact, war is America's favorite and most lucrative pastime and the one killing spree that remains sacrosanct in the hearts and minds of Americans, especially their historians, is World War II. Well, folks, don your helmets and slip on your Kevlar®, Swanson takes on the "good war" with the necessary grim, meat-hook of reality. The book is chock-full of incredible revelations, eye-opening historical facts that wipe out America's house of cards. His argument why WWII did not have to happen is brilliant and bolsters the entire book. As I read Swanson's new book, I was reminded of Rev. William Sloane Coffin when he posed the query, 'If what we're doing in Vietnam is right, what is there left to be called wrong?' The power of Swanson's book asks the same question of the so-called 'good war.' *Leaving World War II Behind* is worth every minute of your time. —Stephen Vittoria, documentary filmmaker and co-author with Mumia Abu-Jamal of *Murder Incorporated: Empire, Genocide, and Manifest Destiny*

"Though I have been an antiwar activist for many years, I admit I haven't always been able to deftly handle the 'What about Hitler?' argument, in part because I had never been taught the truth. Like Howard Zinn's, *A People's History of the United States*, David Swanson's book reveals the ugly truth about WWII, and in doing so repudiates all possible arguments supporting the characterization of WWII as 'just.'" —Leah Bolger, President of the Board of World BEYOND War

"In a well-constructed and compassionate book, David Swanson delivers something that's sorely missing in the age of alternate facts and social media flame wars: He respects and trusts his readers. *Leaving World War II Behind* connects the dots across an incredible range of topics. In doing so, Swanson meticulously provides us with the documented evidence we need to begin questioning embedded myths and thus accessing our better selves." —Mickey Z., author of *Saving Private Power: The Hidden History of "The Good War"*

"As David Swanson points out in this important book, World War II was the most destructive event in human history. And he also shows us that it was not necessary and that it has led to profound brokenness in the 75 years since it ended. Given the enormity of the evils wrought by that worst of all wars, people in the United States are remarkably uninformed about its true history. Thankfully, Swanson gives us a wide-ranging and clearly presented antidote for our ignorance." —Ted Grimsrud, Senior Professor of Peace Theology at Eastern Mennonite University and author of *The Good War That Wasn't—And Why It Matters: World War II's Moral Legacy*

"David Swanson has written an excellent book that should occupy a designated spot in every household and library with a copy of Tom Brokaw's *The Greatest Generation* directly abutting that treacly tome. Swanson deserves credit for shredding the most common fallback argument of those who call history's most bloody conflict 'the Good War,' namely the false ex-post-facto claim that WWII was 'justified' because it was necessary to 'save the Jews' from Nazi extermination. In fact, virtually nothing was done to save the Jews until the very final months of the war, by which time Hitler had managed to murder 6 million Jews, hundreds of thousands of Romani people, and countless Communists and physically and mentally disabled people. As Swanson documents, far from saving Jews, the U.S., Britain, and other nations, when they had a chance to rescue German and Austrian Jewry in 1938, rejected a call to open their borders to threatened

populations. Of 32 nations meeting in Evian, France to discuss the humanitarian threat, only two — Costa Rica and the Dominican Republic — agreed to increase their Jewish immigration quotas." —Dave Lindorff, independent journalist, winner of 2019 Izzy Award

"War is organized insanity played out with mass murder. Nobody knows this better than David Swanson. In this book, revealing the hidden history of even our so-called 'just war,' Swanson will hopefully shock and awaken enough of us to reject war for all time." —Thom Hartmann, author and radio host

"David Swanson provides an abundant amount of well-supported facts that deconstruct the myth about the necessity of World War II and the resulting misguided national and global priorities. Once you see how Swanson lays the false notions about WWII to rest, it becomes much easier to be against war, against all wars." —Patrick Hiller, Executive Director of the War Prevention Initiative

"*Leaving World War II Behind*, is a fascinating scholarly account of killing, orchestrated by wealthy corporations and industrialists. Read it to know why America has been and is the world's leading killer in the name of money." —Helen Caldicott, Founder of Physicians for Social Responsibility

"There is no more important time in world affairs to face the truth about 'the good war' and get beyond the myths that continue to obstruct sensible conflict resolution. I am confident that my father, who fought in it, would agree. Read Swanson's book— and talk to your neighbours about it!" — William S. Geimer, author of *Canada: The Case for Staying Out of Other People's Wars*

"In *Leaving World War II Behind*, David Swanson brilliantly destroys the myth that even if war is generally a bad thing World War II was the good war. In a stunning, fact-laden exposition, Swanson demonstrates the systemic failures of the western governments together with their corporate enablers that generated the practices of genocide, ethnic cleansing, and concentration camps, empowering Hitler. Swanson shows incontrovertibly that it was an underlying drive to preserve capitalism and destroy communist encroachment that led to support for Hitler when he was eminently stoppable. Every serious citizen should read this book. There is well-documented information here you have probably never heard reported before, about the myths of war as well as solutions that will surely transform your view of the world." —Alice Slater, UN NGO Representative of the Nuclear Age Peace Foundation, Board Member of World BEYOND War, Global Network Against Weapons and Nuclear Power in Space, and Global Council of Abolition 2000.

"David Swanson puts little known facts about the origins of World War II into a compelling argument that there are alternatives to wars, if the war money-makers don't influence the politicians who can pursue the alternatives. He documents that the World War II 'good' war wasn't as 'good' as our history books tell us, detailing the U.S. targeting of civilians; firebombing cities in Germany and Japan; insisting on total, unconditional surrender that lengthened the war with Japan; refusing to take steps to save the victims of the Holocaust in the concentration camps; and developing and using nuclear weapons that did not shorten the war and continue to threaten human existence." —Ann Wright, co-author of *Dissent: Voices of Conscience.*

"David Swanson's latest, revelatory book, *Leaving World War II Behind*, challenges a long list of pervasive myths enshrined in both U.S. history books and Hollywood movies. Like a present-day Morpheus, Swanson invites readers to choose the 'red pill' that strips away the false matrix of morality from 'The Great War.' Swanson's 18 chapters (backed with more than 500 footnotes) expose scores of uncomfortable truths. Some examples: Hitler's rise was abetted by some of America's most powerful corporations and businesses. The U.S. ignored Japan's repeated offers to surrender in order to demonstrate the power of its new nuclear weapons. Wars are no longer waged for territory, Swanson notes: 'they're waged for weapons sales, fossil fuels, lusts for power, and bragging rights.'" —Gar Smith, author of *Nuclear Roulette* and *The War and Environment Reader*

"David Swanson's new book on World War II is both about the potency of myth and the dynamism of choice. The myth of the 'Good War' has been powerfully destructive, and Swanson devastatingly demonstrates how dangerous the consequences of this myth have been. But as the book unveils example after example of U.S. militarism and environmental destruction, we are reminded that at every step along the way, people have had the power of choice. Sometimes that choice may be blunted by group psychological processes, but it still exists, omnipresently in the background. Swanson's book is an impassioned plea to choose nonviolence and pacifism as against war and aggression. Revulsion against fascism fueled U.S. national interests in promoting WWII as a progressive cause. If nothing else, *Leaving World War II Behind* shatters the illusions that buttress such a myth, as well as subsidiary narratives that promote other U.S. imperialist wars from the Philippines to Vietnam to Iraq. With the U.S. moving towards war with Russia or China or both, this is a book every activist and antiwar partisan will want on their bookshelf." —Jeffrey Kaye, author and psychologist

"My only regret of David Swanson's *Leaving World War II Behind* is that it was not available during the decades I taught high school social studies. Every American student should be exposed to the myths of World War II. Swanson's *Leaving World War II Behind* offers teachers and students the opportunity to unmask accepted textbook falsehoods of the most damaging war ever." —Jack Gilroy, Maine-Endwell High School, Endwell NY (retired)

"David Swanson's *Leaving World War II Behind* not only debunks many of the myths surrounding WWII as the 'good' war, it thoroughly eviscerates them. One doesn't have to agree with every facet of Swanson's interpretation or even his conclusions to realize that this book makes profound moral and historical arguments that need to be thought about, debated, and learned from if we are ever to end the vicious cycle of violence, bloodshed, suffering, and retribution that has marked our world since long before the Second World War and continues to pose an existential threat to humanity today." —Peter Kuznick, Professor of History and Director of the Nuclear Studies Institute at American University and co-author (with Oliver Stone) of *The Untold History of the United States* (books and documentary film series)

"In this age of endless wars, David Swanson's mission to put an end to war has taken on a new urgency. He calls his latest book a moral argument, but he backs it up with carefully documented historical evidence derived from others and then shapes the evidence into a new polemic: Was the epitome of a good war (WWII) really that great — and thus a reason why more 'good wars' are likely to be necessary? How many Americans know that Hitler studied some of the evils perpetuated in the US — genocide of Indians, reservations (models for concentration camps) slavery, westward expansion, and racist laws to name a few—and incorporated them into his own diabolical vision of Aryan greatness? ('Go East Young Man' a German newspaper proclaimed). Or that powerful US corporations and their leaders collaborated with Nazis *before, during and after the war* to achieve a desired goal: the defeat of the Soviet Union? This, Swanson states confidently, is the 'dirty little secret' hiding in World War II: 'the top enemy of the West ....was the Russian communist menace.' And isn't it still so? Swanson forces us to come to grips with the myths and lies that abound in *all* wars, including the supposed good war in Afghanistan, and challenges us to join him in peace activism because 'mass murder is horrible,' a notion that led him to becoming a determined peace activist in the first place. Perhaps Covid-19, which has stripped away the veneer of America's exceptional 'greatness,' in so many way, will also yield a Renaissance of new thinking about the imperative to end all wars and use the savings to create a new, more just world. To this end, David Swanson has shown us the way and done so brilliantly." —Charlotte Dennett, author of *The Crash of Flight 3804: A Lost Spy, A Daughter's Quest, and the Deadly Politics of the Great Game for Oil*

"I like the logic here. Swanson lays out the logic of pacifism in a couple hundred pages without mentioning the word. If you don't have time to read the book, see if you can read Chapter 18, "WWII and the case for war abolition." If you can't make the time for this prescient and timely selection, take an entire minute to contemplate these 64 words from the final chapter that succinctly identify the myths about war and the reasons to end it forever: 'The myths are that war is, or can be, inevitable, necessary, beneficial, or just. The reasons to end war are that war is immoral; war endangers rather than protects; war destroys the natural environment; war erodes liberties; war impoverishes; war promotes bigotry; and the resources spent on war could do incredible good if spent elsewhere — far more good even than the good of preventing wars.' That's 4 myths about war and 7 reasons to end it. Don't bogart this book, my friend. Pass it on." —Pat Elder, signer of the Declaration of Peace *https://worldbeyondwar.org/individual*

"All wars are lies. David Swanson shows that World War II was no exception. We must not allow the power holders to continue to argue that WWII — the 'good war' — justifies the idea that fighting wars and preparing for ever more wars as the way to fight the 'next Hitler' can create security for our country and the world. Without the idea of 'the good war,' the notion of war as a means of resolving conflicts and achieving 'security' goes out the window. Too bad for the war profiteers! Why did the United States pass up so many opportunities to stop U.S. companies investing in and helping arm Germany in preparation of WWII? Why did the U.S. and other countries

refuse to accept Jewish refugees fleeing Germany? Why did the U.S. delay making peace with Japan before the bombing of Hiroshima and Nagasaki even though Japan indicated offers to surrender and end the war earlier? Was preparing for a future war with the Soviet Union the real reason for many U.S. actions during and after WWII? The U.S. did NOT pursue all peaceful means to resolve conflicts with either Germany or Japan before the war, but by their actions, chose to prepare for war and do those things which made war more likely. Through WWII, the U.S. became addicted to militarism, and wars, and preparations for more wars. But this addiction is our choice. We can choose to end our addiction to war and pursue peaceful means to achieve security — not only for ourselves, but for the whole world. Swanson holds out the vision of creating real security by spending one trillion dollars a year (which we are presently spending on wars) to create a good and decent life for every American and people all over the world – and create REAL SECURITY for the American people rather than the FAKE SECURITY of endless wars and creating ever more enemies. People all over the world should read *Leaving World War II Behind*, give up our addiction to war, and get involved with World BEYOND War to help end all wars. Very highly recommended if you want a future of peace and well being for your children, grandchildren, and future generations!"
—David Hartsough, Co-Founder World BEYOND War and Nonviolent Peaceforce, author of *Waging Peace: Global Adventures of a Lifelong Activist*

"In *Leaving World War II Behind*, David Swanson continues his chronicle of the full costs of militarization. His new work centers on a fundamental dimension of those costs, the many-sided environmental consequences of war and perpetual preparations for war. For the public that hardly understands the links between military operations and environmental damage, this book is a major contribution." —Richard Tucker, editor of *Nature at War: American Environments and World War II*

For Anna, Wes, and Ollie.

Leaving World War II Behind

By David Swanson

Charlottesville, Virginia
First edition—2020

Also by David Swanson

20 Dictators Currently Supported by the U.S. (2020)

Peace Almanac (2019)

Curing Exceptionalism (2018)

War Is Never Just (2016)

War Is A Lie (2010, 2016)

Killing Is Not A Way of Life (2014)

War No More: The Case For Abolition (2013)

Iraq War Among World's Worst Events (2013)

Tube World (2012)

The Military Industrial Complex at 50 (2011)

When The World Outlawed War (2011)

Daybreak: Undoing the Imperial Presidency and Forming a More Perfect Union (2009)

The 35 Articles of Impeachment (Introduction, 2008)

Swanson, David, 1969 Dec. 1-
Leaving World War II Behind
Book design by David Swanson

Cover image: The author, at lower right, and friends raised a peace flag at the Iwo Jima Memorial near the end of a bicycle trip that World War II veteran and peace activist Sam Winstead led from North Carolina to Washington, D.C. several years ago. The photographer is unknown.
Printed in the USA First Edition / September 2020
ISBN: 978-1-7347837-5-9

Contents

1. What WWII has to do with military spending

"I'm going to perform a magic trick by reading your mind," I tell a class of students or an auditorium or video call full of people. I write something down. "Name a war that was justified," I say. Someone says "World War Two." I show them what I wrote: "WWII." Magic![1]

If I insist on additional answers, they're almost always wars even further in the past than WWII.[2] If I ask why WWII is the answer, the response is virtually always "Hitler" or "Holocaust" or words to that effect.

This predictable exchange, in which I get to pretend to have magical powers, is part of a lecture or workshop that I typically begin by asking for a show of hands in response to a pair of questions:

"Who thinks war is never justified?"

and

"Who thinks some sides of some wars are sometimes justified, that engaging in a war is sometimes the right thing to do?"

Typically, that second question gets the majority of the hands.

Then we talk for an hour or so.

Then I ask the same questions again at the end. At that point, the first question ("Who thinks war is never justified?") gets the vast majority of the hands.[3]

Whether that shift in position by certain participants lasts through the next day or year or lifetime I do not know.

I have to perform my WWII magic trick fairly early in the lecture, because if I don't, if I talk too long about defunding militarism and investing in peace, then too many people will have already interrupted me with questions like "What about Hitler?" or "What about WWII?" It never fails. I talk about the unjustifiability of war, or the desirability of ridding the world of wars and war budgets, and somebody brings up WWII as a counter-argument.

What does WWII have to do with military spending? In the minds of many it demonstrates the past and potential need for military spending to pay for wars that are as justified and necessary as WWII.

I'll return to the question of why this matters in the final chapter of this book, but let me sketch it out briefly here. Over half of the U.S. federal discretionary budget — the money the Congress decides what to do with each year, which excludes some major dedicated funds for retirement and healthcare — goes to war and war preparations.[4] Polls show that most people are unaware of this.[5]

The U.S. government spends vastly more than any other country on militarism, as much as most other major militaries combined[6] — and most of those are pressured by the U.S. government to buy more U.S. weapons[7]. While most people do not know this, a majority does think that at least some money should be moved from militarism to things like healthcare, education, and environmental protection.

In July 2020, a public opinion poll found a strong majority of U.S. voters in favor of moving 10% of the Pentagon's budget to urgent human needs.[8] Then both houses of the U.S. Congress voted down just that proposal by strong majorities.[9]

This failure of representation should not surprise us. The U.S. government hardly ever acts against powerful, wealthy interests simply because a majority favors something in poll results.[10] It's even very common for elected officials to brag about ignoring polls in order to follow their principles.

To motivate the Congress to change its budgetary priorities, or to motivate major media corporations to tell people about them, would require a lot more than giving the right answer to a pollster. Shifting 10% out of the Pentagon would require huge numbers of people passionately demanding and protesting for a much larger shift than that. The 10% would have to be a compromise, a bone tossed to a mass movement insisting on 30% or 60% or more.

But there's a big hurdle on the way to building such a movement. When you start talking about a major conversion to peaceful enterprises, or nuclear abolition, or the eventual abolition of militaries, you run headfirst into a surprising topic that has very little to do with the world you currently live in: WWII.

It's not an insurmountable hurdle. It's always there, but most minds, in my experience, can be moved to some degree in under an hour. I'd like to move more minds and to make sure the new understanding sticks. That's where this book comes in.

This book lays out the case for why misconceptions about World War II and its relevance today should not be shaping public budgets. When less than 3% of U.S. military spending could end starvation on earth[11], when the choice of where to put resources shapes more lives and deaths than all the wars[12], it matters that we get this right.

It ought to be possible to propose returning military spending to the level of 20 years ago[13], without a war from 75 years ago becoming the focus of the conversation. There are far better objections and concerns that one might raise than "What about WWII?"

Is a new Hitler coming? Is a surprise recurrence of something resembling WWII likely or possible? The answer to each of those questions is no. To understand why, it may help to develop a better understanding of what World War II was, as well as to examine how much the world has changed since WWII.

My interest in World War II is not driven by a fascination with war or weaponry or history. It's driven by my desire to discuss demilitarization without having to hear about Hitler over and over and over again. If Hitler hadn't been such a horrible person I'd still be sick and tired of hearing about him.

This book is a moral argument, not a work of historical research. I have not successfully pursued any Freedom of Information Act requests, discovered any diaries, or cracked any codes. I will be discussing a great deal of history in the pages that follow. Some of it is very little known. Some of it runs counter to very popular misunderstandings. But virtually none of it is seriously disputed or controversial among historians. I have sought not to include anything without serious documentation, and where I am aware of any controversy over any details, I have been careful to note it. I don't think the case against WWII as a motivation for further war funding requires anything more than facts we can all agree on. I just think those facts lead very clearly to some surprising and even disturbing conclusions.

2. WWII was not fought to save anyone from death camps

If you were to listen to people justifying WWII today, and using WWII to justify the subsequent 75 years of wars and war preparations, the first thing you would expect to find in reading about what WWII actually was would be a war motivated by the need to save Jews from mass murder. There would be old photographs of posters with Uncle Sam pointing his finger, saying "I want you to save the Jews!"

In reality, the U.S. and British governments engaged for years in massive propaganda campaigns to build war support but never made any mention of saving Jews.[14] And we know enough about internal governmental discussions to know that saving Jews (or anyone else) was not a secret motivation kept hidden from antisemitic publics (and if it had been, how democratic would that have been in the great battle for democracy?). So, right away we're faced with the problem that the most popular justification for WWII wasn't invented until after WWII. Was WWII an accidentally just war? Or was it justified by other factors that people understood and acted on at the time, but which have become confused in the retelling? Let's keep these questions in the back of our heads, while making sure we fully understand what's wrong with the popular story.

Antisemitism was mainstream in U.S. and British culture at the time of WWII and in the decades leading up to it, including among elites and top elected officials. Franklin Roosevelt in 1922 had taken it upon himself to convince the Harvard Board of Supervisors to gradually reduce the number of Jews admitted to Harvard University.[15] Winston Churchill in 1920 had authored a newspaper article warning of the "sinister confederacy" of international Jewry, which he called a "world-wide conspiracy for the overthrow of civilisation and for the reconstitution of society on the basis of arrested development, of envious malevolence, and impossible equality."[16] Churchill identified Karl Marx, among others, as representative of the Jewish threat to civilization.

"Marxism represents the most striking phase of the Jewish endeavour to eliminate the dominant significance of personality in every sphere of human life and replace it by the numerical power of the masses." That line comes, not from Churchill, but from the 1925 book, *My Struggle,* by Adolf Hitler.[17]

U.S. immigration policy, crafted largely by antisemitic eugenicists such as Harry Laughlin — themselves sources of inspiration to Nazi eugenicists — severely limited the admission of Jews into the United States before and during World War II.[18] Some segment of the U.S. population is aware of this, I've found. The U.S. Holocaust Museum's website informs visitors: "Though at least 110,000 Jewish refugees escaped to the United States from Nazi-occupied territory between 1933 and 1941, hundreds of thousands more applied to immigrate and were unsuccessful."[19]

But very few, I've found, are aware that the policy of Nazi Germany for years was to pursue the expulsion of the Jews, not their murder, that the world's governments held public conferences to discuss who would accept the Jews, that those governments — for open and shamelessly antisemitic reasons — refused to accept the Nazis' future victims, and that Hitler openly trumpeted this refusal as agreement with his bigotry and as encouragement to escalate it.

When a resolution was introduced in the U.S. Senate in 1934 expressing "surprise and pain" at Germany's actions, and asking that Germany restore rights to Jews, the State Department stopped it from emerging out of committee.[20]

By 1937 Poland had developed a plan to send Jews to Madagascar, and the Dominican Republic had a plan to accept them as well. Prime Minister Neville Chamberlain of Great Britain came up with a plan to send Germany's Jews to Tanganyika in East Africa. None of these plans, or numerous others, came to fruition.

In Évian-les-Baines, France, in July 1938, an early international effort was made, or at least feigned, to alleviate something more common in recent decades: a refugee crisis. The crisis was the Nazi treatment of Jews. The representatives of 32 nations and 63 organizations, plus some 200 journalists covering the event, were well aware of the Nazis' desire to expel all Jews from Germany and Austria, and somewhat aware that the fate that awaited them if not expelled was likely going to be death. The decision of the conference was essentially to leave the Jews to their fate. (Only Costa Rica and the Dominican Republic increased their immigration quotas.) The decision to abandon the Jews was driven primarily by antisemitism, which was widespread among the diplomats in attendance and among the publics they represented. Video footage from the conference is available on the website of the U.S. Holocaust Museum.[21]

These nations were represented at the Évian Conference: Australia, the Argentine Republic, Belgium, Bolivia, Brazil, United Kingdom, Canada, Chile, Colombia, Costa Rica, Cuba, Denmark, Dominican Republic, Ecuador, France, Guatemala, Haiti, Honduras, Ireland, Mexico, the Netherlands, New Zealand, Nicaragua, Norway, Panama, Paraguay, Peru, Sweden, Switzerland, the United States, Uruguay, and Venezuela. Italy refused to attend.

Australian delegate T. W. White said, without asking the native people of Australia: "as we have no real racial problem, we are not desirous of importing one."[22]

The dictator of the Dominican Republic viewed Jews as racially desirable, as bringing whiteness to a land with many people of African descent. Land was set aside for 100,000 Jews, but fewer than 1,000 ever arrived.[23]

In "The Jewish Trail of Tears: The Évian Conference of July 1938," Dennis Ross Laffer concludes that the conference was set up to fail and put on for show. Certainly it was proposed by and chaired by a representative of U.S. President Franklin Roosevelt who chose not to make the necessary efforts to aid Jewish refugees, before, during, or after the conference.[24]

On the Fourth of July, 1938, *New York Times* foreign correspondent, columnist, and Pulitzer Prize winner Anne O'Hare McCormick wrote: "A great power free to act has no alibi for not acting. . . . [I]t may devolve upon this country to save the ideas embodied in the Declaration; not by war, which saves nothing, solves nothing, is only, in the words of Thomas Mann, 'a cowardly escape from the problems of peace,' . . . by taking positive and practical action to solve the problems of peace. The American government is taking the initiative in dealing with the most urgent of these problems. On the invitation of Washington representatives of thirty governments will meet at Evian on Wednesday . . . . It is heartbreaking to think of the queues of desperate human beings around our consulates in Vienna and other cities, waiting in suspense for what happens at Evian. But the question they underline is not simply humanitarian. It is not a question of how many more unemployed this country can safely add to its own unemployed millions. It is a test of civilization. How deeply do we believe in our Declaration of the elementary rights of man? Whatever other nations do, can America live with itself if it lets Germany get away with this policy of extermination . . . ?"[25]

"At stake at Évian were both human lives – and the decency and self-respect of the civilized world," writes Walter Mondale. "If each nation at Évian had agreed on that day to take in 17,000 Jews at once, every Jew in the Reich could have been saved."[26] Of course, with German expansion in the years ahead, the number of Jews and non-Jews subject to murder by the Nazis would grow to much more than 17,000 times 32 (for the 32 nations represented at Évian).

Ervin Birnbaum was a leader on the *Exodus 1947*, a ship that carried Holocaust survivors to Palestine, a Professor of Government in New York, Haifa, and Moscow Universities, and Director of Projects at Ben Gurion's College of the Negev. He writes that, "the fact that the Évian Conference did not pass a resolution condemning the German treatment of Jews was widely used in Nazi propaganda and further emboldened Hitler in his assault on European Jewry leaving them ultimately subject to Hitler's 'Final

Solution to the Jewish Question."[27] The U.S. Congress also failed to pass such a resolution.

Hitler had said when the Évian Conference had been proposed: "I can only hope and expect that the other world, which has such deep sympathy for these criminals [Jews], will at least be generous enough to convert this sympathy into practical aid. We, on our part, are ready to put all these criminals at the disposal of these countries, for all I care, even on luxury ships."[28]

Following the conference, in November of 1938, Hitler escalated his attacks on Jews with *Kristallnacht* or Crystal Night — a nighttime state-organized riot, destroying and burning Jewish shops and synagogues, during which 25,000 people were sent off to concentration camps. The name *Kristallnacht* referred to the smashing of windows, put a positive spin on rioting, and likely derived from Minister of Propaganda Paul Joseph Goebbels' favorite book on propaganda, Austrian-American Edward Bernays' *Crystallizing Public Opinion.*[29] To his credit, Bernays declined to himself do public relations work for the Nazis, but the Nazis did, in 1933, hire a major New York public relations firm, Carl Byoir & Associates, to portray them in a positive light.[30]

Speaking on January 30, 1939, Hitler claimed justification for his actions from the outcome of the Évian Conference:

"It is a shameful spectacle to see how the whole democratic world is oozing sympathy for the poor tormented Jewish people, but remains hard-hearted and obdurate when it comes to aiding them — which is surely, in view of its attitude, an obvious duty. The arguments that are brought up as excuses for not helping them actually speak for us Germans and Italians. For this is what they say:

"1. 'We,' that is the democracies, 'are not in a position to take in the Jews.' Yet in these empires there are not even ten people to the square kilometer. While Germany, with her 135 inhabitants to the square kilometer, is supposed to have room for them!

"2. They assure us: We cannot take them unless Germany is prepared to allow them a certain amount of capital to bring with them as immigrants."[31]

The problem at Évian was, sadly, not ignorance of the Nazi agenda, but failure to prioritize preventing it. This remained a problem through the course of the war. It was a problem found in both politicians and in the public at large. In 2018, the Gallup polling company looked back at and tried to explain its own polling:

"[E]ven though nearly all Americans condemned the Nazi regime's terror against Jews in November 1938, that very same week, 72% of Americans said 'No' when Gallup asked: 'Should we allow a larger number of Jewish exiles from Germany to come to the United States to live?' Just 21% said 'Yes.' . . . Prejudice against Jews in the U.S. was evident in a number of ways in the 1930s. According to historian Leonard Dinnerstein, more than 100 new anti-Semitic organizations were founded in the U.S. between 1933 and 1941. One of the most influential, Father Charles Coughlin's National Union for Social Justice, spread Nazi propaganda and accused all Jews of being communists. Coughlin broadcast anti-Jewish ideas to millions of radio listeners, asking them to 'pledge' with him to 'restore America to the Americans.' Further to the fringes, William Dudley Pelley's Silver Legion of America ('Silver Shirts') fashioned themselves after Nazi Stormtroopers ('brownshirts'). The German American Bund celebrated Nazism openly, established Hitler Youth-style summer camps in communities across the United States, and hoped to see the dawn of fascism in America. Even if the Silver Shirts and the Bund did not represent the mainstream, Gallup polls showed that many Americans held seemingly prejudicial ideas about Jews. A remarkable survey conducted in April 1938 found that more than half of Americans blamed Europe's Jews for their own treatment at the hands of the Nazis. This poll showed that 54% of Americans agreed that 'the persecution of Jews in Europe has been partly their own fault,' with 11% believing it was 'entirely' their own fault. Hostility to refugees was so ingrained that just two months after Kristallnacht, 67% of Americans opposed a bill in the U.S. Congress intended to admit child refugees from Germany. The bill never made it to the floor of Congress for a vote."[32]

Gallup might well have noted the international appeal of fascism, which achieved political success in Spain, Italy, and Germany, but which had prominent proponents in other countries, including France, where the fascist movement was of particular inspiration to a group of Wall Street plotters who in 1934 sought unsuccessfully to organize a fascist coup against Roosevelt.[33] In 1940, Cornelius Vanderbilt Jr. alerted Eleanor Roosevelt to another such plot from New York tycoons and army officers.[34] In 1927, Winston Churchill had commented on his visit to Rome: "I could not help being charmed by Signor Mussolini's gentle and simple bearing, and by his calm, detached poise in spite of so many burdens and dangers." Churchill found in fascism the "necessary antidote to the Russian virus."[35]

Five days after Crystal Night, President Franklin Roosevelt said he was recalling the ambassador to Germany and that public opinion had been "deeply shocked." He did not use the word "Jews." A reporter asked if anywhere on earth might accept many Jews from Germany. "No," said Roosevelt. "The time is not ripe for that." Another reporter asked if Roosevelt would relax immigration restrictions for Jewish refugees. "That is not in contemplation," the president responded.[36] Roosevelt refused to support the child refugee bill in 1939, which would have allowed 20,000 Jews under the age of 14 to enter the United States, and it never came out of committee.[37] Senator Robert Wagner (D., N.Y.) said, "Thousands of American families have already expressed their willingness to take refugee children into their homes." First Lady Eleanor Roosevelt set aside her antisemitism to support the legislation, but her husband successfully blocked it for years. America rejected the 1939 Wagner-Rogers bill to admit more Jewish and non-Aryan refugees, but passed the 1940 Hennings Bill to allow unlimited numbers of British Christian children into the United States.[38]

While many in the United States, as elsewhere, tried heroically to rescue Jews from the Nazis, including by volunteering to take them in, majority opinion was never with them. In 2015, Gallup polling looked back at a January 1939 U.S. poll:

"The basic question Gallup asked related specifically to refugee children: 'It has been proposed that the government permit 10,000 refugee children from Germany to be brought into this country and taken care of in American homes. Do you favor this plan?' A second question asked of a different sample was basically the same as above, but included the phrase 'most of them Jewish' and ended with, 'should the government permit these children to come in?' It didn't matter much whether or not the refugee children were identified as Jewish. A clear majority, 67% of Americans, opposed the basic idea, and a lower 61% were opposed in response to the question that included the phrase 'most of them Jewish.' . . . A separate Gallup question in June 1940 . . . asked if Americans would be willing to take care of one or more refugee children from England and France in their home until the war was over. Attitudes in response to this question were more mixed, but still with a slight plurality saying they opposed — 46% against, 41% in favor."[39] Of course 46% declining to themselves host a child from England or France is a different thing from 67% or 61% opposing anybody hosting children from Germany.

In June 1939, the *St. Louis*, a German ocean liner carrying over 900 Jewish refugees from Germany was turned away by Cuba. The ship sailed up the Florida coast, followed by the U.S. Coast Guard, which had been dispatched by Secretary of the Treasury Henry Morgenthau Jr. to keep track of the ship in case the U.S. government could be persuaded to allow it to dock. The government was not persuaded, the ship returned to Europe, and over 250 of its passengers perished in the Holocaust.[40]

As the fate of the Jews worsened in Europe, openness to accepting them into the United States did not significantly increase. One reason was fear of enemy spies. According to *Time Magazine*, looking back from 2019, "After the rapid German conquest of France, pervasive concerns about American security fostered a fearful and resentful climate of opinion; Roper Poll in June 1940 found that only 2.7% of Americans thought the government was doing enough to counteract a Nazi 'Fifth Column' operating in the U.S. German Jews were not immune from these suspicions. Some Americans thought Jews could be coerced into spying for Germany based on threats to their relatives in Germany; others, including a former undersecretary of state, thought that inherent 'Jewish greed' might lead refugees and immigrants to work for the Nazi cause. By mid-1941 the State Department instructed consuls to deny visas to applicants who had relatives living in the totalitarian countries of Germany, the Soviet Union, and Italy—and then Congress passed a bill directing consuls abroad to refuse a visa to any alien who might endanger public safety."[41]

In fact, in June 1940, Assistant U.S. Secretary of State for Immigration Breckenridge Long circulated a memo proposing that the United States indefinitely delay the admission of immigrants: "We can do this by simply advising our consuls to put every obstacle in the way and to require additional evidence and to resort to various administrative devices which would postpone and postpone and postpone the granting of visas." The restrictive U.S. quotas, with millions of lives in the balance, were one thing, but 90% of the allowed places were not filled, condemning 190,000 people to their fate.[42] There were over 300,000 people on the waiting list in early 1939.[43]

Dick Cheney's and Liz Cheney's 2015 book, *Exceptional: Why the World Needs a Powerful America*, is one of countless accounts of U.S. superiority that finds the historical and moral greatness of the United States in WWII and in contrast to the Nazis.[44] Featured, as is often the case, is the death of Anne Frank. There is no mention of the fact that Anne Frank's family applied for visas to the United States, jumped through numerous hoops, found people to vouch for them, pulled strings with well-connected U.S. big-shots, produced funds, forms, affidavits, and letters of recommendation — and it wasn't enough. Their visa applications were denied.[45]

In July 1940, Adolf Eichmann, a major planner of the holocaust, intended to send all Jews to Madagascar, which now belonged to Germany, France having been occupied. The ships would need to wait only until the British, which now meant Winston Churchill, ended their blockade. That day never came.[46] On November 25, 1940, the French ambassador asked the U.S.

Secretary of State to consider accepting German Jewish refugees then in France.[47] On December 21st, the Secretary of State declined.[48] On October 19, 1941, former U.S. President Herbert Hoover, in a speech on the radio, said over 40 million children in German-invaded democracies were dying as a result of the British blockade. He denounced it as a "holocaust."[49]

On July 25, 1941, the British Ministry of Information created a policy of using material on Nazi atrocities sparingly and only regarding "indisputably innocent" victims. "Not with violent political opponents. And not with the Jews."[50]

By 1941, the Nazis had arrived at their decision to murder the Jews rather than expel them to a world that wouldn't take them or even let them out of Europe. *Time Magazine* notes that "From October 1941 on, [Germany] formally blocked the legal emigration of Jews from its territories, and it called on allies and satellite countries to turn over their Jews. Most German Jews who made it through the difficult security screening in the U.S. came from neutral countries."[51]

On July 29, 1942, Eduard Schulte, the chief executive of a German mining company, risked his life to take knowledge of the mass murder underway in German camps to Switzerland to get it into the hands of Gerhart Riegner of the World Jewish Congress. For Riegner to get it to the president of his organization, Rabbi Stephen Wise, in New York, he had to ask the U.S. diplomats in Bern to send it. The U.S. State Department buried the report, sharing it with neither Wise nor President Roosevelt. After a month's delay, Wise received the report through the British government. He announced that Germany had killed 2 million Jews and was at work killing the rest. The *New York Times* put that story on page 10.[52]

The Office of Strategic Services (OSS, a forerunner of the CIA) had its own sources on the genocide in progress, as well as having been in possession of Schulte's report. An official word from the State Department or the OSS might have moved the story to page 1, but neither said a word. Allen Dulles of the OSS — future director of the CIA — met Schulte in Zurich in the spring of 1943 but was interested in learning about the Nazis, not their victims. When German foreign service official Fritz Kolbe risked his life repeatedly to bring Dulles information on Nazi crimes, Dulles repeatedly ignored it. In April 1944, Kolbe alerted Dulles that Hungary's Jews were about to be rounded up and sent to death camps. Dulles' report on that meeting ended up on Roosevelt's desk but made no mention of Hungary's Jews or of the proposals urged by Schulte and others to bomb the rail lines to the camps or the camps themselves.[53]

The U.S. military bombed other targets so close to Auschwitz that the prisoners saw the planes pass over, and erroneously imagined they were about to be bombed. Hoping to stop the work of the death camps at the cost of their own lives, prisoners cheered for bombs that never came. The U.S. military never took any serious action against the construction and operation of the camps or in support of their expected victims. Former U.S. Senator and presidential candidate George McGovern, who was a B-24 pilot during the war, and who flew missions in the vicinity of Auschwitz, testified that it would have been easy to add the camp and the rail lines to target lists.[54]

Jessie Wallace Hughan, founder of the War Resisters League, was very concerned in 1942 by stories of Nazi plans, no longer focused on expelling Jews but turning toward plans to murder them. Hughan believed that such a development appeared "natural, from their pathological point of view," and that it might really be acted upon if World War II continued. "It seems that the only way to save thousands and perhaps millions of European Jews from destruction," she wrote, "would be for our government to broadcast the promise" of an "armistice on condition that the European minorities are not molested any further. . . . It would be very terrible if six months from now we should find that this threat has literally come to pass without our making even a gesture to prevent it." When her predictions were fulfilled only too well by 1943, she wrote to the U.S. State Department and the *New York Times*: "two million [Jews] have already died" and "two million more will be killed by the end of the war." She warned that military successes against Germany would just result in further scapegoating of Jews. "Victory will not save them, for dead men cannot be liberated," she wrote.[55]

British Foreign Secretary Anthony Eden met on March 27, 1943, in Washington, D.C., with Rabbi Wise and Joseph M. Proskauer, a prominent attorney and former New York State Supreme Court Justice who was then serving as President of the American Jewish Committee. Wise and Proskauer proposed approaching Hitler to evacuate the Jews. Eden dismissed the idea as "fantastically impossible."[56] But the very same day, according to the U.S. State Department, Eden told Secretary of State Cordell Hull something different:

"Hull raised the question of the 60 or 70 thousand Jews that are in Bulgaria and are threatened with extermination unless we could get them out and, very urgently, pressed Eden for an answer to the problem. Eden replied that the whole problem of the Jews in Europe is very difficult and that we should move very cautiously about offering to take all Jews out of a country like Bulgaria. If we do that, then the Jews of the world will be wanting us to make similar offers in Poland and Germany. Hitler might well take us up on any such offer and there simply are not enough ships and means of transportation in the world to handle them."[57]

Churchill agreed. "Even were we to obtain permission to withdraw all the Jews," he wrote in reply to one pleading letter, "transport alone presents a problem which will be difficult of solution." Not enough shipping and transport? At the battle of Dunkirk, the British had evacuated nearly 340,000 men in just nine days. The U.S. Air Force had many thousands of new planes. During even a brief armistice, the U.S. and British could have airlifted and transported huge numbers of refugees to safety.[58]

Not everyone was too busy fighting a war. Particularly from late 1942 on, many in the United States and Britain demanded that something be done. On March 23, 1943, the Archbishop of Canterbury pleaded with the House of Lords to assist the Jews of Europe. So, the British government proposed to the U.S. government another public conference at which to discuss what might be done to evacuate Jews from neutral nations. But the British Foreign Office feared that the Nazis might cooperate in such plans despite never being asked to, writing: "There is a possibility that the Germans or their satellites may change over from the policy of extermination to one of extrusion, and aim as they did before the war at embarrassing other countries by flooding them with alien immigrants."[59]

The concern here was not with saving lives so much as with avoiding the embarrassment and inconvenience of saving lives.

The U.S. government just sat on the proposal until Jewish leaders held a mass demonstration at Madison Square Garden. At that point, the State Department made plans for the Bermuda Conference of April 19-29, 1943, plans that ensured it would be no more than a publicity stunt. No Jewish organizations were included, the location served to keep people out, the conference was assigned to merely make recommendations to a committee, and those recommendations were not to include increased immigration to the United States or to Palestine. The Bermuda Conference, in the end, recommended that "no approach be made to Hitler for the release of potential refugees." There were also some suggestions for helping refugees leave Spain, and a declaration on the postwar repatriation of refugees.[60]

According to Rafael Medoff of the David S. Wyman Institute for Holocaust Studies, "Until the Bermuda conference, most American Jews and most Members of Congress had accepted FDR's 'rescue through victory' approach — the claim that the only way to aid the Jews of Europe was to defeat the Nazis on the battlefield. This long, slow strategy that included blockade and starvation — and the delay of the D-Day invasion for years — condemned large numbers to their fate and has disturbing parallels with the later U.S. practice of imposing economic sanctions on whole nations for long periods of time. But in the wake of Bermuda, there was a growing conviction that by the time the war was won, there might be no European Jews left to save." Public activism increased significantly, to the point where it seemed possible that even the U.S. Congress might act. Before it could, Roosevelt created the War Refugee Board, which may have saved as many as 200,000 people during the last year-and-a-half of the war.[61]

While the United States was failing to rescue most of the Jews of Europe,

Britain was refusing to allow larger numbers of them to settle in Palestine. Given all the injustice and violence generated by the eventual creation of Israel, and the fact that a major concern of the British was Arab protests, the policy should not be simply condemned. But it was condemned by Jewish groups during World War II, and there is no question that the promise of a land in Palestine, combined with its denial, and combined with the failure of the world's governments to follow through on numerous other possible destinations for refugees, created great suffering.

In 1942, a small ship called the Struma sailed from a Romanian port on the Black Sea with 769 refugees trying to reach Palestine. After reaching Istanbul, the ship was in no shape to go on. But Turkey refused to admit the refugees unless Britain would promise that they could enter Palestine. Britain refused. Turkey towed the ship out to sea, where it broke apart. There was one survivor.[62]

Opposition to mass immigration into Palestine came not only from the people who lived there, but also from the King of Saudi Arabia, Ibn Saud, whose oil was important to the Allies, and who hoped to build a pipeline to the Mediterranean. The Saudi King preferred Sidon, Lebanon, to Haifa, Palestine, as an end-point for the desired pipeline.[63] In 1944, his opposition to Jewish immigration to Palestine was "well known" according to U.S. Secretary of State Edward Reilly Stettinius Jr. who on December 13, 1944, warned President Roosevelt that pro-Zionist statements could have "a very definite bearing upon the future of the immensely valuable American oil concession in Saudi Arabia."[64]

Detractors of Franklin Roosevelt blame him for not doing more, arguing that he could have seen to it that Jews found safe haven in Cuba or the Virgin Islands or Santo Domingo or Alaska, or — if Jews were really unwelcome as free citizens of the United States — then in refugee camps. Of course, the same complaint can be lodged against the U.S. Congress. There were 425,000 German prisoners of war in the United States during the war, but only one camp for refugees, in Oswego, N.Y., which held about 1,000 Jews.[65] Were Nazi soldiers 425 times more welcome than Jewish refugees?

Well, perhaps in some sense they were. Prisoners of war are temporary and isolated. Here's what Gallup says of its polling results, even after the war, even after widespread awareness of the horrors that would become the top retroactive justification of the war in decades to follow:

"After the war ended, Gallup asked several questions about the very large number of Jewish and other European refugees who were situated in the ravaged postwar Europe and seeking a home. Gallup found net opposition in response to each of the three ways the questions were worded. The least opposition was in response to a June 1946 question asking Americans if they approved or disapproved of 'a plan to require each nation to take in a given number of Jewish and other European refugees, based upon the size and population of each nation.' . . . The responses were 40% in favor, 49% opposed. . . . In August, a separate question invoked the name of President Harry Truman, saying that the president planned to ask Congress to allow more Jewish and other European refugees to come to the U.S. to live than are allowed under the current law. This idea did not sit well at all with the public, some 72% of whom said that they disapproved. A 1947 question localized the issue to the state level, stating, 'The Governor of Minnesota has said that the Middlewest could take several thousands of displaced (homeless) persons from refugee camps in Europe,' and asking the respondents if they would approve or disapprove of their own state taking about 10,000 of these 'displaced persons from Europe.' A majority, 57%, said no — 24% yes, with the rest evincing uncertainty."[66]

For those interested in more information on U.S. immigration policy and the Holocaust, there's a section on the website of the U.S. Holocaust Museum.[67]

In the end, those left alive in the concentration camps were liberated — though in many cases not very quickly, not as anything resembling a top priority. Some prisoners were kept in horrible concentration camps at least up through September of 1946. General George Patton urged that nobody should "believe that the Displaced person is a human being, which he is not, and this applies particularly to the Jews who are lower than animals."

President Harry Truman admitted at that time that "we apparently treat the Jews the same way as the Nazis did, with the sole exception that we do not kill them."[68]

Of course, even were that not an exaggeration, not killing people is a very important exception. The United States had fascist tendencies but did not succumb to them as Germany did. But neither was there any all-out capital-R Resistance crusade to save those threatened by fascism — not on the part of the U.S. government, not on the part of the U.S. mainstream. Many made heroic efforts, with limited success, but they were in a minority. A Dr. Seuss cartoon showed a woman reading her children a story called "Adolf the Wolf." The caption was: ". . . and the wolf chewed up the children and spit out their bones . . . But those were foreign children and it really didn't matter."[69]

In July 2018, with anti-immigrant sentiments less acceptable but still raging, the singer Billy Joel told the *New York Times*, "My father's family left Germany in '38, after Kristallnacht, but they couldn't get into the United States. There was a quota on European Jews, and if you couldn't get in here, you were shipped back, then you were rounded up and sent to Auschwitz — which is what happened to my father's family. They were all killed at Auschwitz, except my father and his parents. So this anti-immigration stuff strikes a very dark tone with me."[70]

Was WWII a just war by accident because it ended before all the Jews had been killed? That's a tough case to make, since efforts could have been made, in combination with the war or instead of it, to save millions who died. In fact, it wouldn't have taken much effort, just a willingness to say "welcome" or, perhaps to say something like this:

"Give me your tired, your poor,
Your huddled masses yearning to breathe free,
The wretched refuse of your teeming shore.
Send these, the homeless, tempest-tossed to me,
I lift my lamp beside the golden door!"

Perhaps WWII was a just war; but we'll have to find another reason why. The popular notion of a war to save Jews is fiction. The variation in which the war is justified simply because the enemy killed Jews is weak if the war was not aimed at stopping that evil. The political or propagandistic nature of popular myths and misconceptions can be easily illustrated by a couple of facts. First, the victims of the Nazi concentration camps and other deliberate murder campaigns included at least as many non-Jews as Jews; these other victims were targeted for other reasons, yet are sometimes not even mentioned or considered.[71] Second, Hitler's war efforts were aimed at killing and did kill many more people than the camps killed. In fact, numerous nations in both the European and Pacific wars killed many more people than were killed in the camps, and the war as a whole killed several times the number killed in the camps, making the war an odd cure for the genocide disease.[72]

3. *WWII did not have to happen*

"One day President Roosevelt told me that he was asking publicly for suggestions about what the war should be called. I said at once, 'The Unnecessary War.' There never was a war more easy to stop than that which has just wrecked what was left of the world from the previous struggle." — Winston Churchill[73]

World War II grew out of World War I, and almost nobody tries to argue that World War I was just or glorious. Generally it's treated, even in school history texts, as pointless and even barbaric. Barbara Tuchman's Pulitzer-Prize-winning 1962 book *The Guns of August* tells the story of the slow launching of WWI, driven by war planners and the momentum of their plans. Erich Maria Remarque's 1929 novel *All's Quiet on the Western Front* described WWI so well that the Nazis banned and burned it. By behaving more wisely, governments could have chosen not to launch World War I, or not to end World War I in a manner that had people predicting WWII on the spot. A war that could have been avoided is only a justifiable war if actually desirable, if actually preferable to peace — a position generally limited to sadists and weapons dealers. Of course what was still avoidable in 1939 might not be the same as what was avoidable in 1919, and we'll come to that (see Chapter 12 below, but please read the intervening chapters first). Let's start with the full 20 years of completely unnecessary actions. If we went back an additional 20 years to the proposals for peace discussed at the Hague in 1899 but never acted upon, our case would be that much stronger.[74]

Jane Addams and her colleagues not only predicted in 1919 that a second world war would come, but also detailed what would need to be changed about the Treaty of Versailles and the League of Nations in order to avoid it — and launched a global peace organization to advocate toward that end. That organization, which is still around, the Women's International League for Peace and Freedom (WILPF), posted on its website in 2019 an account of what had been said one century earlier.[75] The famous 14 points promoted by President Woodrow Wilson, nine of which WILPF took credit for having proposed to him, were largely lost in the Treaty of Versailles, replaced by brutal punishment and humiliation for Germany. Addams warned that this would lead to another war.[76]

Months before the treaty negotiations, Wilson had told Congress, "Food relief is now the key to the whole European situation and to the solution of peace." But a commission led by Winston Churchill recommended maintaining the blockade against Germany, because "it would be inadvisable to remove the menace of starvation by a too sudden and abundant supply of foodstuffs."[77] One wouldn't want starvation to stop too suddenly! And it certainly didn't. As Adolf Hitler later gained power, he made frequent reference to his own experience with hunger, which he blamed not on England, France, Italy, or the United States, but on a global Jewish conspiracy. The very next day after Germany had ratified the Treaty of Versailles, Hitler had begun attending Army propaganda classes aimed at repressing revolutionary tendencies and at promoting antisemitism. The endless "we're about to win" WWI coverage of the German media — which resembled, in reverse, that of the British and Americans[78] — made defeat and the subsequent demand for reparations payments shocking to the German public, made it easy to blame a treasonous scapegoat.[79]

The British economist John Maynard Keynes wrote in 1919 in _The Economic Consequences of the Peace_, "If we aim deliberately at the impoverishment of Central Europe, vengeance, I dare predict, will not limp. Nothing can then delay for very long that final civil war between the forces of Reaction and the despairing convulsions of Revolution, before which the horrors of the late German war will fade into nothing, and which will destroy, whoever is victor, the civilization and the progress of our generation."[80] There are many far less sensible things that Keynes wrote that were taken far more seriously than this warning was.

Thorstein Veblen, in a highly critical review of Keynes' book, also predicted the Treaty of Versailles leading to more war, though he understood the basis of the treaty to be animosity toward the Soviet Union, against which, it should be noted, the United States and allied nations were fighting a war in 1919 that rarely shows up in U.S. history books.[81] Veblen believed that reparations could have easily been taken from wealthy German property owners without imposing suffering on all of German society, but that the primary goal of those making the treaty had been to uphold property rights and to use Germany as a force against the communist Soviet Union.

Woodrow Wilson had promised "peace without victory," but, in the treaty negotiations, given in to French and British vengeance toward Germany. Afterwards, he predicted World War II unless the United States joined the League of Nations. The United States did not join, and World War II came. Whether joining the League as it then existed would have prevented World War II is hard to guess. WILPF wanted the League transformed into a league for peace, rather than for war alliances. WILPF thought disarmament was needed, and that no league could prevent war while its members all armed themselves in frantic anticipation of more slaughter. In 1928, the powerful nations of the world outlawed war with the Kellogg-Briand Pact, but didn't stop arming and didn't prosecute violators.[82] Would the League have done the trick?

Veblen thinks Wilson didn't cave in and compromise at the treaty negotiations, but rather prioritized enmity toward the Soviet Union. However, Veblen, unlike Keynes, wasn't there. And those who were there knew that Wilson began by forcefully arguing against vindictive punishment of Germany, but that Wilson was struck down by the so-called Spanish flu, that he was weakened severely, that he spoke as though delusional, and that he quickly agreed to abandon much of what he had promised the world.[83] The Spanish flu (so called because, although it probably came from U.S. military bases to the European war, Spain allowed its newspapers to write about unpleasant news, a forbidden practice in nations at war) had infected the White House.[84] The previous fall, on September 28, 1918, Philadelphia had held a massive pro-war parade that included flu-infected troops just back from the war. Doctors had warned against it, but politicians had announced that nothing would go wrong if everyone refrained from coughing, sneezing, and spitting. They didn't. The flu spread.[85] Wilson got it. He didn't do what he might have done in Paris. It's not inconceivable that World War II could have been avoided had a parade in Philadelphia been avoided. That may sound crazy, but the parade in Philadelphia, as we will see, was just one stupid thing in an ocean of stupid things that didn't have to be done. Nobody could have predicted World War II as a result of that parade, but such a prediction was possible and in fact made about many other of the unnecessary and foolish actions in the years between the wars.

William Geimer, drawing on the research of Margaret MacMillan, writes that "There were those on the allied side," at the negotiations of the Treaty of Versailles, "notably Lloyd George, who saw the future danger of the treaty and saw the need for modifications. A member of his delegation said, *We came to Paris confident that the new order was about to be established; we left convinced that the new order had merely fouled the old.* Herbert Hoover, the American administrator of relief for Europe, recognized *that the consequences of many parts of the proposed Treaty would ultimately bring destruction.*"[86] In Geimer's analysis, much of the harm was in how the treaty was negotiated, with Germany and Russia excluded from the process and from the League of Nations, with Germany blamed, declared guilty, punished, and humiliated. Additional harm came from drawing borders that divided numerous ethnic groups, including dividing German-speaking and German-identifying people from Germany, and splitting one piece of Germany off from another.

Ferdinand Foch, a Frenchman, was Supreme Allied Commander. He accepted the German surrender in World War I. He refused to allow an immediate ceasefire, preferring a six-hour delay, which resulted in the war ending upon the eleventh hour of the eleventh day of the eleventh month. I do not know whether he found it numerically pleasing that the delay cost 11,000 additional lives. Foch was very disappointed with the Treaty of Versailles. "This is not peace," he exclaimed. "It is an armistice for 20 years." World War II began 20 years and 65 days later. Foch's concern was not that Germany was punished too severely. Foch wanted Germany's territory limited on the west by the Rhine River.[87]

With widespread agreement that all governments would arm and prepare for more wars, predicting that Germany would be embittered by too much punishment or that too little punishment could allow Germany to launch a new attack were both safe predictions. With the ideas of prosperity without armament, the rule of law without violence, and humanity without tribalism still so marginal, Foch's prediction made as much sense as Jane Addams'.

After WWII, Winston Churchill said, "Last time I saw it all coming and I cried aloud to my own fellow-countrymen and to the world, but no one paid any attention. . . . There never was a war in history easier to prevent by timely action than the one which has just desolated such great areas of the globe. It could have been prevented in my belief without the firing of a single shot, and Germany might be powerful, prosperous and honored today; but no one would listen and one by one we were all sucked into the awful whirlpool."[88] Churchill meant that more armaments, more show of force, more threats and provocations could have prevented WWII, and that the same would prevent war with the Soviet Union. Churchill also put it this way:

"President Roosevelt one day asked what this War should be called. My answer was, 'The Unnecessary War.' If the United States had taken an active part in the League of Nations, and if the League of Nations had been prepared to use concerted force, even had it only been European force, to prevent the re-armament of Germany, there was no need for further serious bloodshed. If the Allies had resisted Hitler strongly in his early stages, even up to his seizure of the Rhineland in 1936, he would have been forced to recoil, and a chance would have been given to the sane elements in German life, which were very powerful especially in the High

Command, to free Germany of the maniacal Government and system into the grip of which she was falling. Do not forget that twice the German people, by a majority, voted against Hitler, but the Allies and the League of Nations acted with such feebleness and lack of clairvoyance, that each of Hitler's encroachments became a triumph for him over all moderate and restraining forces until, finally, we resigned ourselves without further protest to the vast process of German re-armament and war preparation which ended in a renewed outbreak of destructive war. Let us profit at least by this terrible lesson. In vain did I attempt to teach it before the war."[89]

While Churchill seems not to be describing a stable peaceful world, so much as a delicate and increasingly dangerous imperial balance, there is no way to know that he's mistaken. There was great opposition to Nazism in Germany, and some shift in history — whether a greater understanding of the tools of nonviolent action, or a more Churchillian militaristic resolve, or an assassination or coup (there were a number of failed plots) — might have defeated it.

But the point here is not that the world might have gotten lucky, or as we will discuss further, might have acted very differently. Rather, the world acted foolishly, both by the standards of the time, and even more so by today's. The Marshall Plan following WWII, for all its deep flaws, was an effort not to repeat the stupid way in which WWI had been ended. People were too much aware immediately after WWII of how they had created it after WWI.

The Treaty of Versailles was only one thing among many that did not have to happen. The people of Germany did not have to allow the rise of Nazism. Nations and businesses around the world did not have to fund and encourage the rise of Nazism. Scientists and governments did not have to inspire the Nazi ideology. Governments did not have to prefer armaments to the rule of law, and did not have to wink at German outrages while encouraging a German attack on the Soviet Union. We'll get to each of these topics. I'd like to focus in the next several chapters on some of the ways in which the United States did not have to contribute to Nazism.

4. The United States did not have to develop and promote the dangerous bunk science of eugenics

Eugenics had British and U.S. roots and was popularized by Americans in the first two decades of the Twentieth Century, despite various scientists pointing out the lack of evidence for its claims. It took until the 1930s for most scientists to finally reject it, but much longer for the public and governments to catch on. Eugenics was so American that one of its big promoters was John Harvey Kellogg, the same guy who invented corn flakes. Eugenics was so loony that its proponents developed intelligence tests no more scientific than any eugenic claims, and those tests were used to classify half of U.S. draftees in World War I as "morons."[90] A moron was someone smarter than an "idiot" or an "imbecile" but not smart enough for morality.

Eugenics was so American that Margaret Sanger promoted birth control by describing it as a tool for eugenics. The latter was acceptable, the former scandalous. During the 1920s and right up through WWII, at state fairs in the United States, families competed in "Better Babies" and "Fitter Families" contests (sometimes limited to whites only), exhibiting humans in competitions analogous to those for various farm animals. African American author and brilliant opponent of racism WEB Dubois even suggested that the talented tenth Negroes should breed for a better race. That's how saturated the society was with eugenics. Even those opposing bigotry thought in its terms. The NAACP held better babies contests to fund campaigns against lynching.[91]

Eugenics was funded by the Carnegie Institution, the Rockefeller Foundation, and the Harriman railroad fortune. Members of the American

Breeders' Association (still around but renamed the American Genetic Association) included Alexander Graham Bell. The League of Women Voters promoted eugenic public policies. Witnesses on the evolution side of the Scopes Monkey Trial were eugenicists.

U.S. eugenicist Charles Davenport wrote a letter to U.S. eugenicist and white supremacist Madison Grant arguing for the need to "build a wall" to "keep out the cheaper races."[92] Grant's book, *The Passing of the Great Race*, invented a race called The Nordic Race that had a lot in common with the race later promoted by the Nazis.[93] Edwin Black writes:

"[T]he concept of a white, blond-haired, blue-eyed master Nordic race didn't originate with Hitler. The idea was created in the United States, and cultivated in California, decades before Hitler came to power."[94]

U.S. eugenicist Harry Laughlin shaped U.S. immigration policy with pseudo-science about the inferiority of races, in particular Jews. Various people — non-morons, I guess you'd call them — including various Jews, pointed out at the time that Laughlin had fixed the facts around the policy and not pursued actual scientific findings.[95] The U.S. Congress didn't have to ignore those wiser voices.

Most eugenicists supported strict and racist immigration laws, as well as sterilization and the prevention of reproduction through the segregation of "feeble-minded" men and women into separate asylums. Eugenics was also used to support anti-miscegenation laws. Some eugenicists also promoted the idea of extermination. A report by the Carnegie Institute in 1911 proposed euthanasia.[96] While eugenicide never gained mainstream popularity, it was practiced. According to Edwin Black:

"The most commonly suggested method of eugenicide in the United States was a 'lethal chamber' or public, locally operated gas chambers. In 1918, [Paul] Popenoe, the Army venereal disease specialist during World War I, co-wrote the widely used textbook, 'Applied Eugenics,' which argued, 'From an historical point of view, the first method which presents itself is execution . . . Its value in keeping up the standard of the race should not be underestimated.' . . . Eugenic breeders believed American society was not ready to implement an organized lethal solution. But many mental institutions and doctors practiced improvised medical lethality and passive euthanasia on their own. One institution in Lincoln, Ill., fed its incoming patients milk from tubercular cows believing a eugenically strong individual would be immune. Thirty to 40 percent annual death rates resulted at Lincoln. Some doctors practiced passive eugenicide one newborn infant at a time. Others doctors at mental institutions engaged in lethal neglect."[97]

Straying for a moment from eugenics to gas chambers, here's a passage from a long article about Hitler in *The New Yorker* in 2018:

"In 1924, the first execution by gas chamber took place, in Nevada. In a history of the American gas chamber, Scott Christianson states that the fumigating agent Zyklon-B, which was licensed to American Cyanamid by the German company I. G. Farben, was considered as a lethal agent but found to be impractical. Zyklon-B was, however, used to disinfect immigrants as they crossed the border at El Paso—a practice that did not go unnoticed by Gerhard Peters, the chemist who supplied a modified version of Zyklon-B to Auschwitz. Later, American gas chambers were outfitted with a chute down which poison pellets were dropped. Earl Liston, the inventor of the device, explained, 'Pulling a lever to kill a man is hard work. Pouring acid down a tube is easier on the nerves, more like watering flowers.' Much the same method was introduced at Auschwitz, to relieve stress on S.S. guards."[98]

When the U.S. Supreme Court ruled in 1927, in the case of *Buck v. Bell* (which has yet to be overturned), that a healthy and intelligent rape victim abused by her society could be forcibly sterilized, the ruling was reported in the press as a step toward "a super race."[99]

When Hitler came to power, he put in place a sterilization law based on a model law written by Harry Laughlin and the laws that 27 U.S. states had put in place. Hitler had read Madison Grant and written him a fan letter, and referred to his book as "my Bible." Hitler had written in *Mein Kampf* that Germany must follow the United States in immigration and segregation:

"At present there exists one State which manifests at least some modest attempts that show a better appreciation of how things ought to be done in this matter. It is not, however, in our model German Republic but in the U.S.A. that efforts are made to conform at least partly to the counsels of commonsense. By refusing immigrants to enter there if they are in a bad state of health, and by excluding certain races from the right to become naturalized as citizens, they have begun to introduce principles similar to those on which we wish to ground the People's State."[100]

"I have studied with great interest," Hitler told a fellow Nazi, "the laws of several American states concerning prevention of reproduction by people whose progeny would, in all probability, be of no value or be injurious to the racial stock."[101]

Laughlin bragged about his role in creating the 1935 Nuremberg racial hygiene laws, and in 1936 was given an award by the Nazis.[102]

U.S. eugenicist Paul Popenoe published a report on forced sterilizations in California that was widely cited by the Nazis.[103] Many eugenicists in California promoted their work in Germany. The Rockefeller Foundation, as well as Carnegie, funded and helped develop German eugenics programs, including the one that Josef Mengele worked in before he worked at Auschwitz gassing people to death and experimenting on them, as well as the German Psychiatric Institute where Ernst Rüdin worked before he became the architect of Hitler's eugenics program. Edwin Black recounts that:

"In 1934, as Germany's sterilizations were accelerating beyond 5,000 per month, the California eugenics leader C. M. Goethe, upon returning from Germany, ebulliently bragged to a colleague, 'You will be interested to know that your work has played a powerful part in shaping the opinions of the group of intellectuals who are behind Hitler in this epoch-making program. Everywhere I sensed that their opinions have been tremendously stimulated by American thought . . . I want you, my dear friend, to carry this thought with you for the rest of your life, that you have really jolted into action a great government of 60 million people.'"[104]

Winston Churchill was an honorary vice president of the British Eugenics Society and a true believer in its power to solve "race deterioration." In 1910, he proposed sterilizing 100,000 "mental degenerates," and confining tens of thousands more to state-run labor camps.[105]

It took Nazism to give eugenics a bad name in the United States, but neither Nazism nor the prosecution of its members for crimes including forced sterilization ended such practices in the United States, where over 60,000 people were forcibly sterilized up through 1963, a third of them in California. In fact, eugenics saw something of a revival in the United States after WWII under the banner of "neo-eugenics," targeted at the poor and minorities, with possibly 80,000 people forcibly sterilized in the United States in the late 1960s and 1970s (up through 1981 in Oregon), and many more sterilized without consent up to the current day.[106] From the 1930s to 1970s a third of the female population in Puerto Rico was sterilized.[107] In the 1970s, 40% of Native American women and 10% of Native American men were sterilized.[108] Even in recent years, such as 2013 in California, scandals pop up revealing the sterilization of prisoners without proper consent.[109]

After WWII, eugenics organizations and associations in the United States, Germany, and elsewhere were renamed using the term "genetics." Nazi scientists resumed respectable careers and international collegiality. But the dark sides of the work, and the reliance on dubious science, never disappeared. Humans have only about one-fifth as many DNA sequences as wheat, and 90 percent of them identical to those of mice. Claims that DNA determines your future are extremely weak but extremely widespread, especially among those seeking to use "genetics" — rather than, say, the distribution of money — to solve such problems as poverty.[110]

Human experimentation, like eugenics, and often connected to it, also had a home in the United States before, during, and after WWII. Non-consensual experimentation on institutionalized children and adults was common in the United States before, during, and even more so after the U.S.

and its allies prosecuted Nazis for the practice in 1947, sentencing many to prison and seven to be hanged. The tribunal created the Nuremberg Code, standards for medical practice that were immediately ignored back home. Some American doctors considered it "a good code for barbarians."[111]

The code begins: "Required is the voluntary, well-informed, understanding consent of the human subject in a full legal capacity." A similar requirement is included in the CIA's rules, but has not been followed, even as doctors have assisted with such torture techniques as waterboarding. Thus far, the United States has never really accepted the Nuremberg Code. While the code was being created, the U.S. was giving people syphilis in Guatemala.[112] It did the same at Tuskegee. Also during the Nuremberg trial, children at the Pennhurst school in southeastern Pennsylvania were given hepatitis-laced feces to eat.[113]

Other sites of experimentation scandals have included the Jewish Chronic Disease Hospital in Brooklyn, the Willowbrook State School on Staten Island, and Holmesburg Prison in Philadelphia. And, of course, the CIA's Project MKUltra (1953-1973) was a smorgasbord of human experimentation. The United States military, during WWII, experimented on its own troops with gas chambers, segregating the troops, as always, by race, and pursuing pseudo-scientific racial ideas.[114]

Robert Jackson, Chief U.S. Prosecutor at the trials of Nazis for war and related crimes held in Nuremberg, Germany, following WWII, set a standard for the world: "If certain acts of violation of treaties are crimes, they are crimes whether the United States does them or whether Germany does them, and we are not prepared to lay down a rule of criminal conduct against others which we would not be willing to have invoked against us."[115]

Among the trials held in Nuremberg was one of Nazi doctors accused of human experimentation and mass murder. This trial lasted from December 9, 1946, to August 20, 1947. An important witness provided by the American Medical Association was Dr. Andrew C. Ivy. He explained that Nazi doctors' actions "were crimes because they were performed on prisoners without their consent and in complete disregard for their human rights. They were not conducted so as to avoid unnecessary pain and suffering."[116]

In the April 27, 1947, *New York Times*, that newspaper's science editor Waldemar Kaempffert wrote that human experiments with syphilis would be valuable but "ethically impossible."[117] Dr. John C. Cutler read the short article. He was at the time engaged in giving syphilis to unsuspecting victims in Guatemala. He was doing this with the funding, knowledge, and support of his superiors at the U.S. Public Health Service. He called the *Times* article to the attention of Dr. John F. Mahoney, his director at the Venereal Diseases Research Laboratory of the Public Health Service. Cutler wrote to Mahoney that in light of the *Times* article, Cutler's work in Guatemala should be guarded with increased secrecy.

Cutler had gone to Guatemala because he believed it was a place where he could get away with intentionally infecting people with syphilis in order to experiment with possible cures and placebos. He did not believe he could get away with such actions in the United States. In February 1947, Cutler had begun infecting female prostitutes with syphilis and using them to infect numerous men. In April he began infecting men directly.[118]

For more information about eugenics, I recommend the PBS film "American Experience: The Eugenics Crusade."[119]

The eugenics of the Nazis was far more murderous than that of other nations, and — as responsibility is not a finite quantity — any blame given to others diminishes the responsibility of the Nazis for their actions not a speck. But without the development of eugenics by the Americans, Nazism would not have resembled what Nazism was. The United States provided the pseudo-scientific rationale for mass-expulsion of the Jews, and then refused to accept the Jews, leading to mass eugenicide.

5. The United States did not have to develop the practice of racist segregation

James Q. Whitman is an American lawyer, Ford Foundation Professor of Comparative and Foreign Law at Yale University, and a Fellow of the American Academy of Arts and Sciences. His critically acclaimed 2017 book is well researched. Its title is *Hitler's American Model: The United States and the Making of Nazi Race Law.*[120]

Whitman's book provides an understanding of U.S. influences on the drafting of Nazi race laws. No, there were no U.S. laws in the 1930s establishing mass murder by poison gas in concentration camps. But neither were the Nazis looking for such laws. Nazis lawyers were looking for models of functioning laws on race, laws that effectively defined race in some way despite the obvious scientific difficulties, laws that restricted immigration, citizenship rights, and interracial marriage. In the early 20th century the recognized world leader in such things was the United States.

Whitman quotes from the transcripts of Nazi meetings, internal documents, and published articles and books. There is no doubt of the role that U.S. (state, not just federal) legal models played in the development of the Nuremberg Laws. The 1930s was a time, we should recall, when Jews in Germany and African Americans (primarily, but others too) in the United States were lynched. It was also a time when U.S. immigration laws used national origin as a means of discrimination that Hitler praised in *Mein Kampf.*

It was also a time of de facto second-class citizenship in the United States for blacks, Chinese, Filipinos, Puerto Ricans, Japanese, and others. Thirty U.S. states had systems of laws banning interracial marriage of various sorts — something the Nazis could find nowhere else and studied in comprehensive detail, among other things for the examples of how the races were defined. The U.S. had also shown how to conquer territories of undesirables, such as in the Philippines or Puerto Rico, incorporate them into an empire that denied them first-class citizenship rights, but present itself to the world as a model of democracy. Up until 1930 a U.S. woman could lose her citizenship if she married a non-citizen Asian man.

The most radical of the Nazis, not the moderates, in their deliberations were the advocates for the U.S. models. But even they believed some of the U.S. systems simply went too far. The "one-drop" rule for defining a colored person was considered too harsh, for example, as opposed to defining a Jew as someone with three or more Jewish grandparents (how those grandparents were defined as Jewish is another matter; it was the willingness to ignore logic and science in all such laws that was most of the attraction). The Nazis also defined as Jewish someone with only two Jewish grandparents who met other criteria. In this broadening of the definition of a race to things like behavior and appearance, the U.S. laws were also a model.

One of many U.S. state laws that Nazis examined was this from Maryland:

"All marriages between a white person and a Negro, or between a white person and a person of Negro descent, to the third generation, inclusive, or between a white person and a member of the Malay race or between a Negro and a member of the Malay race, or between a person of Negro descent to the third generation, inclusive, and a member of the Malay race ... [skipping over many variations] ... are forever prohibited ... punished by imprisonment in the penitentiary for not less than eighteen months nor more than ten years."

The Nazis of course examined and admired the Jim Crow laws of segregation as well but determined that such a regime would only work against an impoverished oppressed group. German Jews, they reasoned, were too rich and powerful to be segregated. Some of the Nazi lawyers in the 1930s, before Nazi policy had become mass murder, also found the extent of the U.S. segregation laws too extreme. But Nazis admired racist statements from contemporary U.S. pundits and authorities back at least to Thomas Jefferson. Some argued that because segregation was de facto established in the U.S. South despite a Constitution mandating equality, this proved that segregation was a powerful, natural, and inevitable force. In other words, U.S. practice allowed Nazis to more easily think of their own desired practices in the early years of their madness as normal.

In 1935, a week after Hitler had proclaimed the Nuremberg Laws, a group of Nazi lawyers sailed to New York to study U.S. law. There, they were protested by Jews but hosted by the New York City Bar Association.

U.S. laws on miscegenation lasted until the 1967 *Loving v. Virginia* ruling by the U.S. Supreme Court. Vicious and bigoted U.S. policies on immigration and refugees are alive and well today. Whitman examines the U.S. legal tradition, noting much that is to admire in it, but pointing to its political or democratic nature as something that the Nazis found preferable to the inflexibility of an independent judiciary. To this day, the U.S. elects prosecutors, imposes Nazi-like habitual offender (or three-strikes-you're-out) sentences, uses the death penalty, employs jailhouse snitches' testimony in exchange for release, locks up more people than anywhere else on earth, and does so in an extremely racist manner. To this day, racism is alive in U.S. politics. What right-wing dictators admire in Donald Trump's nation is not all new and not all different from what fascists admired 80 or 90 years ago.

It's worth repeating the obvious: the United States was not and is not Nazi Germany. And that is a very good thing. But what if a Wall Street coup had succeeded? What if the United States had been bombed flat and faced defeat from abroad while demonizing a domestic scapegoat? Who can really say it couldn't have or still couldn't happen here?

Whitman suggests that Germans do not write about foreign influence on Nazism so as not to appear to be shifting blame. For similar reasons many Germans refuse to oppose the slaughter of and mistreatment of Palestinians. We can fault such positions as going overboard. But why is it that U.S. writers rarely write about U.S. influence on Nazism? Why, for that matter, do we not learn about U.S. crimes, like slavery or Native American genocide, in the way that Germans learn about German crimes?

Another book worth reading for a grasp of U.S. race relations at the time of World War II and in the years leading up to it is Douglas Blackmon's *Slavery By Another Name: The Re-Enslavement of Black Americans from the Civil War to World War II.* Blackmon documents how the institution of slavery in the U.S. South largely ended for as long as 20 years in some places upon completion of the U.S. Civil War. And then it was back again, in a slightly different form, reduced but still widespread, publicly known and accepted in certain places — right up to World War II.[121]

During widely publicized trials of slave owners for the crime of slavery in 1903 — trials that did virtually nothing to end the pervasive practice — the *Montgomery Advertiser* editorialized: "Forgiveness is a Christian virtue and forgetfulness is often a relief, but some of us will never forgive nor forget the damnable and brutal excesses that were committed all over the South by negroes and their white allies, many of whom were federal officials, against whose acts our people were practically powerless." This was a publicly acceptable position in Alabama in 1903: slavery should be tolerated because of the evils committed by the North during the war and during the occupation that followed.

Across much of the Deep South, a system of petty, even meaningless, crimes, such as "vagrancy," created the threat of arrest for any black person. Upon arrest, a black man would be presented with a debt to pay through years of hard labor. The way to protect oneself from being put into one of the hundreds of forced labor camps was to put oneself in debt to and under the protection of a white owner. The 13th Amendment sanctions slavery for convicts, and no statute prohibited slavery until the 1950s. All that was needed for the pretense of legality was the equivalent of today's plea bargain.

Not only did slavery not fully end following the U.S. Civil War, but for many thousands it was worsened. The antebellum slave owner typically had a financial interest in keeping an enslaved person alive and healthy enough to work. A mine or mill that purchased the work of hundreds of convicts had no interest in their futures beyond the term of their sentences. In fact, local governments would replace a convict who died with another, so there was no economic reason not to work them to death. Mortality rates for leased-out convicts in Alabama were as high as 45 percent per year.

Enslaved Americans after the "ending of slavery" were bought and sold, chained by the ankles and necks at night, whipped to death, waterboarded, and murdered at the discretion of their owners, such as U.S. Steel Corporation which purchased mines near Birmingham where generations of "free" people were worked to death underground.

The threat of that fate hung over every black man not enduring it, as well as the threat of lynching that escalated in the early 20th century along with newly pseudo-scientific justifications for racism. "God ordained the southern white man to teach the lessons of Aryan supremacy," declared Woodrow Wilson's friend Thomas Dixon, author of the book and play *The Clansman,* which became the film *Birth of a Nation.*

Five days after the Japanese attack on Pearl Harbor, the U.S. government finally decided to take prosecuting slavery seriously, to counter possible criticism from Germany or Japan.

The vicious racism and antisemitism and homophobia and assorted other bigotries of the Nazis are fully the fault of the Nazis. But blame is unlimited. Giving it to someone does not take it away from anyone else. It's hard to know how the laws stripping Jews of rights would have been developed in Germany without the American model. It's easy to grasp that the United States did not need to create that model, that it could have done better and can do better in the future. As I write this, California is using prisoners to fight forest fires, paying them $1 an hour, and public scandals over police murders of black men are frequent occurrences.

As racist as the U.S. was prior to WWII, it was made more racist by WWII — something that happens with each major war. In 2018, Frontline PBS and ProPublica reporter A. C. Thompson produced a film called "Documenting Hate: New American Nazis," in which Thompson interviewed professor Kathleen Belew, author of *Bring the War Home: The*

White Power Movement in Paramilitary America.[122]

KATHLEEN BELEW: One thing to understand is that throughout American history there's always a correlation between the aftermath of warfare and this kind of vigilante and revolutionary white power violence. So if you look, for instance, at the surges in Ku Klux Klan membership, they align more consistently with the return of veterans from combat and the aftermath of war than they do with anti-immigration, populism, economic hardship or any of the other factors that historians have typically used to explain them. Nationalist fervor, populist movements—those are all worse predictors than the aftermath of war.

A. C. THOMPSON: Postwar periods tend to correspond then with an upsurge in white power, white supremacist activity?

KATHLEEN BELEW: Always. Yes.

A. C. THOMPSON: Wow.

A. C. THOMPSON: Belew outlines a long history of military men who became key figures in the white power movement: George Lincoln Rockwell, World War II veteran and founder of the American Nazi Party; Richard Butler, World War II veteran and founder of the Aryan Nations; Louis Beam, Vietnam veteran and grand dragon of the KKK; Timothy McVeigh, Gulf War veteran and Oklahoma City bomber.

KATHLEEN BELEW: It's important to remember, too, that returning veterans that join this movement, and active-duty troops, we're talking about a tiny, not even statistically significant, percentage of veterans. But within this movement, those people who did serve are playing an enormously important role in instruction of weapons, in creating paramilitary activist mentality and training.

It's not hard to understand how wars feed off racism and feed back into it. William Halsey, who commanded the United States' naval forces in the South Pacific during WWII, thought of his mission as "Kill Japs, kill Japs, kill more Japs," and had vowed that when the war was over, the Japanese language would be spoken only in hell.[123] *LIFE* magazine showed a picture of a Japanese person burning to death and commented: "This is the only way."[124] Dr. Seuss, whose *The Butter Battle Book* depicts war as idiocy, and who thought child refugees should be saved, churned out racist war propaganda, including a cartoon depicting Germans and Japanese as insects being sprayed with insecticide by Uncle Sam,[125] and another with the caption "Slap that Jap! Bugswatters cost money!"[126]

A U.S. Army poll in 1943 found that roughly half of all GIs believed it would be necessary to kill every Japanese on earth.[127] War correspondent Edgar L. Jones wrote in the February 1946 *Atlantic Monthly,* "What kind of war do civilians suppose we fought anyway? We shot prisoners in cold blood, wiped out hospitals, strafed lifeboats, killed or mistreated enemy civilians, finished off the enemy wounded, tossed the dying into a hole with the dead, and in the Pacific boiled flesh off enemy skulls to make table ornaments for sweethearts, or carved their bones into letter openers."[128]

In 1942, with the assistance of the Census Bureau, the United States locked up 110,000 Japanese Americans and Japanese in various internment camps, primarily on the West Coast, where they were identified by numbers rather than names. This action, taken by President Roosevelt, was supported two years later by the U.S. Supreme Court.[129]

In 1943 off-duty white U.S. troops attacked Latinos and African Americans in Los Angeles' "zoot suit riots," stripping and beating them in the streets in a manner that would likely have made Hitler proud. The Los Angeles City Council, in a remarkable effort to blame the victims, responded by banning the style of clothing worn by Mexican immigrants called the zoot suit.[130]

When U.S. troops were crammed onto the Queen Mary in 1945 headed for the European war, blacks were kept apart from whites and stowed in the depths of the ship near the engine room, as far as possible from fresh air, in the same location in which blacks had been brought to America from Africa centuries before.[131]

African American soldiers who survived World War II could not legally return home to many parts of the United States if they had married white women overseas. Black soldiers who returned to the Southern United

States sometimes found themselves required to sit in the back of streetcars so that Nazi prisoners of war could sit in the front.[132] White soldiers who had married Asians were up against the same anti-miscegenation laws in 15 states.

Whatever the United States fought WWII for — and we've seen that it wasn't to save the Jews — it surely wasn't to oppose any sort of racist injustice. Nor was it to put an end to the imperial conquest of territory.

During World War II the U.S. Navy seized the small Hawaiian island of Koho'alawe for a weapons testing range and ordered its inhabitants to leave. The island has been devastated. In 1942, the U.S. Navy displaced Aleutian Islanders. President Harry Truman made up his mind that the 170 native inhabitants of Bikini Atoll had no right to their island in 1946. He had them evicted and dumped as refugees on other islands without means of support. In the coming years, the United States would remove 147 people from Enewetak Atoll and all the people on Lib Island. U.S. atomic and hydrogen bomb testing rendered various depopulated and still-populated islands uninhabitable, leading to further displacements. Up through the 1960s, the U.S. military displaced hundreds of people from Kwajalein Atoll. A super-densely populated ghetto was created on Ebeye.

Also during WWII, the United States evicted all native people, but not whites, from their homes in the Aleutian Islands of Alaska, and put them into camps lacking food, water, or basic hygiene. Ten percent of them died.[133] In Hawaii, the U.S. government declined to remove the workforce desired by wealthy, white plantation owners, but did impose martial law and lock up 2,000 people of Japanese descent.[134]

On Vieques, off Puerto Rico, the U.S. Navy displaced thousands of inhabitants between 1941 and 1947, announced plans to evict the remaining 8,000 in 1961, but was forced to back off and — in 2003 — to stop bombing the island. On nearby Culebra, the Navy displaced thousands between 1948 and 1950 and attempted to remove those remaining up through the 1970s.[135]

Beginning during World War II but continuing right through the

1950s, the U.S. military displaced a quarter million Okinawans, or half the population, from their land, forcing people into refugee camps and shipping thousands of them off to Bolivia — where land and money were promised but not delivered.[136]

In 1953, the United States made a deal with Denmark to remove 150 Inughuit people from Thule, Greenland, giving them four days to get out or face bulldozers. They are being denied the right to return.[137]

Between 1968 and 1973, the United States and Great Britain exiled all 1,500 to 2,000 inhabitants of Diego Garcia, rounding people up and forcing them onto boats while killing their dogs in a gas chamber and seizing possession of their entire homeland for the use of the U.S. military. They are being denied the right to return.[138]

When I say that WWII was not fought to save the Jews or to oppose racism or imperialism, I mean both that the U.S. government was not so motivated and that the U.S. public and U.S. recruits were not so motivated. The public actually had very little say in the matter. President Franklin Roosevelt had blocked passage of the Ludlow Amendment that would have put the decision to go to war to a public vote. As a result, the public got no vote and did not even have to be persuaded of a justification. As Jacques R. Pauwels puts it in *The Myth of the Good War*,

"A Gallup poll of September 1942 revealed that 40 per cent of Americans had no idea at all why their country was involved in the war, and that less than one-quarter of Americans had ever heard of the Atlantic Charter. Only 7 per cent were able to name one of the 'four freedoms.' For the American people, the war was not a crusade for freedom and democracy but simply, as *Fortune* magazine wrote, 'a painful necessity' — a deplorable but inescapable misfortune."[139]

6. The United States did not have to develop practices of genocide, ethnic cleansing, and concentration of people on reservations

Jeffrey Ostler is Beekman Professor of Northwest and Pacific History at the University of Oregon. His 2019 book, *Surviving Genocide: Native Nations and the United States from the American Revolution to Bleeding Kansas*, tells a complex and nuanced story of what overall and in many particular parts fits the UN definition of, as well as the popular conception of, genocide.[140]

In Ostler's account, the U.S. government had a clear policy from the start, not just in 1830, of moving Native Americans west of the Mississippi, and enacted that policy. Yet, between the 1780s and 1830, the population of Native Americans east of the Mississippi increased. The formalized and accelerated policy of removal put in place in 1830 was driven by greed for land and racist hatred, not by any humanitarian impulse to help native peoples survive by moving them to better locations where they wouldn't supposedly face inevitable demise. They would have survived better if left alone, rather than being forced on difficult journeys into already occupied lands and lands without the means to sustain them.

Greed for land — or what might be called *Lebensraum* — really seems to have been the dominant motivation. Smaller groups of Native Americans in the East not occupying highly desirable territory were allowed to remain, and in some cases have remained to this day. Others that put up too great a fight were allowed to remain for a time. Others that adopted European ways of agriculture and all the trappings of what was called "civilization" (including slavery) were allowed to remain until their land became too desirable. The supposed failure of native nations to become "civilized" seems to have no more basis in reality as a motivation for expelling them than does their supposed dying out. Neither does the supposed need to make peace among them. Nations fought each other as they were driven into each other's territories by the U.S. settler colonists.

The United States did sometimes make peace between warring nations, but only when it served some purpose, such as facilitating the displacement of more people into their land. The work of empire was not the work of brute force alone. Much "diplomacy" was needed. Treaties had to be secretly made with minority groups within native nations. Treaties had to be secretly worded to mean the opposite of what it appeared. Leaders had to be bribed or coaxed into meeting, and then captured or killed. Carrots and sticks had to be applied until people "voluntarily" chose to abandon their homes. Propaganda had to be developed to whitewash atrocities.

There was plenty of brute force. Ostler shows that U.S. officials developed the policy that "wars of extermination" were "not only necessary, but ethical and legal." Causes of decline among Native peoples included direct killing, other traumatizing violence prominently including rape, the burning of towns and crops, forcible deportation, and the intentional and non-intentional spreading of diseases and of alcoholism to weakened populations. Ostler writes that the most recent scholarship finds the devastation caused by European diseases resulted less from Native Americans' lack of immunity, and more from the weakness and starvation created by the violent destruction of their homes.

The American War for Independence (for the independence of one elite from another at the expense of native and enslaved people) involved more destructive assaults on Native Americans than had the preceding wars in which George Washington had acquired the name Town Destroyer. The outcome of the war was even worse news. Assaults on native peoples would come from the U.S. government, state governments, and ordinary people. Settlers would push the conflicts forward, and in settled parts of the East where Native Americans remained, individuals would steal their land, kill, and harass them. There were groups like the Quakers who dealt much less cruelly with indigenous people. There were ebbs and flows, and every nation has a different story. But fundamentally, the United States intended to get rid of Native Americans and got rid of many of them and took most of the land they lived on.

The Nazis, and pre-Nazi Germans, were impressed. The Nazis, as we have seen, resorted to mass murder when mass expulsion didn't work. But they had resorted to mass expulsion only after successfully driving large numbers of Jews to voluntarily flee. Those who didn't voluntarily flee the *Reich* could be driven into ghettos, starved, and made ill. They could be manipulated with false promises. They could be made to look like wild beasts. Non-Jews could be ordered to ride on Jews in the street as though they were horses, much as Native Americans in California could be made to eat from troughs like pigs.[141] Once a population had been dehumanized and demonized, riots and lynchings could be set loose upon them.

In a 2020 article about the removal of a Teddy Roosevelt statue in New York, Jon Schwarz wrote:

"In a 1928 speech, Adolf Hitler was already speaking approvingly of how Americans had 'gunned down the millions of Redskins to a few hundred thousands, and now keep the modest remnant under observation in a cage.' In 1941, Hitler told confidants of his plans to 'Europeanize' Russia. It wasn't just Germans who would do this, he said, but Scandinavians and Americans, 'all those who have a feeling for Europe.' The most important thing was to 'look upon the natives as Redskins.'"[142]

Alex Ross wrote in *The New Yorker* in 2018: "The Nazis idolized many aspects of American society: the cult of sport, Hollywood production values, the mythology of the frontier. From boyhood on, Hitler devoured the Westerns of the popular German novelist Karl May. In 1928, Hitler remarked, approvingly, that white settlers in America had 'gunned down the millions of redskins to a few hundred thousand.' When he spoke of *Lebensraum*, the German drive for 'living space' in Eastern Europe, he often had America in mind. . . . His two abiding obsessions were violent anti-Semitism and *Lebensraum*. As early as 1921, he spoke of confining Jews to concentration camps, and in 1923 he contemplated—and, for the moment, rejected—the idea of killing the entire Jewish population. The Holocaust was the result of a hideous syllogism: if Germany were to expand into the East, where millions of Jews lived, those Jews would have to vanish, because Germans could not coexist with them."[143]

That is the syllogism of Manifest Destiny. In 2011, Carroll P. Kakel published *The American West and the Nazi East: A Comparative and Interpretive Perspective*. Kakel finds that Hitler frequently compared his war for *Lebensraum* with nineteenth century wars waged by the United States. He believed his mission inevitably destined the Slavic and Jewish peoples, or "natives," to destruction along the lines of what had been done to the Native Americans. "A similar process will repeat itself for a second time as in the conquest of America," he said of what Nazis called "the German East" or "the Wild East," meaning the eastern provinces of Germany, Poland, the Baltic States, Ukraine, Belarus, and Russia.[144]

While there were numerous models of imperialist, colonialist, and genocidal campaigns by European nations that could inspire, and did inspire Hitler, it was the U.S. campaign against its natives that provided the clearest model, in Kakel's view, of what Hannah Arendt later called "continental imperialism," meaning expansion into lands adjacent to the imperial homeland, not across distant seas and continents. This sort of imperialism required extreme race hatred. Kakel finds virtually identical language to that of the Nazis in U.S. justifications of westward expansion for "living space" for "white" settlers "cleansing" the territory. The Nazis spoke of "massacres" and colonial "settlement" of the "Wild East" by "Aryans."

Friedrich Ratzel, the Social Darwinist who coined the term *Lebensraum*, published a book by that title in 1901, and promoted eastward settler-colonialism, citing the North American example, as well as the examples of southern Brazil, Tasmania, and New Zealand. Ratzel had traveled to the United States and was not only inspired by Frederick Jackson Turner's "frontier thesis" of U.S. history, but corresponded with Turner and U.S.

historian Alfred Thayer Mahan, as well as Halford Mackinder in Great Britain and Rudolf Kjellén in Sweden. *Lebensraum* was part of German imperialist thinking from the 1890s on, and in other languages part of Euro-American imperialist thinking for longer than that. Kakel finds striking parallels and roots in many U.S. authors, most notably Thomas Jefferson, whose idyllic, agrarian, genocidal vision of expansion shows up in Hitler.

Karl Haushofer, the son of a colleague of Ratzel, became a leading proponent of Lebensraum. In 1924, he visited Hitler in prison numerous times to educate him. The results show up in *Mein Kampf*. After 1933, Haushofer worked for the Nazis, devising pseudo-scientific slogans. Kakel explains:

"In *Mein Kampf*, Hitler invoked the American conquest of 'the West' as a model for Nazi continental territorial expansion in 'the East.' In his view, the Nazis must lead the German people 'from its present restricted living space to new land and soil'; this was necessary to free [Germany] from danger of vanishing from the earth or of serving others as a slave nation'. As an example, Hitler looked to 'the American Union which possesses its own [land] base in its own continent'; from this continental land base, he continued, 'comes the immense inner strength of this state'. As the 'Aryans' of the American continent cleared the 'wild soil' and made a 'stand against the natives', he noted, 'more and more [white] settlements sprang up in the land'. Germans should look to this historical experience for 'proof', since its population of 'largely Germanic elements mixed little with lower colored peoples.'"[145]

Hitler's understanding of the North American genocide was dependent both on its celebration in popular novels and on the racist theories of the eugenicists. In a speech on May 1, 1939, Hitler declared that the "Anglo-Saxon" was "nothing other than a branch of our German *Volk*," and that it was a "tiny Anglo-Saxon tribe [which] set out from Europe, conquered England, and later helped to develop the American continent."[146]

This racist theory had earlier been developed in the United States.

The "Aryans" had supposedly come from the Middle East to Germany and from there to England in the form of the Anglo-Saxons. America's Manifest Destiny was understood by many in the United States as thus being global in scope. In one vision, the Anglo-Saxons had come west to the New World, would move west to the Pacific (slaughtering/benefitting anyone in the way) and proceed west through the Pacific and Asia, coming full-circle to the supposed birthplace of the "race" near an area that some in Washington D.C. still obsess over to this day, a nation whose name derives from Aryan: Iran.[147]

A believer in this theory, Teddy Roosevelt, played dress-up in Brooks Brothers-designed uniforms not just as politics, but also to model a superior racial specimen eager for war. The same racist theories maintained that the process of warmaking and conquering was necessary for the health of the race. When the Aryans had reached the Pacific, the mission had to continue, not just to fulfill a prophecy or to open markets or to win elections, but so that the race might not degenerate in the dangerous luxury of peace. General Douglas MacArthur, years later, would attack WWI veterans with chemical weapons in the streets of Washington where they were demanding bonus pay[148], take part (according to the Congressional testimony of Smedley Butler) in planning a coup against Franklin Roosevelt[149], be removed as army chief of staff by President Roosevelt and sent off to the Philippines[150], allow the destruction of U.S. airplanes in the Philippines by the Japanese on the original "Pearl Harbor Day,"[151] effectively rule over Japan[152], help provoke and escalate a war in Korea[153], and get fired by President Truman. That MacArthur's father, General Arthur MacArthur, was himself, for a time, the ruler of the Philippines, and explained to a U.S. Senate committee:

"Many thousands of years ago our Aryan ancestors raised cattle, made a language, multiplied in numbers, and overflowed. By due process of expansion to the west they occupied Europe, developed arts and sciences, and created a great civilization, which, separating into innumerable currents, inundated and fertilized the globe with blood and ideas, the primary basis of all human progress, incidentally crossing the Atlantic and thereby reclaiming, populating, and civilizing a hemisphere. As to why the United States was in the Philippines , the broad actuating laws which underlie all these wonderful phenomena are still operating with relentless vigor and have recently forced one of the currents of this magnificent Aryan people across the Pacific — that is to say, back almost to the cradle of its race."[154]

In a 1910 lecture at Oxford, Teddy Roosevelt argued that recent white gains might be more temporary than those of the past, because modern Anglo-Saxons had allowed captive races to (partially) survive, whereas "all of the world achievements worth remembering are to be credited to the people of European descent . . . the intrusive people having either exterminated or driven out the conquered peoples." Roosevelt praised this as "ethnic conquest."[155]

Sven Lindqvist's 1992 book, *"Exterminate All the Brutes": One Man's Odyssey into the Heart of Darkness and the Origins of European Genocide*, after delicately pointing out the painfully obvious fact that no two events are identical, traces the Nazi genocide to some of its sources in the past exterminations that Teddy Roosevelt so admired. These include the German extermination of the Herero people in southwest Africa (Namibia) when Hitler was a child, as well as various exterminations of peoples by the British, French, and Americans, all justified by what Lindqvist says was a mainstream European belief in the early twentieth century that the inferior "races" of the world were doomed to go extinct, as predicted in 1871 in *The Descent of Man* by Charles Darwin.[156]

Europeans massacred non-European peoples, not just in North America, but also in the Congo, in South Africa, in the South Sea Islands, in Australia, in New Zealand, in Argentina. The Guanches of the Canary Islands were wiped out. The people of Tasmania were wiped out. The last Tasmanian died in 1876, and her skeleton is displayed in the Tasmanian Museum in Hobart. In 2020, statues of King Leopold of Belgium are being vandalized and removed. What he did to the people of the Congo is an acceptable topic of conversation today, even if its connection to a common pattern that includes Nazism is still taboo.

Carl Peters, German commissioner of an East Africa colony, brutally slaughtered the people who lived there. In 1897, he was brought to court in Berlin following his murder of a black mistress. "What was actually being condemned," writes Lindqvist, "was not the murder but the sexual relationship. The innumerable murders Peters had committed during the conquest of the German East Africa colony were considered quite natural and went unpunished."

The dominant model of overseas exterminations came from the British empire. Germany was not uninfluenced. "As lecturer in German at Glasgow (1890-1900)," writes Lindqvist, "Alexander Tille became familiar with British imperial ideology. He 'Germanized' it by linking Darwin's and Spencer's theories to Nietzsche's superman morality into a new 'evolutionary ethic'. . . . In Southwest Africa in 1904, the Germans demonstrated that they too had mastered an art that Americans, British, and other Europeans had exercised all through the nineteenth century — the art of hastening the extermination of a people of 'inferior culture'. . . . The Hereroes were not particularly warlike. Their leader, Samuel Maherero, over two decades had signed one treaty after another with the Germans and ceded large areas of land to avoid war. But just as the Americans did not feel themselves bound by their treaties with the Indians, equally, the Germans did not think that as a higher race they had any need to abide by treaties they made with the natives."

Hitler and his fellow Nazis referred to Ukrainian peoples as "Indians." On September 18, 1941, Hitler proposed, presumably jokingly, to send to Ukraine "kerchiefs, glass beads, and other things colonial peoples like."[157] He wasn't joking about devaluing those people. Hitler made frequent mention of the American West in the early months of the Soviet invasion, according to Alex Ross. "The Volga would be 'our Mississippi,' he said. Europe — and not America — will be the land of unlimited possibilities. Poland, Belarus, and Ukraine would be populated by pioneer farmer-soldier families. Autobahns would cut through fields of grain. The present occupants of those lands — tens of millions of them — would be starved to death."[158]

Leading Nazi Heinrich Himmler described eastern *Lebensraum* as "black earth that could be a paradise, a California of Europe." A German newspaper headline during the war read "Go East, Young Man!"[159]

How the Nazis treated prisoners of war depended on who those prisoners were. Only 3.5% of English and American prisoners of the Nazis died in captivity, compared to 57% of Soviet prisoners of war.[160]

On October 21, 1939, the *New York Times* reported that 2,000 Viennese Jews were on their way to a "reservation" near Lublin, in Poland. "They left here aboard special trains last night for their new and permanent homes in an area described as being similar to an American Indian reservation. It was understood that this was the first of a series of mass migrations that eventually may include all Austrian, or perhaps all German Jews."[161]

The reason that concentration camps were described as being similar to American Indian reservations was not that they were identical or served the same purpose, but that they were similar and were inspired by them. It was Spain, in Cuba, that had first used something it called concentration camps. The United States had condemned that outrage and then duplicated it in the Philippines. Britain and Germany had used similar camps under similar names in Africa.[162] Hitler was aware of all of these precedents.

Some 50 to 60 million indigenous people were killed — intentionally or by disease (or by intentional deprivation combined with disease) in the Americas. Some 10 to 12 million of those were north of Mexico. And this was over a comparatively very long period of time.[163]

Some 70 to 85 million people were killed worldwide in WWII. Of that total, 19 to 28 million deaths were due to disease or famine. Also of the same total, 50 to 55 million were civilians. Of the military deaths, some 5 million were prisoners of war. Still from within the same total, 20 to 27 million of the dead were from the Soviet Union, 15 to 20 million from China, 6.9 to 7.4 million from Germany, 5.9 to 6 million from Poland, 3 to 4 million from the Dutch East Indies, 2.5 to 3.1 million from Japan, 2.2 to 3 million from India, 1 to 1.7 million from Yugoslavia, 1 to 2.2 million from French Indochina, 0.6 million from France, 0.5 million from the Philippines, 0.5 to 0.8 million from Greece, 0.5 million from Romania, 0.4 to 0.5 million from Italy, 0.4 to 0.5 million from Korea, and 0.4 million from each of Hungary, the United Kingdom, and the United States.[164]

Some 6 million Jews were killed, many of them in death camps, by the Nazi Holocaust. An equal or even greater number of non-Jews were similarly killed in the camps or by execution or deliberate famine, including Roma, homosexuals, the handicapped, political opponents, religious dissenters, and others. Millions more were killed as part of a racially-motivated war, including Soviet and Polish civilians and prisoners of war.[165]

Some 5 to 8 million died of violence or disease (or deprivation combined with disease) in the Congo under the rule of Belgium, 1885 to 1908.[166]

Some 2.7 to 5.4 million died in the Democratic Republic of the Congo as a result of the Second Congo War (1998 to 2008).[167]

Some 1 million were killed by the 2003-begun war on Iraq.[168]

Some 34,000 to 110,000 people were murdered in the Herero and Namaqua genocide.[169]

Some 480,000 to 600,000 people were murdered in the Dzungar genocide.[170]

Some 3.8 million died violent war deaths in the U.S. war on Vietnam, not counting the dead in Laos or Cambodia.[171]

Some 0.4 to 1.5 million were killed or expelled in the Circassian genocide.[172]

Some 450,000 to 750,000 died in the Greek genocide.[173]

Some 1.5 million were killed in the Armenian genocide.[174]

Some 1.5 to 2 million died in the Cambodian genocide.[175]

Some 390,000 died, 380,000 of them on the Ethiopian side, when Mussolini's Italy attacked Ethiopia in 1935, yet not a single person at one of my events has ever asked "But what about Mussolini?"[176]

This is a small sampling. We could add other types of horrors to it.

As of this writing, some 0.7 million people, and rising fast, have died from coronavirus.

Those who die from poverty on a wealthy planet dwarf all of these numbers. According to UNICEF, 291 million children under age 15 died from preventable causes between 1990 and 2018.[177]

How do we compare such horrors?

I'm not sure why that has to be a difficult question, why the very question should offend us or threaten our sense of identity. We compare various horrors by looking at all the similarities and differences among them. Ignoring some atrocities does not help us better appreciate others.

While no two horrors are the same, some came before others and set precedents. Hitler believed the world's failure to seriously protest the Armenian genocide gave him license to commit his own.[178]

While genocide in Western Europe was unusual, genocide committed by Western Europeans was not. Prior to "settling" the United States, some of the early settlers had previously "settled" Ireland, where the British had paid rewards for Irish heads and body parts, just as they later would for Native American scalps.[179]

Hitler's war on the Slavic East was planned to violently kill and starve vast numbers of people. It did kill many more people than were killed in the Holocaust. The war, considering all sides, killed several times what the Holocaust killed, and killed mostly civilians. Most of the members of the militaries killed on all sides were low ranking draftees.

Why in current U.S. culture is the immediate go-to example of evil "Hitler" or "the Holocaust"? I mean, why isn't that one of dozens of possibilities? Why is it almost always the one and only example of ultimate evil? Why, for that matter, is there a U.S. Holocaust Museum featuring a Holocaust in Germany, and the more recently built Washington, D.C., museums of "The American Indian" and "African American History and Culture," but no museum of U.S. Genocide and Slavery? Is it "relativizing" something sacredly and supremely and separately evil to mention U.S. slavery in the same sentence with the Holocaust? Why? Isn't it exactly as nonsensical to claim that it is "relativizing" something sacredly and supremely and separately evil to mention the Holocaust in the same sentence with U.S. slavery? Aren't both things hideous enough to demand respect for irrational attitudes toward them?

Isn't the current U.S. practice of separating immigrant families and locking up children in cages, or the sheriff in Texas who recently set up what he called a concentration camp for Latinos and was pardoned for his crimes by President Donald Trump, combined with centuries of similar precedents reason enough to not always — perhaps just sometimes — reach over to Germany to find an example of evil public policy?

WWII had long precedents but occurred in just a handful of years. It is, as a chapter yet to come will establish, the worst thing that humanity has done to itself and the earth in any short period of time. Probably just the European or Pacific half of it alone would also meet that threshold. But WWII was committed by numerous nations and was much larger than the Holocaust.

How necessary was the developed Euro-American model of racist extermination to the development of Nazism and to the ability of the Nazis to justify their statements and attract more followers? Well, we can't run an experiment in which Europeans don't assault the globe, in order to see whether Germany still invades Poland. But I think the preceding pages have shown the connections between Nazism and what came before it to have been critical to its creation. The next chapter covers some additional things without which WWII could not have happened: raw materials, war supplies, and money.

7. The United States did not have to fund and arm the Nazis

The Nazis could not have waged war or genocide as they did without the collaboration of certain major U.S. corporations, bankers, lawyers, and plutocrats who saw Nazi Germany as one more place (or — it was hoped — an especially easy place) to make a buck, and who in some cases saw it as in their interest to promote Nazism. Nor could Nazism have advanced to the extent it did without the U.S. government that, to a significant extent, let U.S. corporate powers get away with their support for the Nazis.

IBM

IBM was the least of it, but is a good place for us to start. IBM's is a story well told in Edwin Black's 2001 book, *IBM and the Holocaust: The Strategic Alliance Between Nazi Germany and America's Most Powerful Corporation.* The Nazi Holocaust was greatly enhanced by IBM and its chairman Thomas J. Watson. The company knowingly and enthusiastically custom designed the censuses and punch-cards and proto-computers that were used to identify, organize, abuse, sterilize, transport, and exterminate people — including initially producing the numbers tattooed on victims' arms. IBM leased the machines to the Nazis, trained them in their use, and regularly serviced the machines, knowing perfectly well what they were being used for.[180]

The punch-card-machine technology had originally been developed by the creator of IBM for the U.S. Census Bureau, which was of course used by the government of Franklin Roosevelt to compile a list of all U.S. citizens with Japanese ancestry. Some of the technology was also used for Social

Security in the U.S. and developed at U.S. taxpayer expense. Now it was knowingly deployed in Germany by IBM to identify who should be worked to death at what sort of job and who should simply be murdered.

When it became illegal for IBM to oversee these operations from its New York office, it did so from its Swiss office. The drive was part belief in Nazism, part pure amoral capitalist greed. Watson appreciated the profits available through fascism, but his admiration went beyond that. IBM was a company where employees wore uniforms, sang songs, and were expected to exhibit total loyalty. Watson praised Benito Mussolini for, among other things, his emphasis on loyalty. IBM's punch card tabulators served numerous corporations in Nazi Germany and the Nazi government in numerous ways, including making the trains run on time, including the trains to the death camps.

In 1937, Watson was president of the International Chamber of Commerce which held its meeting in Berlin. Ninety-five U.S. business executives made the trip. There were 2,500 delegates. Watson brought with him a friendly message to the meeting from President Franklin Roosevelt. Watson had tea with Hitler prior to the meeting which took place in the German Opera House that doubled as the *Reichstag* with Nazi flags fluttering from the balconies. Hitler arrived, took his place in the royal box, and was saluted by the crowd, delegates rising to their feet and shouting "Heil" while reaching for the sky with their right arms. Herman Goering spoke, as did *Reichsbank* President Hjalmar Schacht. Josef and Magda Goebbels entertained the Watsons at the Opera House. The Schachts invited the Watsons and delegates to the Berlin Palace. The Goerings hosted a banquet for the Watsons at the Charlottenburg Palace.

Goebbels spent 4 million *Reichsmarks* on a Venetian Nights-themed party on Peacock Island where an elaborate dinner was served to over 3,000 guests. The crowning moment came when Hitler's medal was bestowed upon Watson: an eight-pointed gold-framed cross of white enamel embedded with German eagles and Nazi emblems held around the neck by a red, black, and white ribbon, plus a six-pointed star over the left breast. Watson left Berlin to meet with Mussolini in Italy. He planned the International Chamber of Commerce's next meeting for 1939 in Tokyo. Germany and Japan had signed the Anti-Comintern pact to oppose communism and the Soviet Union in 1936. In 1940, under pressure from the U.S. government, Watson gave Hitler the medal back, but he didn't stop working with or profiting from the Nazis.[181]

FORD

The *New York Times* on December 20, 1922, reported that Henry Ford was funding Hitler and that Hitler's office displayed a photograph of Henry Ford and a pile of books by Henry Ford.[182] Hitler was a fan of Ford's *The International Jew: The World's Foremost Problem*. Ford supported Hitler's cause, but his greatest loyalty may have been to amassing ever more money. According to his biographer David Lanier Lewis, Ford during the war "expressed the hope that neither the Allies nor the Axis would win," and suggested that the United States supply both sides "the tools to keep on fighting until they both collapse." Ford did his part, supplying both sides, even after the United States entered the war.[183]

For an account of the behavior of the Ford Motor company leading up to and during WWII, I recommend an article in the January 24, 2000, issue of *The Nation* magazine by Ken Silverstein.[184] Here are a few excerpts:

"When Ford was considering a run for the presidency . . . ," Hitler told the *Chicago Tribune*, 'I wish that I could send some of my shock troops to Chicago and other big American cities to help.'

". . . In *Mein Kampf*, written two years later, Hitler singled Ford out for praise. . . . In 1938, long after the vicious character of Hitler's government had become clear, Ford accepted the Grand Cross of the German Eagle, the Nazi regime's highest honor for foreigners.

". . . Ford Motor set up shop in Germany in 1925, . . . and, . . . the value of the German subsidiary more than doubled during the course of the war. . . . Ford eagerly collaborated with the Nazis, which greatly enhanced its business prospects and at the same time helped Hitler prepare for war (and after the 1939 invasion of Poland, conduct it). In the mid-thirties, Dearborn helped boost German Ford's profits by placing orders with the Cologne plant for direct delivery to Ford plants in Latin America and Japan. In 1936, . . . the Nazi government blocked the German subsidiary from buying needed raw materials. Ford headquarters in Dearborn responded — just as the Nazis hoped it would — by shipping rubber and other materials to Cologne.

". . . Ford began producing vehicles of a strictly military nature for the Reich even before the war began. By 1941 Ford of Germany had stopped manufacturing passenger vehicles and was devoting its entire production capacity to military trucks. . . . Of the 350,000 trucks used by the motorized German Army as of 1942, roughly one-third were Ford-made. . . . Ford's cooperation with the Nazis continued until at least August 1942 — eight months after the United States entered the war — through its properties in Vichy France.

". . . While Ford Motor enthusiastically worked for the Reich, the company initially resisted calls from President Roosevelt and British Prime Minister Churchill to increase war production for the Allies.

". . . In May of 1942, the Superior Court of Cologne finally put Ford Werke in "trusteeship" . . . . Dearborn maintained its 52 percent share through the duration of the war. Ford Werke even set aside dividend payments due to Dearborn, which were paid after the war. . . . By 1943 half of Ford Werke's work force comprised foreign captives. . . . Ford's worker-inmates toiled for twelve hours a day with a fifteen-minute break. They were given 200 grams of bread and coffee for breakfast, no lunch, and a dinner of spinach and three potatoes or soup made of turnip leaves. . . . An account by Robert Schmidt, the man appointed to run Ford Werke in 1939, states that the company used forced laborers even before the Nazis put the plant in trusteeship. . . . Robert Schmidt so successfully converted the plant to a war footing that the Nazi regime gave him the title of *Wehrwirtschaftsführer*, or Military Economic Leader.

". . . Before its fall, the Nazi regime had given Ford Werke about $104,000 in compensation for damages caused by Allied bombings (Ford also got money for bombing damages from the Vichy government). Dearborn was not satisfied with that amount. In 1965 Ford went before the Foreign Claims Settlement Commission of the US to ask for an additional $7 million. (During the hearings, commission attorney Zvonko Rode pointed to the embarrassing fact — which Ford's attorney did not dispute — that most of the manufactured products destroyed during the bombings had been intended for the use of the Nazi armed forces.) In the end, the commission awarded the company $1.1 million."

This outrageous conduct by Ford Motor before, during, and after the war, combined with the antisemitism and Nazism of Henry Ford, and with the fact that Ford's major factory in Cologne, Germany, survived the war largely unscathed despite heavy bombing of that city, has long fueled speculation that the allies chose not to bomb the Ford facility. As far as I know, this is only speculation and likely false. According to Michael Parenti, who is apparently mistaken, "Pilots were given instructions not to hit factories in Germany that were owned by U.S. firms. Thus Cologne was almost leveled by Allied bombing but its Ford plant, providing military equipment for the Nazi army, was untouched; indeed, German civilians began using the plant as an air raid shelter."[185] The only damage done to the Ford Werke plant, other authors falsely assert, was done by the retreating German military. Otherwise, it was "undamaged by bombs or shell fire," according to a March 11, 1945 survey.[186] But Jason Weixelbaum persuasively documents a different account.[187]

Weixelbaum identifies British and U.S. military planning and bombing-mission reports that establish that the British prioritized the Ford plant as a target (though the British were never much for daytime or precision bombing), that the U.S. deprioritized it due to reports of its reduced relevance, that the U.S. repeatedly attempted to bomb it but encountered smoke and bad weather, that the U.S. in fact did bomb it but tragically hit the barracks of forced laborers rather than the production facilities, that the U.S. intentionally bombed other Ford facilities in Europe, and that the U.S. strategized in secret documents as to how and why to bomb the Ford plant but never — so far as we know — how to avoid bombing it or feign bombing it. It seems quite likely that the Ford factory in Cologne survived by luck, not by intention. This rather tangential question should not, I think, distract us from Ford's well-established complicity with Nazism.

DUPONT AND GENERAL MOTORS

The DuPonts were one of the wealthiest families in the United States. Irénée Dupont was President of the DuPont Company and head of the DuPont trust. He was a believer in eugenics and white supremacy and a funder of rightwing groups. DuPont had profited massively from WWI and worked to prevent disarmament agreements in the years that followed. It would profit from both sides of WWII. In his 1983 book, *Trading With the Enemy*, Charles Higham wrote:

"Irénée du Pont was the most imposing and powerful member of the clan. He was obsessed with Hitler's principles. He keenly followed the career of the future Führer in the 1920s, and on September 7, 1926, in a speech to the American Chemical Society, he advocated a race of supermen, to be achieved by injecting special drugs into them in boyhood to make their characters to order. He insisted his men reach physical standards equivalent to that of a Marine and have blood as pure as that in the veins of the Vikings. Despite the fact that he had Jewish blood in his own veins, his anti-Semitism matched that of Hitler."[188]

Dupont had a controlling interest in General Motors (GM). In 1933, the DuPonts and GM started funding U.S. fascist groups, such as the American Liberty League, Clark's Crusaders, and the Black Legion — the murderous KKK splinter group that sought to prevent union organizing and which Malcolm X believed murdered his father. GM poured millions into plants of the German chemical conglomerate IG Farben and its own Opel plants in Germany, and funded the Nazi Party before it came to power.[189] In 1937, GM signed a statement of commitment to the Nazi cause.[190] GM manufactured trucks, armored cars, and tanks for the Nazis. The head of its European operations, James D. Mooney, was awarded the Order of the Golden Eagle by Hitler.[191] According to the 2000 book by a group of German historians, *Working for the Enemy: Ford, General Motors and Forced Labor in Germany During the Second World War*, GM and Ford produced "most of the trucks ordered by the German armed forces" between 1933 and 1939, and Opel began making war-plane parts and engines in the first months of the war.[192]

DuPont signed agreements with IG Farben that, according to Nadan Feldman, "gave IG Farben critical knowledge for war production, enabling Nazi Germany to start the war. . . . Amazingly," he added, "Dupont continued [ties] ... even after Germany declared war on the United States in December 1941." DuPont also had stakes in two companies (also part of IG Farben) responsible for making the gas Zyklon B, which was used to murder over a million people.[193] DuPont also profited from investments and patents in Nazi-occupied France.[194]

In December of 1999, the German government and numerous companies that had used slave and forced labor during WWII — including Bayer, BMW, Volkswagen and Daimler-Chrysler —established a $5.1 billion fund to pay victims. Opel (GM) was one of the companies that announced it would contribute to the fund.[195]

It's possible that General Motors would have conducted itself toward the Nazis approximately as it did, purely from a profit motive, if that motive can be separated cleanly from ideological support for Nazism (an ideology dedicated to, among other things, corporate profit). In a 2018 op-ed in the *Washington Post*, Jason Weixelbaum provides a summary of GM's conduct in which its choices are all driven by financial greed.[196]

In 1928, GM bought Opel, the largest carmaker in Europe, going into $42 million in debt. Then the Nazis prevented the transfer of profits out of Germany. GM was interested in the Nazi Volkswagen project to create an inexpensive car, but failed to win that contract. But Opel took on Nazi military contracts, though it couldn't transfer the profits to GM, choosing instead to invest its profits in more Nazi military production. In 1937, GM chief Alfred Sloan visited Germany and decided that GM should sell all or part of Opel to German nationals and cut its losses. Yet, in 1938, Sloan reversed that decision after meeting with Nazi officials who reportedly persuaded him that GM's investment would be profitable to it in the long-run. Opel quickly took on larger Nazi military contracts. GM retained ownership of Opel right through the war, after which it found its factories bombed and its bank accounts full of worthless currency. It did, however, pick up a $10 million bailout from the U.S. government to compensate for allied bombings of the factories of Opel, a leading Nazi military supplier. Of course, the fact that GM made a risky and losing investment in the Nazis raises the possibility that part of its motivation was attraction to the Nazi cause. Regardless of motivation, what GM did to support Nazism was not required by any law of physics; it was a human choice, and a terrible one.

The most pro-GM account of its conduct with the Nazis, that of Henry Ashby Turner, Jr., who was chosen by GM to research its past, does not dispute that GM chose to keep ownership of Opel and build Nazi weaponry. It merely claims that GM was obliged to do so, out of its responsibility to maximize profits for share-holders.[197]

IG FARBEN

IG Farben at the time of WWII was the biggest chemical manufacturing enterprise on earth. It had U.S. directors. It had Wall Street funding. It had U.S. affiliates. Among the directors of American IG Farben were Edsel Ford, C.E. Mitchell of the Federal Reserve Bank of New York, and Walter Teagle of Standard Oil, who was also the director of the Federal Reserve Bank of New York and the president of Franklin Roosevelt's Georgia Warm Springs Foundation.[198]

In the view of a report presented to Congress by the U.S. War Department in 1945, "Without I. G.'s immense productive facilities, its intense research, and vast international affiliations, Germany's prosecution of the war would have been unthinkable and impossible; Farben not only directed its energies toward arming Germany, but concentrated on weakening her intended victims."[199]

One example of how this worked is the case of synthetic rubber. It was badly desired by all sides. IG Farben worked with Standard Oil of New Jersey to block any other U.S. companies from researching synthetic rubber development.[200] This left the Allies so far behind the Nazis in rubber, that the United States took numerous steps that included belatedly researching synthetic rubber, pursuing more petroleum, instituting recycling programs, lowering speed limits, creating new rubber plantations in Central America, and concocting a plan to invade Brazil called "Plan Rubber." The invasion didn't happen, because the President of Brazil was persuaded that the Allies would win the war. Instead of a military invasion of the coast of Brazil, an army of workers invaded the rainforests of the Amazon to extract as much rubber as possible.[201]

In Jason Weixelbaum's account of Peter Hayes' *Industry and Ideology*, which Weixelbaum characterizes as being written from a corporate-friendly perspective, and for which Hayes received undefined "ancillary support" from IG Farben, we nonetheless read that IG Farben "constructed the notorious Auschwitz concentration camp, . . . shared a cartel with other large American chemical producers, managed American subsidiaries, and retained the legal advice of American corporate lawyer and policymaker, John Foster Dulles, . . . [while it also] benefitted greatly from its relationship with the Nazis: it enjoyed low labor overhead, courtesy of 'leased' slave labor, monopolistic protection, huge government contracts, and opportunities to expand into conquered nations."[202] Who needs non-corporate-friendly perspectives?

ITT

The U.S.-based International Telephone and Telegraph Corporation (ITT) funded the Gestapo and had the head of the Gestapo's counterintelligence service on its board. Founder Sosthenes Behn was friends with leading Nazi Hermann Göring. ITT acquired 28% of the Focke-Wulf company and improved the bombers that would later be fueled with the help of other U.S. companies to bomb London. After the United States entered the war, ITT entered into a partnership with the Nazi government in order to avoid being acquired by it.[203]

ITT manufactured for the German military, while the U.S. military was at war with it, the following products: "switchboards, telephones, alarm gongs, buoys, air raid warning devices, radar equipment," and fuses for artillery shells, as well as ingredients for rocket bombs, radio equipment, and various other tools of war without which the German air force could not have functioned.[204]

THE BANKS

Loans provided by U.S. and international banks were as critical to the rise of the Nazis as any punch card or fuel additive. Without massive amounts of money, no war can be prepared for. Central to funding the Nazis with U.S. and British funds was the Bank for International Settlements (BIS) which had been set up to handle German reparations payments for WWI, but which was effectively controlled by the Nazi Party and its international allies. Hermann Schmitz of IG Farben, an associate of Allen Dulles of the OSS, was one of five directors of BIS who would be charged with war crimes. BIS laundered hundreds of millions of dollars in looted gold.[205] The BIS had a British director and the approval of the British government, even while Britain and Germany were at war, even though BIS was chiefly funneling money to Hitler.[206]

Chase National Bank and National City Bank, among others, also played major roles and had clearly been misnamed. They were U.S. banks that helped fund the Nazis.[207] Chase Manhattan's French branch, during the war, froze the accounts of Jews and worked with German officials to finance war production for the Nazi Army.[208]

As critical to all of this as bankers were lawyers. Law firms like Sullivan and Cromwell, which employed Allen Dulles and John Foster Dulles, helped keep U.S. investments in Nazi Germany. Many top Nazis were longtime friends of the Dulles brothers, for whom the real enemy was always the Soviet Union.[209] Jason Weixelbaum reviews Nancy Lisagor's and Frank Lipsius' 1988 book, *The Untold Story of Sullivan and Cromwell*, finding that "under the direction of John Foster Dulles from the early 1920s through the end of World War II, the firm helped create a network of holding companies, corporate managers, and lawyers, to facilitate corporate development within Germany."[210] Weixelbaum continues:

"Although Lisagor and Lipsius meant to simply produce a history of the firm from its inception to the 1980s, this work inadvertently presents a significant challenge to historians who would argue that American corporate cooperation with the Third Reich was uncoordinated and small scale. The authors demonstrate that Sullivan & Cromwell specialized in both maintaining managerial control and obscuring overseas corporate operations in providing legal representation for nearly all the businesses discussed here: Ford, GM, IBM, the BIS, IG Farben, ITT, Chase Bank, JP Morgan, and Standard Oil. Additionally, the authors show that influential policymakers, John Foster Dulles and Allen Dulles on the American side, and Heinrich Albert and Gerhard Westrick on the German side, were intimately involved in these business relationships."[211]

THE BROADER PICTURE

The above is a small sample of the conduct of some 150 U.S. companies that did business with Nazi Germany, often right through the war, often in blatant violation of laws that were often not enforced. Other U.S. companies that worked with Nazi Germany included Coca Cola, Union Carbide, Westinghouse, General Electric, Goodrich, Singer, Eastman Kodak, Texaco, Alcoa, and Chrysler. At the time that the United States entered the war, U.S. companies had some $475 million invested in Hitler's

Third Reich.[212]

The U.S. ambassador to Germany from 1933 to 1937 was William Dodd, a man with many flaws, but generally too good for the job and far more decent and responsible than the norm. Among the many dangers he tried to alert the U.S. government to was that of U.S. corporations and plutocrats funding Nazism in Germany and Nazi-like groups in the United States. In a letter to President Franklin Roosevelt on October 19, 1936, Dodd wrote that over 100 U.S. corporations had subsidiaries or cooperative understandings with Germany. "The DuPonts have three allies in Germany that are aiding in the armaments business. Their chief ally is the I. G. Farben Company, a part of the government which gives 200,000 marks a year to one propaganda organization operating on American opinion. Standard Oil Company (New York sub-company) sent $2,000,000 here in December 1933 and has made $500,000 a year helping Germans make Ersatz gas for war purposes . . . . The International Harvester Company president told me their business here rose 33% a year (arms manufacture, I believe)."[213]

The U.S. government knew what was going on but did not make any all-out effort to stop it. The same companies that were central to the workings of Nazi Germany were central to the workings of the United States, politically powerful, and too big to fail. These companies' owners praised the low-wage non-union workers found in Nazi Germany and fascist Italy. They did their part to promote and to profit from those states. They met in Switzerland or Sweden while the war raged. They got rich and rooted for one side or the other or neither. They were little disturbed, even tacitly supported, by the U.S. government,[214] even as President Franklin Roosevelt warned of a "European model" and "fascist" concentration of wealth and power in corporate monopolies and cartels, brought about by the Harding-Coolidge-Hoover era.[215] (That concentration was indeed extreme, but did not approach current levels as I write this in 2020.)[216]

"The alliance between American capitalism and Nazi Germany," says Nadan Feldman, "helped Hitler implement an armaments program that was unprecedented at the time, and to begin the world war. . . . [W]ithout the mobilization of corporate America for Nazi Germany, it is very doubtful whether Hitler could have started the war, doubtful whether he would have succeeded in rehabilitating the German economy."[217] Of course, he could have rehabilitated the German economy without the war, even if neither the war nor the rehabilitation would have been possible without U.S. investment.

Albert Speer, Hitler's architect and wartime armaments minister said that without synthetic fuels that were made available by U.S. companies, Hitler "would never have considered invading Poland."[218]

U.S. businesses, through the Lend Lease program and otherwise, invested even more heavily in Britain. Germany eventually shut smaller, less-connected foreign businesses out of Germany in favor of a Germany-first approach. In addition, Germany presented U.S. businesses with competition in Latin America. When the United States went to war with Germany, that wasn't completely at odds with U.S. business interests. Many of them would get rich providing for the U.S. military. No war is ever at odds with the (short-sighted) interests of war profiteers. France and Britain also armed Germany.[219] The United States also armed Japan.[220] In Jason Weixelbaum's account of Neil Forbes' *Doing Business With the Nazis*, Forbes presents an openly pro-business account, and blames "self-interest and political naiveté, rather than capriciousness" for the collaboration of British corporations with the Nazis. But Forbes does not dispute that they so collaborated — which action, rather than capriciousness, is the serious offense at issue here.[221]

8. The United States did not have to prioritize opposing the Soviet Union

Hitler was clearly preparing for war long before he started it. Hitler remilitarized the Rhineland, annexed Austria, and threatened Czechoslovakia. High-ranking officials in the German military and "intelligence" plotted a coup. But Hitler gained popularity with every step he took, and the lack of any sort of opposition from Britain or France surprised and demoralized the coup plotters. The British government was aware of the coup plots and was aware of the plans for war, yet chose not to support political opponents of the Nazis, not to support the coup plotters, not to enter the war, not to threaten to enter the war, not to blockade Germany, not to get serious about ceasing to arm and supply Germany, not to uphold the Kellogg-Briand Pact through court proceedings like those that would happen after the war in Nuremberg but could have happened before the war (at least with defendants *in absentia*) over Italy's attack on Ethiopia or Germany's attack on Czechoslovakia, not to demand that the United States join the League of Nations, not to demand that the League of Nations act, not to propagandize the German public in support of nonviolent resistance, not to evacuate those threatened with genocide, not to propose a global peace conference or the creation of the United Nations, and not to pay any attention to what the Soviet Union was saying.

The Soviet Union was proposing a pact against Germany, an agreement with England and France to act together if attacked. England and France were not even slightly interested. The Soviet Union tried this approach for years and even joined the League of Nations. Even Poland was uninterested. The Soviet Union was the only nation that proposed to go in and fight for Czechoslovakia if Germany attacked it, but Poland — which ought to have known it was next in line for a Nazi assault — denied the Soviets passage to reach Czechoslovakia. Poland, later also invaded by the Soviet Union, may have feared that Soviet troops would not pass through it but occupy it. While Winston Churchill seems to have been almost eager for a war with Germany, Neville Chamberlain not only refused to cooperate with the Soviet Union or to take any violent or nonviolent step on behalf of Czechoslovakia, but actually demanded that Czechoslovakia not resist, and actually handed Czechoslovakian assets in England over to the Nazis. Chamberlain seems to have been on the side of the Nazis beyond what would have made sense in the cause of peace, a cause that the business interests he usually acted on behalf of did not completely share. For his part, Churchill was such an admirer of fascism that historians suspect him of later contemplating installing the Nazi-sympathizing Duke of Windsor as a fascist ruler in England, but Churchill's more dominant inclination for decades seems to have been for war over peace.

The position of most of the British government from 1919 until the rise of Hitler and beyond was fairly consistent support for the development of a rightwing government in Germany. Anything that could be done to keep communists and leftists out of power in Germany was supported. Former British Prime Minister and Leader of the Liberal Party David Lloyd George on September 22, 1933, remarked: "I know there have been horrible atrocities in Germany and we all deplore and condemn them. But a country passing through a revolution is always liable to ghastly episodes owing to the administration of justice being seized here and there by an infuriated rebel." If the Allied powers overthrew Nazism, Lloyd George warned, "extreme communism" would take its place. "Surely that cannot be our objective," he remarked.[222]

So, that was the trouble with Nazism: a few bad apples! One must be understanding during times of revolution. And, besides, the British were tired of war after WWI. But the funny thing is that immediately upon the conclusion of WWI, when nobody could have possibly been more tired of war due to WWI, a revolution happened — one with its share of bad apples that could have been magnanimously tolerated: the revolution in Russia. When the Russian revolution happened, the United States, Britain, France, and allies sent first funding in 1917, and then troops in 1918, into Russia to support the anti-revolutionary side of the war. Through 1920 these understanding and peace-loving nations fought in Russia in a failed effort to overthrow the Russian revolutionary government. While this war rarely makes it into U.S. text books, Russians tend to remember it as the beginning of over a century of opposition and insistent enmity from the United States and Western Europe, the alliance during WWII notwithstanding.

In 1932, Cardinal Pacelli, who in 1939 would become Pope Pius XII, wrote a letter to the *Zentrum* or Center Party, the third largest political party in Germany. The Cardinal was worried about the possible rise of communism in Germany, and advised the Center Party to help make Hitler chancellor. From then on the *Zentrum* supported Hitler.[223]

President Herbert Hoover, who lost Russian oil holdings to the Russian revolution, believed that the Soviet Union needed to be crushed.[224]

The Duke of Windsor, who was King of England in 1936 until he abdicated to marry the scandalously previously married Wallis Simpson from Baltimore, had tea with Hitler at Hitler's Bavarian mountain retreat in 1937. The Duke and Duchess toured German factories that were manufacturing weapons in preparation for WWII, and "inspected" Nazi troops. They dined with Goebbels, Göring, Speer, and Foreign Minister Joachim von Ribbentrop. In 1966, the Duke recalled that, "[Hitler] made me realize that Red Russia was the only enemy, and that Great Britain and all of Europe had an interest in encouraging Germany to march against the east and to crush communism once and for all . . . . I thought that we ourselves would be able to watch as the Nazis and the Reds would fight each other."[225]

Is "appeasement" the proper denunciation for people so enthused about becoming spectators to mass slaughter?[226]

There's a dirty little secret hiding in WWII, a war so dirty that you wouldn't think it could have a dirty little secret, but it's this: the top enemy of the West before, during, and after the war was the Russian communist menace. What Chamberlain was after in Munich was not only peace between Germany and England, but also war between Germany and the Soviet Union. It was a longstanding goal, a plausible goal, and a goal that was in fact eventually achieved. The Soviets tried to make a pact with Britain and France but were turned away. Stalin wanted Soviet troops in Poland, which Britain and France (and Poland) would not accept. So, the Soviet Union signed a non-aggression pact with Germany, not an alliance to join in any war with Germany, but an agreement not to attack each other, and an agreement to divide up Eastern Europe. But, of course, Germany didn't mean it. Hitler simply wanted to be left alone to attack Poland. And so he was. Meanwhile, the Soviets sought to create a buffer and expand their own empire by attacking the Baltic states, Finland, and Poland.

The Western dream of bringing down the Russian communists, and using German lives to do it, seemed ever closer. From September of 1939 to May of 1940, France and England were officially at war with Germany, but not actually waging much war. The period is known to historians as "the Phoney War." In fact, Britain and France were waiting for Germany to attack the Soviet Union, which it did, but only after attacking Denmark, Norway, Holland, Belgium, France, and England. Germany fought WWII on two fronts, the western and the eastern, but mostly the eastern. Some 80% of German casualties were on the eastern front. The Russians lost, according to Russia's calculations, 27 million lives.[227] The communist menace, however, survived.

When Germany invaded the Soviet Union in 1941, U.S. Senator Robert Taft articulated a view held across the political spectrum and by civilians and officials in the U.S. military when he said that Joseph Stalin was "the most ruthless dictator in the world," and claimed that "the victory of communism . . . would be far more dangerous than the victory of fascism."[228]

Senator Harry S Truman took what might be called a balanced perspective, though not so balanced between life and death: "If we see that Germany is winning we ought to help Russia and if Russia is winning we ought to help Germany, and that way let them kill as many as possible, although I don't want to see Hitler victorious under any circumstances."[229]

In line with Truman's view, when Germany moved swiftly into the Soviet Union, President Roosevelt proposed sending aid to the Soviet Union, for which proposal he received vicious condemnation from those on the right in U.S. politics, and resistance from within the U.S. government.[230] The United States promised aid to the Soviets, but three-quarters of it — at least at this stage — didn't arrive.[231] The Soviets were doing more damage to the Nazi military than all other nations combined, but were struggling in the effort. In lieu of promised aid, the Soviet Union asked for approval to keep, after the war, the territories it had seized in Eastern Europe. Britain urged the United States to agree, but the United States, at this point, refused.[232]

In lieu of promised aid or territorial concessions, Stalin made a third request of the British in September 1941. It was this: fight the damn war! Stalin wanted a second front opened against the Nazis in the west, a British invasion of France, or alternatively British troops sent to assist in the east. The Soviets were denied any such assistance, and interpreted this refusal as a desire to see them weakened. And weakened they were; yet they prevailed. In the fall of 1941 and the following winter, the Soviet Army turned the tide against the Nazis outside of Moscow. The German defeat began before the United States had even entered the war, and before any western invasion of France.[233]

That invasion was a long, long time in coming. In May of 1942 Soviet Minister of Foreign Affairs Vyacheslav Molotov met with Roosevelt in Washington, and they announced plans for the opening up of a western front that summer. But it was not to be. Churchill persuaded Roosevelt to instead invade North Africa and the Middle East where the Nazis were threatening British colonial and oil interests.

Remarkably, however, in the summer of 1942, the Soviet struggle against the Nazis received such favorable media coverage in the United States, that a strong plurality favored a U.S. and British opening of a second front immediately. U.S. cars carried bumper stickers reading "Second Front

Now." But the U.S. and British governments ignored the demand. The Soviets, meanwhile, kept pushing the Nazis back.[234]

If you learned about WWII from Hollywood movies and popular U.S. culture, you would have no idea that the vast bulk of the fighting against the Nazis was done by the Soviets, that if the war had any top victor it was certainly the Soviet Union. Nor would you know that huge numbers of Jews survived because they migrated east within the Soviet Union prior to WWII or escaped east within the Soviet Union as the Nazis invaded. Through 1943, at enormous cost to both sides, the Russians pushed the Germans back toward Germany, still without serious help from the west. In November of 1943, in Tehran, Roosevelt and Churchill promised Stalin an invasion of France the following spring, and Stalin promised to fight Japan as soon as Germany was defeated. Yet, it was not until June 6, 1944, that Allied troops landed at Normandy. By that point, the Soviets had occupied much of Central Europe. The United States and Britain had been happy for the Soviets to do most of the killing and dying for years, but did not want the Soviets arriving in Berlin and declaring victory alone.

The three nations agreed that all surrenders must be total and must be made to all three of them together. However, in Italy, Greece, France, and elsewhere the United States and Britain cut Russia out almost completely, banned communists, shut out leftist resisters to the Nazis, and re-imposed rightwing governments that the Italians, for example, called "fascism without Mussolini."[235] After the war, into the 1950s, the United States, in "Operation Gladio," would "leave behind" spies and terrorists and saboteurs in various European countries to fend off any communist influence.

Originally scheduled for the first day of Roosevelt's and Churchill's meeting with Stalin in Yalta, the U.S. and British bombed the city of Dresden flat, destroying its buildings and its artwork and its civilian population, apparently as a means of threatening Russia.[236] The United States then developed and used on Japanese cities nuclear bombs, a decision driven, in part, by the desire to see Japan surrender to the United States alone, without the Soviet Union, and by the desire to threaten the Soviet Union.[237]

Immediately upon German surrender, Winston Churchill proposed using Nazi troops together with allied troops to attack the Soviet Union, the nation that had just done the bulk of the work of defeating the Nazis.[238] This was not an off-the-cuff proposal. The U.S. and British had sought and achieved partial German surrenders, had kept German troops armed and ready, and had debriefed German commanders on lessons learned from their failure against the Russians. Attacking the Russians sooner rather than later was a view advocated by General George Patton, and by Hitler's replacement Admiral Karl Donitz, not to mention Allen Dulles and the OSS. Dulles made a separate peace with Germany in Italy to cut out the Russians, and began sabotaging democracy in Europe immediately and empowering former Nazis in Germany, as well as importing them into the U.S. military to focus on war against Russia.[239]

When U.S. and Soviet troops first met in Germany, they hadn't been told they were at war with each other yet. But in the mind of Winston Churchill they were. Unable to launch a hot war, he and Truman and others launched a cold one. The United States worked to make sure that West German companies would rebuild quickly but not pay war reparations owed to the Soviet Union. While the Soviets were willing to withdraw from countries like Finland, their demand for a buffer between Russia and Europe hardened as the Cold War grew and came to include the oxymoronic "nuclear diplomacy." The Cold War was a regrettable development, but could have been much worse. While it was the sole possessor of nuclear weapons, the U.S. government, led by Truman, drew up plans for an aggressive nuclear war on the Soviet Union, and began mass-producing and stockpiling nuclear weapons and B-29s to deliver them. Before the 300 desired nuclear bombs were ready, U.S. scientists secretly gave bomb secrets to the Soviet Union — a move that may have accomplished just what the scientists said they intended, the replacement of mass slaughter with a standoff.[240] Scientists today know much more about the likely results of dropping 300 nuclear bombs, which include a worldwide nuclear winter and mass starvation for humanity.

The hostility, the nuclear weapons, the war preparations, the troops in Germany, are all still there, and now with weapons in Eastern Europe right up to the border of Russia. World War II was an incredibly destructive force, yet despite the role played in it by the Soviet Union it did little or no lasting damage to anti-Soviet sentiment in Washington. The later demise of the Soviet Union and end of communism had a similarly negligible effect on ingrained and profitable hostility toward Russia.

9. The United States did not have to develop the pledge of allegiance and the one-arm salute

If you do a web search for images of "Bellamy salute" you find countless black-and-white photographs of U.S. children and adults with their right arms raised stiffly out in front of them in what will strike most people as a Nazi salute. From the early 1890s through 1942 the United States used the Bellamy salute to accompany the words written by Francis Bellamy and known as the Pledge of Allegiance. In 1942, the U.S. Congress instructed Americans to instead place their hands over their hearts when swearing allegiance to a flag, so as not to be mistaken for Nazis.[241]

Jacques-Louis David's 1784 painting *The Oath of the Horatii* is believed to have begun the fashion that lasted for centuries of depicting ancient Romans as making a gesture very similar to the Bellamy or Nazi salute.[242]

A U.S. stage production of *Ben Hur*, and a 1907 film version of the same, made use of the gesture. Those using it in U.S. dramatic productions of that period would have been aware of both the Bellamy salute and the tradition of depicting a "Roman salute" in neoclassical art. As far as we know, the "Roman salute" was never actually used by the ancient Romans.

Of course, it's a very simple salute, not hard to think up; there are only so many things humans can do with their arms. But when Italian fascists picked it up, it had neither survived from ancient Rome nor been newly invented. It had been seen in *Ben Hur*, and in several Italian films set in ancient times, including *Cabiria* (1914), written by Gabriele D'Annunzio.

From 1919 to 1920 D'Annunzio made himself the dictator of something called the Italian Regency of Carnaro, which was the size of one small city. He instituted many practices that Mussolini would soon appropriate, including the corporate state, public rituals, black-shirted thugs, balcony speeches, and the "Roman salute," which he would have seen in *Cabiria.*

By 1923, Nazis had picked up the salute for greeting Hitler, presumably copying the Italians. In the 1930s fascist movements in other countries and various governments around the world picked it up. Hitler himself recounted a medieval German origin for the salute, which, as far as we know, is no more real that the ancient Roman origin.[243] Hitler certainly knew of Mussolini's use of the salute and almost certainly knew of the U.S. use. Whether the U.S. connection inclined him in favor of the salute or not, it seems not to have dissuaded him from adopting the salute.

The official salute of the Olympics is also very similar to these other ones, though rarely used because people don't want to look like Nazis. It was widely used at the 1936 Olympics in Berlin, and confused a lot of people then and ever since as to who was saluting the Olympics and who was saluting Hitler. Posters from the 1924 Olympics show the salute with the arm almost vertical. A photograph from the 1920 Olympics shows a somewhat different salute.

It seems that a number of people had a similar idea around the same time, perhaps influenced by each other. And it seems that Hitler gave the idea a bad name, leading everybody else to drop, modify, or downplay it from that point forward.

What difference does it make? Hitler could have instituted that salute without the United States existing. Or if he couldn't have, he could have instituted some other salute that would have been no better or worse. Yes, of course. But the problem is not where the arm is placed. The problem is the mandatory ritual of militarism and blind, servile obedience.

It was strictly required in Nazi Germany to give the salute in greeting, accompanied by the words Hail Hitler! or Hail Victory! It was also required when the National Anthem or the Nazi Party Anthem was played. The national anthem celebrated German superiority, machismo, and war.[244] The Nazi anthem celebrated flags, Hitler, and war.[245]

When Francis Bellamy created the Pledge of Allegiance, it was presented as part of the following program for schools:[246]

"The schools should assemble at 9 A.M. in their various rooms. At 9:30 the detail of Veterans is expected to arrive. It is to be met at the entrance of the yard by the Color-Guard of pupils,—escorted with dignity to the building, and presented to the Principal. The Principal then gives the signal, and the several teachers conduct their students to the yard, to beat of drum or other music, and arrange them in a hollow square about the flag, the Veterans and Color-Guard taking places by the flag itself. The Master of Ceremonies then gives the command 'Attention!' and begins the exercises by reading the Proclamation.

"1. READING OF THE PRESIDENT'S PROCLAMATION — by the Master of Ceremonies

"At the close of the reading he announces, 'In accordance with this recommendation by the President of the United States, and as a sign of our devotion to our country, let the Flag of the Nation be unfurled above this School.'

"2. RAISING OF THE FLAG—by the Veterans

"As the Flag reaches the top of the staff, the Veterans will lead the assemblage in 'Three Cheers for "Old Glory." '

"3. SALUTE TO THE FLAG—by the Pupils

"At a signal from the Principal the pupils, in ordered ranks, hands to the side, face the Flag. Another signal is given; every pupil gives the flag the military salute—right hand lifted, palm downward, to a line with the forehead and close to it. Standing thus, all repeat together, slowly, 'I pledge allegiance to my Flag and the Republic for which it stands; one Nation indivisible, with Liberty and Justice for all.' At the words, 'to my Flag,' the right hand is extended gracefully, palm upward, toward the Flag, and remains in this gesture till the end of the affirmation; whereupon all hands immediately drop to the side. Then, still standing, as the instruments strike a chord, all will sing AMERICA—'My Country, 'tis of Thee.'

"4. ACKNOWLEDGMENT OF GOD—Prayer or Scripture

"5. SONG OF COLUMBUS DAY—by Pupils and Audience . . .

"Dear Country, the star of the valiant and free!

Thy exiles afar are dreaming of thee.

No fields of the Earth so enchantingly shine,

No air breathes such incense, such music as thine. . . .

   "6. THE ADDRESS

   "'The Meaning of the Four Centuries' A Declamation of the Special Address prepared for the occasion by The Youth's Companion.

   "7. THE ODE

   "'Columbia's Banner,' A Reading of the Poem written for the Occasion by Edna Dean Proctor.

   "Here should follow whatever additional Exercises, Patriotic Recitations, Historic Representations, or Chorals may be desired.

   "8. ADDRESSES BY CITIZENS, and National Songs."

   Of course, the current version of the pledge is slightly different from above and reads: "I pledge allegiance to the Flag of the United States of America, and to the Republic for which it stands, one Nation under God, indivisible, with liberty and justice for all."[247]

   Nationalism, militarism, religion, exceptionalism, and a ritual oath of loyalty to a piece of cloth: this is quite a mix. Imposing this on children has got to be among the worst ways to prepare them to oppose fascism. Once you've pledged your allegiance to a flag, what are you to do when someone waves that flag and screams that evil foreigners need to be killed? Rare is the U.S. government whistleblower or war veteran peace activist who won't tell you how much time they spent trying to deprogram themselves of all the patriotism that was put into them as children.

   Some people who visit the United States from other countries are shocked to see children standing, using the modified salute of hand-on-heart, and robotically reciting a loyalty oath to a "nation under God." It seems that the modification of hand position has not succeeded in preventing them looking like Nazis.[248]

   The Nazi salute has not simply been abandoned in Germany; it has been banned. While Nazi flags and chants can occasionally be found at racist rallies in the United States, they are forbidden in Germany, where neo-Nazis sometimes wave the flag of the Confederate States of America as a legal means of making the same point.

10. The United States welcomed Nazis into the U.S. military

How opposed could the U.S. government have been to Nazism, considering what it did in Operation Paperclip?

Annie Jacobsen's 2014 book *Operation Paperclip: The Secret Intelligence Program That Brought Nazi Scientists to America* tells the story. It isn't terribly secret anymore, of course, and it was never very intelligent. Jacobsen has added some details, and the U.S. government is still hiding many more. But the basic facts have been available; they're just left out of most U.S. history books, movies, and television programs.[249]

After WWII, the U.S. military hired sixteen hundred former Nazi scientists and doctors, including some of Adolf Hitler's closest collaborators, including men responsible for murder, slavery, and human experimentation, including men convicted of war crimes, men acquitted of war crimes, and men who never stood trial. Some of the Nazis tried at Nuremberg had already been working for the U.S. in either Germany or the U.S. prior to the trials. Some were protected from their past by the U.S. government for years, as they lived and worked in Boston Harbor, Long Island, Maryland, Ohio, Texas, Alabama, and elsewhere, or were flown by the U.S. government to Argentina to protect them from prosecution. Some trial transcripts were classified in their entirety to avoid exposing the pasts of important U.S. scientists. Some of the Nazis brought over were frauds who had passed themselves off as scientists, some of whom subsequently learned their fields while working for the U.S. military.

The U.S. occupiers of Germany after WWII declared that all military research in Germany was to cease, as part of the process of denazification. Yet that research went on and expanded in secret, under U.S. authority, both in Germany and in the United States, as part of a process that it's possible to view as nazification. Not only scientists were hired. Former Nazi spies, most of them former S.S., were hired by the U.S. in post-war Germany to spy on — and torture — Soviets.

The U.S. military shifted in numerous ways when former Nazis were put into prominent positions. It was Nazi rocket scientists who proposed placing nuclear bombs on rockets and began developing the intercontinental ballistic missile. It was Nazi engineers who had designed Hitler's bunker beneath Berlin, who now designed underground fortresses for the U.S. government in the Catoctin and Blue Ridge Mountains. Known Nazi liars were employed by the U.S. military to draft classified intelligence briefs falsely hyping the Soviet menace. Nazi scientists developed U.S. chemical and biological weapons programs, bringing over their knowledge of tabun and sarin, not to mention thalidomide — and their eagerness for human experimentation, which the U.S. military and the newly created CIA readily engaged in on a major scale. Every bizarre and gruesome notion of how a person might be assassinated or an army immobilized was of interest to their research. New weapons were developed, including VX and Agent Orange. A new drive to visit and weaponize outer space was created, and former Nazis were put in charge of a new agency called NASA.[250]

Permanent war thinking, limitless war thinking, and creative war thinking in which science and technology overshadowed death and suffering, all went mainstream. When a former Nazi spoke to a women's luncheon at the Rochester Junior Chamber of Commerce in 1953, the event's headline was "Buzz Bomb Mastermind to Address Jaycees Today." That doesn't sound terribly odd to us, but might have shocked anyone living in the United States any time prior to World War II.[251]

A Walt Disney television program featuring a former Nazi who worked slaves to death in a cave building rockets is now available on YouTube.[252] Not long after Operation Paperclip, President Dwight Eisenhower would be lamenting that "the total influence — economic, political, even spiritual — is felt in every city, every State house, every office of the Federal government." Eisenhower was not referring to Nazism but to the power of the military-industrial complex. Yet, when asked whom he had in mind in remarking in the same speech that "public policy could itself become the captive of a scientific-technological elite," Eisenhower named two scientists, one of them the former Nazi in the Disney video.[253] The decision to inject 1,600 of Hitler's scientific-technological elite into the U.S. military was driven by fears of the USSR, both arguably plausible and the result of fraudulent fear mongering. The decision evolved over time and was the product of many misguided minds. But the buck stopped with President Harry S Truman. Henry Wallace, Truman's predecessor as vice-president who we like to imagine would have guided the world in a better direction than Truman did as president, actually pushed Truman to hire the Nazis as a jobs program. It would be good for American industry, said our progressive hero. Truman's subordinates debated, but Truman decided. As bits of Operation Paperclip became known, the American Federation of Scientists, Albert Einstein, and others urged Truman to end it. Nuclear physicist Hans Bethe and his colleague Henri Sack asked Truman:

"Did the fact that the Germans might save the nation millions of dollars imply that permanent residence and citizenship could be bought? Could the United States count on [the German scientists] to work for peace when their indoctrinated hatred against the Russians might contribute to increase the divergence between the great powers? Had the war been fought to allow Nazi ideology to creep into our educational and scientific institutions by the back door? Do we want science at any price?"[254]

Less well-known was a separate operation that granted immunity from prosecution to the Japanese scientists of Unit 731 who had worked on biological weapons and a wide variety of horrific human experimentation. General Douglas MacArthur justified this: "Since it is believed that the USSR possesses only a small portion of the technical information, and since any war-crimes action would completely reveal such data to all nations, it is felt that such publicity must be avoided in the interests of defense and security of the U.S. It is believed also that the war-crimes prosecution of Gen. Ishii and his associates would serve to stop the flow of much additional information of a technical and scientific nature."[255] While such a statement would never appear in any museum in the United States, the memo containing it is displayed on the wall of the Unit 731 Museum in Harbin, China.

In 1947 Operation Paperclip, still rather small, was in danger of being terminated. Instead, Truman transformed the U.S. military with the National Security Act, and created the best ally that Operation Paperclip could want: the CIA. Now the program took off, intentionally and willfully, with the full knowledge and understanding of the same U.S. President who had declared as a senator that if the Russians were winning the U.S. should help the Germans, and vice versa, to ensure that the most people possible died, the same president who viciously and pointlessly dropped two nuclear bombs on Japanese cities, the same president who brought us the war on Korea, the war without declaration, the secret wars, the permanent expanded empire of bases, heightened military secrecy in all matters, the imperial presidency, and the military-industrial complex. The U.S. Chemical Warfare Service took up the study of German chemical weapons at the end of the war as a means to continue in existence. George Merck both diagnosed biological weapons threats for the military and sold the military vaccines to handle them. War was business and business was going to be good for a long time to come.

But how big a change did the United States go through after WWII, and how much of it can be credited to Operation Paperclip? Is the firebombing of Japanese cities and the complete leveling of German cities less offensive that the hiring of Nazi scientists? Isn't a government that would give immunity to both Nazi and Japanese war criminals in order to learn their criminal ways already in a bad place? As one of the defendants argued in trial at Nuremberg, the U.S. had already engaged in its own experiments on humans using almost identical justifications to those offered by the Nazis. If that defendant had been aware, he could have pointed out that the U.S. was in that very moment engaged in such experiments in Guatemala. The Nazis, as we have seen, had learned some of their eugenics and other nasty inclinations from Americans. Some of the Paperclip scientists had worked in the U.S. before the war, as many Americans had worked in Germany. These were not isolated worlds.

The former Nazi scientist in the Disney video I mentioned was named Wernher von Braun. There's a monument to him in Huntsville, Alabama. In 2020, as I write this, monuments are being toppled around the United States in protest of racism. I lean more toward moving offensive monuments out of central squares and providing context and explanation in less prominent locations, as well as favoring the creation of numerous non-offensive public artworks. But if you're going to tear anything down (or blast anything into outer space), shouldn't the bust of Wernher von Braun in Huntsville, Alabama, be considered for inclusion on the list?

Out of a long list of major wars there are only a few the United States claims to have ever won. One of those is the U.S. Civil War, from which monuments to the losers later sprouted up like toxic mushrooms. Now they're coming down. Another, although principally won in Europe by the Soviet Union, was WWII. Some of the losers of that one also have monuments in the United States.

The Confederate monuments were put up in the cause of racism. The celebrations of Nazis in Huntsville glorify, not racism, but the creation of the high-tech weaponry of war, which is only offensive if you notice who gets bombed or if you object to murdering anybody.

But we're not dealing here with a view toward truth, reconciliation, and rehabilitation. The bust of Von Braun — or for that matter the U.S. postage stamp of him — is not meant to say: "Yes, this man used slave labor to build weaponry for the Nazis. He and his colleagues fit right into white Huntsville in 1950, from which point on they produced horrible murderous weaponry to kill only the proper people who truly needed killing, plus rockets that went to the moon thereby outdoing the Soviets."

On the contrary, naming things around Huntsville for Von Braun is a way to say "Thou shalt maintain a steadfast ignorance about what this man and his colleagues did in Germany, and squint hard when viewing what they contributed to in places like Vietnam. These people brought federal dollars and symphony orchestras and sophisticated culture to our backwater, and they understood our racist ways as only Nazis could. Remember, we still had slavery and worse in Alabama right up until WWII."

Why does the rocket museum in Huntsville have a "biergarten"? Nobody would guess it was to celebrate Nazis. Any explanation uses only the word "Germans."[256] Look at how a website for Alabama writes about the great Von Braun's former house[257] and memorabilia[258]. Look how the *Chattanooga Times Free Press* writes about a tourist pilgrimage to all the Huntsville sites sanctified by Von Braun.[259] Never a critical or vaguely questioning word anywhere. No discussion of second chances — rather, enforced amnesia.

Confronting racism 160 years after the U.S. Civil War is encouraging, but suggests that perhaps a mere 75 years after WWII is too early to expect people to confront Nazism.

11. The United States did not have to engage in an arms race with Japan

The U.S. government planned, prepared for, and provoked a war with Japan for years, and was in many ways at war already, waiting for Japan to fire the first shot, when Japan attacked the Philippines and Pearl Harbor. What gets lost in the questions of exactly who knew what when in the days before those attacks, and what combination of incompetence and cynicism allowed them to happen, is the fact that major steps had indisputably been taken toward war but none had been taken toward peace.

The Asia pivot of the Obama-Trump era had a precedent in the years leading up to WWII, as the United States and Japan built up their military presence in the Pacific. The United States was aiding China in the war against Japan and blockading Japan to deprive it of critical resources prior to Japan's attack on U.S. troops and imperial territories. The militarism of the United States does not free Japan of responsibility for its own militarism, or vice versa, but the myth of the innocent bystander shockingly assaulted out of the blue is no more real than the myth of the war to save the Jews.

When I ask people to justify WWII, they always say "Hitler," but if the European war was so easily justifiable, why shouldn't the United States have joined it earlier? Why was the U.S. public so overwhelmingly against U.S. entry into the war until after December 7, 1941? Why does a war with Germany that supposedly should have been entered have to be depicted as a defensive battle through the convoluted logic that Japan fired the first shot, thereby (somehow) making the crusade to end the Holocaust in Europe a question of self-defense? Germany declared war on the United States, hoping that Japan would assist Germany in the struggle against the Soviet Union. But Germany did not attack the United States.

Winston Churchill wanted the United States to enter WWII, just as he had wanted the United States to enter WWI. The *Lusitania* was attacked by Germany without warning, during WWI, we're told in U.S. text books, despite Germany literally having published warnings in New York newspapers and newspapers around the United States. These warnings were printed right next to ads for sailing on the *Lusitania* and were signed by the German embassy.[260] Newspapers wrote articles about the warnings. The Cunard company was asked about the warnings. The former captain of the *Lusitania* had already quit — reportedly due to the stress of sailing through what Germany had publicly declared a war zone. Meanwhile Winston Churchill wrote to the President of Britain's Board of Trade, "It is most important to attract neutral shipping to our shores in the hope especially of embroiling the United States with Germany."[261] It was under his command that the usual British military protection was not provided to the *Lusitania*, despite Cunard having stated that it was counting on that protection. That the *Lusitania* was carrying weapons and troops to aid the British in the war against Germany was asserted by Germany and by other observers, and was true. Sinking the *Lusitania* was a horrible act of mass-murder, but it wasn't a surprise assault by evil against pure goodness.

THE 1930s

In September of 1932, Colonel Jack Jouett, a veteran U.S. pilot, began teaching 80 cadets at a new military flying school in China.[262] Already, war was in the air. On January 17, 1934, Eleanor Roosevelt made a speech: "Any one who thinks, must think of the next war as suicide. How deadly stupid we are that we can study history and live through what we live through, and complacently allow the same causes to put us through the same thing again."[263] When President Franklin Roosevelt visited Pearl Harbor on July 28, 1934, General Kunishiga Tanaka wrote in the *Japan Advertiser*, objecting to the build-up of the American fleet and the creation of additional bases in Alaska and the Aleutian Islands: "Such insolent behavior makes us most suspicious. It makes us think a major disturbance is purposely being encouraged in the Pacific. This is greatly regretted."[264]

In October 1934, George Seldes wrote in *Harper's Magazine*: "It is an axiom that nations do not arm for war but for a war." Seldes asked an official at the Navy League:

"Do you accept the naval axiom that you prepare to fight a specific navy?" The man replied "Yes."

"Do you contemplate a fight with the British navy?"

"Absolutely, no."

"Do you contemplate war with Japan?"

"Yes."[265]

In 1935 Smedley Butler, two years after foiling a coup against Roosevelt, and four years after being court martialed for recounting an incident in which Benito Mussolini ran over a girl with his car[266], published to enormous success a short book called *War Is a Racket*.[267] He wrote:

"At each session of Congress the question of further naval appropriations comes up. The swivel-chair admirals don't shout that 'We need lots of battleships to war on this nation or that nation.' Oh, no. First of all, they let it be known that America is menaced by a great naval power. Almost any day, these admirals will tell you, the great fleet of this supposed enemy will strike suddenly and annihilate our 125,000,000 people. Just like that. Then they begin to cry for a larger navy. For what? To fight the enemy? Oh my, no. Oh, no. For defense purposes only. Then, incidentally, they announce maneuvers in the Pacific. For defense. Uh, huh.

"The Pacific is a great big ocean. We have a tremendous coastline in the Pacific. Will the maneuvers be off the coast, two or three hundred miles? Oh, no. The maneuvers will be two thousand, yes, perhaps even thirty-five hundred miles, off the coast. The Japanese, a proud people, of course will be pleased beyond expression to see the United States fleet so close to Nippon's shores. Even as pleased as would be the residents of California were they to dimly discern, through the morning mist, the Japanese fleet playing at war games off Los Angeles."

In March 1935, Roosevelt bestowed Wake Island on the U.S. Navy and gave Pan Am Airways a permit to build runways on Wake Island, Midway Island, and Guam. Japanese military commanders announced that they were disturbed and viewed these runways as a threat. So did peace activists in the United States. By the next month, Roosevelt had planned war games and maneuvers near the Aleutian Islands and Midway Island. By the following month, peace activists were marching in New York advocating friendship with Japan. Norman Thomas wrote in 1935: "The Man from Mars who saw how men suffered in the last war and how frantically they are preparing for the next war, which they know will be worse, would come to the conclusion that he was looking at the denizens of a lunatic asylum."

On May 18, 1935, ten thousand marched up Fifth Avenue in New York with posters and signs opposing the build-up to war with Japan. Similar scenes were repeated numerous times in this period.[268] People made the case for peace, while the government armed for war, built bases for war, rehearsed for war in the Pacific, and practiced blackouts and sheltering from air raids to prepare people for war. The U.S. Navy developed its plans for a war on Japan. The March 8, 1939, version of these plans described "an offensive war of long duration" that would destroy the military and disrupt the economic life of Japan.

The U.S. military even planned for a Japanese attack on Hawaii, which it thought might begin with conquering the island of Ni'ihau, from which flights would take off to assault the other islands. U.S. Army Air Corp. Lt. Col. Gerald Brant approached the Robinson family, which owned Ni'ihau and still does. He asked them to plow furrows across the island in a grid, to render it useless for airplanes. Between 1933 and 1937, three Ni'ihau men cut the furrows with plows pulled by mules or draft horses. As it turned out, the Japanese had no plans to use Ni'ihau, but when a Japanese plane that had just been part of the attack on Pearl Harbor had to make an emergency landing, it landed on Ni'ihau despite all the efforts of the mules and horses.

On July 21, 1936, all the newspapers in Tokyo had the same headline: the

U.S. government was loaning China 100 million yuan with which to buy U.S. weapons.[269] On August 5, 1937, the Japanese government announced that it was disturbed that 182 U.S. airmen, each accompanied by two mechanics, would be flying airplanes in China.[270]

1940

In November 1940, Roosevelt loaned China one hundred million dollars for war with Japan, and after consulting with the British, U.S. Secretary of the Treasury Henry Morgenthau made plans to send the Chinese bombers with U.S. crews to use in bombing Tokyo and other Japanese cities. On December 21, 1940, China's Minister of Finance T.V. Soong and Colonel Claire Chennault, a retired U.S. Army flier who was working for the Chinese and had been urging them to use American pilots to bomb Tokyo since at least 1937, met in Morgenthau's dining room to plan the firebombing of Japan. Morgenthau said he could get men released from duty in the U.S. Army Air Corps if the Chinese could pay them $1,000 per month. Soong agreed.[271]

In 1939-1940, the U.S. Navy built new Pacific bases in Midway, Johnston, Palmyra, Wake, Guam, Samoa, and Hawaii.[272]

In September, 1940, Japan, Germany, and Italy signed an agreement to assist each other in war. This meant that were the United States at war with one of them, it would likely be at war with all three.

On October 7, 1940, the director of the U.S. Office of Naval Intelligence Far East Asia Section Arthur McCollum wrote a memo.[273] He worried about possible future Axis threats to the British fleet, to the British Empire, and to the Allies' ability to blockade Europe. He speculated about a theoretical future Axis attack on the United States. He believed decisive action could lead to the "early collapse of Japan." He recommended war with Japan:

"While . . . there is little that the United States can do to immediately retrieve the situation in Europe, the United States is able to effectively nullify Japanese aggressive action, and do it without lessening U.S. material assistance to Great Britain.

". . . In the Pacific the United States possesses a very strong defensive position and a navy and naval air force at present in that ocean capable of long distance offensive operation. There are certain other factors which at the present time are strongly in our favor, viz:

A.   Philippine Islands still held by the United States.

B.   Friendly and possibly allied government in control of the Dutch East Indies.

C.   British still hold Hong Kong and Singapore and are favorable to us.

D.   Important Chinese armies are still in the field in China against Japan.

E.   A small U.S. Naval Force capable of seriously threatening Japan's southern supply routes already in the theatre of operations.

F.   A considerable Dutch naval force is in the Orient that would be of value if allied to U.S.

"A consideration of the foregoing leads to the conclusion that prompt aggressive naval action against Japan by the United States would render Japan incapable of affording any help to Germany and Italy in their attack on England and that Japan itself would be faced with a situation in which her navy could be forced to fight on most unfavorable terms or accept fairly early collapse of the country through the force of blockade. A prompt and early declaration of war after entering into suitable arrangements with England and Holland, would be most effective in bringing about the early collapse of Japan and thus eliminating our enemy in the pacific before Germany and Italy could strike at us effectively. Furthermore, elimination of Japan must surely strengthen Britain's position against Germany and Italy and, in addition, such action would increase the confidence and support of all nations who tend to be friendly towards us.

"It is not believed that in the present state of political opinion the United States government is capable of declaring war against Japan without more ado; and it is barely possible that vigorous action on our part might lead the Japanese to modify their attitude. Therefore, the following course of action is suggested:

A.   Make an arrangement with Britain for the use of British bases in the Pacific, particularly Singapore.

B.   Make an arrangement with Holland for the use of base facilities and acquisition of supplies in the Dutch East Indies.

C.   Give all possible aid to the Chinese government of Chiang-Kai-Shek.

D.   Send a division of long range heavy cruisers to the Orient, Philippines, or Singapore.

E.   Send two divisions of submarines to the Orient.

F.   Keep the main strength of the U.S. fleet now in the Pacific in the vicinity of the Hawaiian Islands.

G.   Insist that the Dutch refuse to grant Japanese demands for undue economic concessions, particularly oil.

H.   Completely embargo all U.S. trade with Japan, in collaboration with a similar embargo imposed by the British Empire.

"If by these means Japan could be led to commit an overt act of war, so much the better. At all events we must be fully prepared to accept the threat of war."

According to U.S. Army military historian Conrad Crane, "A close reading [of the above memo] shows that its recommendations were supposed to deter and contain Japan, while better preparing the United States for a future conflict in the Pacific. There is an offhand remark that an overt Japanese act of war would make it easier to garner public support for actions against Japan, but the document's intent was not to ensure that event happened."[274]

The dispute between interpretations of this memo and similar documents is a subtle one. Nobody believes the memo quoted above was aimed at negotiating peace or disarmament or establishing the rule of law over violence. Some think the intention was to get a war started but be able to blame it on Japan. Others think the intention was to get ready for a war to start, and take steps that might very well provoke Japan to start one, but might instead — it was just barely possible — frighten Japan out of its militaristic ways. This range of debate turns an Overton window into a keyhole. It's a debate that has also been sidetracked into a focus on whether one of the eight recommendations above — the one about keeping the fleet in Hawaii — was part of a nefarious plot to get more ships destroyed in a dramatic attack (not a particularly successful plot, as only two ships were permanently destroyed).

Not just that one point — which is significant with or without such a plot — but all eight recommendations made in the memo or at least steps similar to them were pursued. These steps were aimed at intentionally or accidentally (the distinction is a fine one) starting a war, and they seem to have worked. Work on the recommendations, coincidentally or not, began on October 8, 1940, the very next day after the memo was written. On that date, the U.S. State Department told Americans to evacuate Eastern Asia. Also on that date, President Roosevelt ordered the fleet kept in Hawaii. Admiral James O. Richardson wrote later that he had strongly objected to the proposal and to its purpose. "Sooner or later," he quoted Roosevelt as having said, "the Japanese would commit an overt act against the United States and the nation would be willing to enter the war."[275]

EARLY 1941

Richardson was relieved of his duties on February 1, 1941, so perhaps he lied about Roosevelt as a disgruntled former employee. Or perhaps getting out of such duties in the Pacific in those days was a popular move by those who could see what was coming. Admiral Chester Nimitz declined to command the Pacific Fleet. His son, Chester Nimitz Jr. later told the History Channel that his father's thinking had been as follows: "It is my guess that the Japanese are going to attack us in a surprise attack. There will be a revulsion in the country against all those in command at sea, and they will be replaced by people in positions of prominence ashore, and I want to be ashore, and not at sea, when that happens."[276]

In early 1941, U.S. and British military officers met to plan their strategy for defeating Germany and then Japan, once the United States was in the war. In April, President Roosevelt started having U.S. ships inform the British military of the locations of German U-boats and planes. Then he started allowing the shipment of supplies to British soldiers in North Africa. Germany accused Roosevelt of "endeavoring with all the means at his disposal to provoke incidents for the purpose of baiting the American people into the war."[277]

In January 1941, the *Japan Advertiser* expressed its outrage over the U.S. military build-up at Pearl Harbor in an editorial, and the U.S. ambassador to Japan wrote in his diary: "There is a lot of talk around town to the effect that the Japanese, in case of a break with the United States, are planning to go all out in a surprise mass attack on Pearl Harbor. Of course I informed my government."[278] On February 5, 1941, Rear Admiral Richmond Kelly Turner wrote to Secretary of War Henry Stimson to warn of the possibility of a surprise attack at Pearl Harbor.

On April 28, 1941, Churchill wrote a secret directive to his war cabinet: "It may be taken as almost certain that the entry of Japan into the war would be followed by the immediate entry of the United States on our side." On May 24, 1941, the *New York Times* reported on U.S. training of the Chinese air force, and the provision of "numerous fighting and bombing planes" to China by the United States and Britain. "Bombing of Japanese Cities is Expected" read the subheadline.[279] On May 31, 1941, at the Keep America Out of War Congress, William Henry Chamberlin gave a dire warning: "A total economic boycott of Japan, the stoppage of oil shipments for instance, would push Japan into the arms of the Axis. Economic war would be a prelude to naval and military war."[280]

By July, 1941, the Joint Army-Navy Board had approved a plan called JB 355 to firebomb Japan. A front corporation would buy American planes to be flown by American volunteers. Roosevelt approved, and his China expert Lauchlin Currie, in the words of Nicholson Baker, "wired Madame Chiang Kai-Shek and Claire Chennault a letter that fairly begged for interception by Japanese spies." The 1st American Volunteer Group (AVG) of the Chinese Air Force, also known as the Flying Tigers, moved ahead with recruitment and training immediately, were provided to China prior to Pearl Harbor, and first saw combat on December 20, 1941.[281]

On July 24, 1941, President Roosevelt remarked, "If we cut the oil off, [the Japanese] probably would have gone down to the Dutch East Indies a year ago, and you would have had a war. It was very essential from our own selfish point of view of defense to prevent a war from starting in the South Pacific. So our foreign policy was trying to stop a war from breaking out there."[282] Reporters noticed that Roosevelt said "was" rather than "is." The next day, Roosevelt issued an executive order freezing Japanese assets. The United States and Britain cut off oil and scrap metal to Japan. Radhabinod Pal, an Indian jurist who served on the war crimes tribunal after the war, found the embargoes a predictably provocative threat to Japan.[283]

On August 7, 1941, the *Japan Times Advertiser* wrote: "First there was the creation of a superbase at Singapore, heavily reinforced by British and Empire troops. From this hub a great wheel was built up and linked with American bases to form a great ring sweeping in a great area southwards and westwards from the Philippines through Malaya and Burma, with the link broken only in the Thailand peninsula. Now it is proposed to include the narrows in the encirclement, which proceeds to Rangoon."[284]

On August 12, 1941, Roosevelt met secretly with Churchill in Newfoundland and drew up the Atlantic Charter, which set out the war aims for a war that the United States was not yet officially in. Churchill asked Roosevelt to join the war immediately, but he declined. Following this secret meeting, on August 18th, Churchill met with his cabinet back at 10 Downing Street in London. Churchill told his cabinet, according to the minutes: "The [U.S.] President had said he would wage war but not declare it, and that he would become more and more provocative. If the Germans did not like it, they could attack American forces. Everything was to be done to force an 'incident' that could lead to war."[285]

British propagandists had also argued since at least 1938 for using Japan to bring the United States into the war.[286] At the Atlantic Conference on August 12, 1941, Roosevelt assured Churchill that the United States would bring economic pressure to bear on Japan.[287] Within a week, in fact, the Economic Defense Board began economic sanctions.[288] On September 3, 1941, the U.S. State Department sent Japan a demand that it accept the principle of "nondisturbance of the status quo in the Pacific," meaning cease turning European colonies into Japanese colonies.[289] By September 1941 the Japanese press was outraged that the United States had begun shipping oil right past Japan to reach Russia. Japan, its newspapers said, was dying a slow death from "economic war."[290] In September, 1941, Roosevelt announced a "shoot on sight" policy toward any German or Italian ships in U.S. waters.

A WAR SALES PITCH

On October 27, 1941, Roosevelt made a speech[291]:

"Five months ago tonight I proclaimed to the American people the existence of a state of unlimited emergency. Since then much has happened. Our Army and Navy are temporarily in Iceland in the defense of the Western Hemisphere. Hitler has attacked shipping in areas close to the Americas in the North and South Atlantic. Many American-owned merchant ships have been sunk on the high seas. One American destroyer was attacked on September fourth. Another destroyer was attacked and hit on October seventeenth. Eleven brave and loyal men of our Navy were killed by the Nazis. We have wished to avoid shooting. But the shooting has started. And history has recorded who fired the first shot. In the long run, however, all that will matter is who fired the last shot. America has been attacked. The *U.S.S. Kearny* is not just a navy ship. She belongs to every man, woman and child in this nation. Illinois, Alabama, California, North Carolina, Ohio, Louisiana, Texas, Pennsylvania, Georgia, Arkansas, New York, Virginia — those are the home states of the honored dead and wounded of the *Kearny*. Hitler's torpedo was directed at every American whether he lives on our sea coasts or in the innermost part of the nation, far from the seas and far from the guns and tanks of the marching hordes of would-be conquerors of the world. The purpose of Hitler's attack was to frighten the American people off the high seas — to force us to make a trembling retreat. This is not the first time he has misjudged the American spirit. That spirit is now aroused."

The ship sunk on September 4th was the *Greer*. The Chief of U.S. Naval Operations Harold Stark testified before the Senate Naval Affairs Committee that the *Greer* had been tracking a German submarine and relaying its location to a British airplane, which had dropped depth charges on the submarine without success. After hours of being tracked by the *Greer*, the submarine turned and fired.

The ship sunk on October 17th, the *Kearny*, was a replay of the *Greer*. It may have mystically belonged to the spirit of every American and so forth, but it was not innocent. It was taking part in a war that the United States had not officially entered, that the U.S. public was adamantly opposed to entering, but that the U.S. president was eager to get on with. That president continued:

"If our national policy were to be dominated by the fear of shooting, then all of our ships and those of our sister Republics would have to be tied up in home harbors. Our Navy would have to remain respectfully-abjectly-behind any line which Hitler might decree on any ocean as his own dictated version of his own war zone. Naturally we reject that absurd and insulting suggestion. We reject it because of our own self-interest, because of our own self-respect, because, most of all, of our own good faith. Freedom of the seas is now, as it has always been, a fundamental policy of your government and mine."

This strawman argument depends on the pretense that innocent ships not participating in the war were attacked, and that one's dignity depends on sending war ships around the world's oceans. It's a ridiculously transparent effort to manipulate the public, for which Roosevelt really ought to have paid royalties to the propagandists of WWI. Now we come to the claim that the President seems to have thought would clinch his case for war. It's a case based almost certainly on a British forgery, which makes it theoretically possible that Roosevelt actually believed what he was saying:

"Hitler has often protested that his plans for conquest do not extend across the Atlantic Ocean. But his submarines and raiders prove otherwise. So does the entire design of his new world order. For example, I have in my possession a secret map made in Germany by Hitler's government — by the planners of the new world order. It is a map of South America and a part of Central America, as Hitler proposes to reorganize it. Today in this area there are fourteen separate countries. The geographical experts of Berlin, however, have ruthlessly obliterated all existing boundary lines; and have divided South America into five vassal states, bringing the whole continent under their domination. And they have also so arranged it that the territory of one of these new puppet states includes the Republic of Panama and our great life line — the Panama Canal. That is his plan. It will never go into effect. This map makes clear the Nazi design not only against South America but against the United States itself."

Roosevelt had edited this speech to remove an assertion as to the map's authenticity. He refused to show the map to the media or the public. He did not say where the map came from, how he connected it to Hitler, or how it depicted a design against the United States, or — for that matter — how one might have sliced up Latin America and not included Panama.

When he had become Prime Minister in 1940, Churchill had set up an agency called British Security Coordination (BSC) with the mission to use any necessary dirty tricks to get the United States into the war. The BSC was run out of three floors of Rockefeller Center in New York by a Canadian named William Stephenson — the model for James Bond, according to Ian Fleming. It ran its own radio station, WRUL, and press agency, the Overseas News Agency (ONA). The hundreds or thousands of BSC staffers, later including Roald Dahl, kept busy sending forgeries to the U.S. media, creating astrologers to predict Hitler's demise, and generating false rumors of powerful new British weapons. Roosevelt was well aware of the BSC's work, as was the FBI.

According to William Boyd, a novelist who has investigated the agency, the "BSC evolved a prankish game called 'Vik' – a 'fascinating new pastime for lovers of democracy'. Teams of Vik players across the USA scored points depending on the level of embarrassment and irritation they caused Nazi sympathisers. Players were urged to indulge in a series of petty persecutions – persistent 'wrong number' calls in the night; dead rats dropped in water tanks; ordering cumbersome gifts to be delivered, cash on delivery, to target addresses; deflating the tyres of cars; hiring street musicians to play 'God Save the King' outside Nazi sympathisers' houses, and so on."[292]

Ivar Bryce, who was Walter Lippman's brother-in-law and Ian Fleming's buddy, worked for the BSC, and in 1975 published a memoir claiming to have produced there the first draft of Roosevelt's phony Nazi map, which had then been approved by Stephenson and arranged to be obtained by the U.S. government with a false story as to its origins.[293] Whether the FBI and/or Roosevelt was in on the trick is not clear. Of all the pranks pulled by "intelligence" agents over the years, this was one of the more successful, and yet least trumpeted, as the British are supposed to be a U.S. ally. U.S. book readers and moviegoers would later dump fortunes into admiring James Bond, even if his real-life model had tried to deceive them into the worst war the world had ever seen.

Of course, Germany was struggling in a drawn-out war with the Soviet Union, and had not dared to invade England. Taking over South America was not going to happen. No record of the phony map has ever turned up in Germany, and speculation that somehow there might have been some shadow of truth to it seems especially strained in the context of the next section of Roosevelt's speech, in which he claimed to possess another document that he also never showed anyone and which may never have existed, and the content of which wasn't even plausible:

"Your government has in its possession another document made in Germany by Hitler's government. It is a detailed plan, which, for obvious reasons, the Nazis did not wish and do not wish to publicize just yet, but which they are ready to impose — a little later — on a dominated world — if Hitler wins. It is a plan to abolish all existing religions — Protestant, Catholic, Mohammedan, Hindu, Buddhist, and Jewish alike. The property of all churches will be seized by the Reich and its puppets. The cross and all other symbols of religion are to be forbidden. The clergy are to be forever silenced under penalty of the concentration camps, where even now so many fearless men are being tortured because they have placed God above Hitler. In the place of the churches of our civilization, there is to be set up an International Nazi Church — a church which will be served by orators sent out by the Nazi Government. In the place of the Bible, the words of Mein Kampf will be imposed and enforced as Holy Writ. And in place of the cross of Christ will be put two symbols — the swastika and the naked sword. A God of Blood and Iron will take the place of the God of Love and Mercy. Let us well ponder that statement which I have made tonight."

Needless to say, this was not based in reality; religion was openly practiced in Nazi-controlled nations, in some cases newly restored after Soviet-imposed atheism, and medals that the Nazis bestowed on their biggest supporters were, as we have seen above, shaped like crosses. But the pitch to enter a war for love and mercy was a nice touch. The next day, a reporter asked to see Roosevelt's map and was turned down. As far as I know, nobody even asked to see this other document. It's possible that people understood this not to be a literal claim to have an actual document in possession, but rather a defense of holy religion against evil — not something to be questioned with skepticism or seriousness. Roosevelt continued:

"These grim truths which I have told you of the present and future plans of Hitlerism will of course be hotly denied tonight and tomorrow in the controlled press and radio of the Axis Powers. And some Americans — not many — will continue to insist that Hitler's plans need not worry us — and that we should not concern ourselves with anything that goes on beyond rifle shot of our own shores. The protestations of these American citizens — few in number — will, as usual, be paraded with applause through the

Axis press and radio during the next few days, in an effort to convince the world that the majority of Americans are opposed to their duly chosen Government, and in reality are only waiting to jump on Hitler's band wagon when it comes this way. The motive of such Americans is not the point at issue."

No, the point seems to have been to limit people to two options and get them into a war.

"The fact is that Nazi propaganda continues in desperation to seize upon such isolated statements as proof of American disunity. The Nazis have made up their own list of modern American heroes. It is, fortunately, a short list. I am glad that it does not contain my name. All of us Americans, of all opinions, are faced with the choice between the kind of world we want to live in and the kind of world which Hitler and his hordes would impose upon us. None of us wants to burrow under the ground and live in total darkness like a comfortable mole. The forward march of Hitler and of Hitlerism can be stopped — and it will be stopped. Very simply and very bluntly — we are pledged to pull our own oar in the destruction of Hitlerism. And when we have helped to end the curse of Hitlerism we shall help to establish a new peace which will give to decent people everywhere a better chance to live and prosper in security and in freedom and in faith. Each day that passes we are producing and providing more and more arms for the men who are fighting on actual battle-fronts. That is our primary task. And it is the nation's will that these vital arms and supplies of all kinds shall neither be locked up in American harbors nor sent to the bottom of the sea. It is the nation's will that America shall deliver the goods. In open defiance of that will, our ships have been sunk and our sailors have been killed."

Here Roosevelt admits that the U.S. ships sunk by Germany were engaged in supporting war against Germany. He just seems to believe it more important to convince the U.S. public that it is already at war than to continue further with the claim that the ships attacked were wholly innocent.

LATE 1941

In late October, 1941, U.S. spy Edgar Mowrer spoke with a man in Manila named Ernest Johnson, a member of the Maritime Commission, who said he expected "The Japs will take Manila before I can get out." When Mowrer expressed surprise, Johnson replied "Didn't you know the Jap fleet has moved eastward, presumably to attack our fleet at Pearl Harbor?"[294]

On November 3, 1941, the U.S. ambassador to Japan, Joseph Grew, tried — not for the first time — to communicate something to his government, a government that was either too incompetent to understand, or too cynically engaged in plotting war, or both, but which certainly was not even considering working for peace. Grew sent a lengthy telegram to the State Department warning that the economic sanctions imposed by the United States might force Japan to commit "national hara-kiri." He wrote: "An armed conflict with the United States may come with dangerous and dramatic suddenness."[295]

On November 6, 1941, Japan proposed an agreement with the United States that included partial Japanese withdrawal from China. The United States rejected the proposal on November 14th.[296]

On November 15, 1941, U.S. Army Chief of Staff George Marshall briefed the media on something we do not remember as "the Marshall Plan." In fact we don't remember it at all. "We are preparing an offensive war against Japan," Marshall said, asking the journalists to keep it a secret, which as far as I know they dutifully did.[297] Marshall told Congress in 1945 that the United States had initiated Anglo-Dutch-American agreements for unified action against Japan and put them into effect before December 7th.[298]

On November 20, 1941, Japan proposed a new agreement with the United States for peace and cooperation between the two nations.[299]

On November 25, 1941, Secretary of War Henry Stimson wrote in his diary that he'd met in the Oval Office with Marshall, President Roosevelt, Secretary of the Navy Frank Knox, Admiral Harold Stark, and Secretary of State Cordell Hull. Roosevelt had told them the Japanese were likely to attack soon, possibly the next Monday, December 1, 1941. "The question,"

Stimson wrote, "was how we should maneuver them into the position of firing the first shot without allowing too much danger to ourselves. It was a difficult proposition."

On November 26, 1941, the United States made a counter-proposal to Japan's proposal of six days earlier.[300] In this proposal, sometimes called the Hull Note, sometimes the Hull Ultimatum, the United States required complete Japanese withdrawal from China, but no U.S. withdrawal from the Philippines or anywhere else in the Pacific. The Japanese rejected the proposal. Neither nation, it seems, invested remotely the resources into these negotiations that they did into preparing for war. Henry Luce referred in *Life* magazine on July 20, 1942, to "the Chinese for whom the U.S. had delivered the ultimatum that brought on Pearl Harbor."[301]

"In late November," according to Gallup polling, 52% of Americans told Gallup pollsters that the United States would be at war with Japan "sometime in the near future."[302] The war was not going to be a surprise to over half the country, or to the U.S. government.

On November 27, 1941, Rear Admiral Royal Ingersoll sent a warning of war with Japan to four naval commands. On November 28, Admiral Harold Rainsford Stark re-sent it with the added instruction: "IF HOSTILITIES CANNOT REPEAT CANNOT BE AVOIDED THE UNITED STATES DESIRES THAT JAPAN COMMIT THE FIRST OVERT ACT."[303] On November 28, 1941, Vice Admiral William F. Halsey, Jr., gave instructions to "shoot down anything we saw in the sky and to bomb anything we saw on the sea."[304] On November 30, 1941, the *Honolulu Advertiser* carried the headline "Japanese May Strike Over Weekend."[305] On December 2, 1941, the *New York Times* reported that Japan had been "cut off from about 75 percent of her normal trade by the Allied blockade."[306] In a 20-page memo on December 4, 1941, the Office of Naval Intelligence warned, "In anticipation of open conflict with this country, Japan is vigorously utilizing every available agency to secure military, naval and commercial information, paying particular attention to the West Coast, the Panama Canal, and the Territory of Hawaii."[307]

As of December 6, 1941, no poll had found majority U.S. public support for entering the war.[308] But Roosevelt had already instituted the draft, activated the National Guard, created a huge Navy in two oceans, traded old destroyers to England in exchange for the lease of its bases in the Caribbean and Bermuda, supplied planes and trainers and pilots to China, imposed harsh sanctions on Japan, advised the U.S. military that a war with Japan was beginning, and — just 11 days before the Japanese attack — secretly ordered the creation of a list of every Japanese and Japanese-American person in the United States. (Hurray for IBM technology!)

On December 7, 1941, following the Japanese attack, President Roosevelt drew up a declaration of war against both Japan and Germany, but decided it wouldn't work and went with Japan alone. On December 8th, Congress voted for war against Japan, with Jeanette Rankin casting the only no vote.

CONTROVERSY AND LACK THEREOF

Robert Stinnett's *Day of Deceit: The Truth About FDR and Pearl Harbor* is controversial among historians, including in its claims about U.S. knowledge of Japanese codes and coded Japanese communications. I don't think, however, that either of the following points should be controversial:

1. The information I've already presented above is already more than sufficient to recognize that the United States was neither an innocent bystander attacked out of the blue nor an engaged party making an all-out effort for peace and stability.

2. Stinnett is right to have put in the efforts he has to declassify and make public government documents, and right that there can be no good excuse for the National Security Agency continuing to keep huge numbers of Japanese naval intercepts secret in the 1941 U.S. Navy files.[309]

While Stinnett believes his most important findings only made it into the 2000 paperback of his book, the *New York Times* review by Richard Bernstein of the 1999 hardcover is notable for how narrowly it defines the questions that remain in doubt:[310]

"Historians of World War II generally agree that Roosevelt believed war with Japan was inevitable and that he wanted Japan to fire the first shot. What Stinnett has done, taking off from that idea, is compile documentary evidence to the effect that Roosevelt, to ensure that the first shot would have a traumatic effect, intentionally left Americans defenseless. . . .

"Stinnett's strongest and most disturbing argument relates to one of the standard explanations for Japan's success in keeping the impending Pearl Harbor attack a secret: namely that the aircraft carrier task force that unleashed it maintained strict radio silence for the entire three weeks leading up to Dec. 7 and thus avoided detection. In truth, Stinnett writes, the Japanese continuously broke radio silence even as the Americans, using radio direction finding techniques, were able to follow the Japanese fleet as it made its way toward Hawaii. . . .

"It is possible that Stinnett might be right about this; certainly the material he has unearthed ought to be reviewed by other historians. Yet the mere existence of intelligence does not prove that that intelligence made its way into the proper hands or that it would have been speedily and correctly interpreted.

"Gaddis Smith, the Yale University historian, remarks in this connection on the failure to protect the Philippines against Japanese attack, even though there was a great deal of information indicating that such an attack was coming. Nobody, not even Stinnett, believes that there was any intentional withholding of information from the American commander in the Philippines, Douglas MacArthur. The information available was for some reason just not put to use.

"In her 1962 book, *Pearl Harbor: Warning and Decision,* the historian Roberta Wohlstetter used the word static to identify the confusion, the inconsistencies, the overall uncertainty that affected intelligence gathering before the war. While Stinnett assumes that most information that now seems important would have gotten speedy attention at the time, the Wohlstetter view is that there was a great avalanche of such evidence, thousands of documents every day, and that the understaffed and overworked intelligence bureaus may simply not have interpreted it correctly at the time."

Incompetence or malevolence? The usual debate. Did the U.S. government fail to know the exact details of the coming attack because it was incapable or because it didn't want to know them, or didn't want certain parts of the government to know them? It's an interesting question, and it's all too easy to underestimate incompetence, and all too reassuring to underestimate malevolence. But there is no question that the U.S. government knew the general outlines of the coming attack and had been knowingly acting for years in ways that made it more likely.

THE PHILIPPINES

As the book review above mentions, the same question about the details of foreknowledge and the same lack of any question about the general outlines of it apply to the Philippines as to Pearl Harbor.

In fact, the case for an intentional act of treason would be easier for historians to speculate about in regard to the Philippines than in regard to Hawaii, if they were so inclined. "Pearl Harbor" is a strange shorthand. Hours after the attack on Pearl Harbor — on the same day but technically December 8th due to the International Date Line, and delayed six hours by the weather — the Japanese attacked the U.S. military in the U.S. colony of the Philippines, fully expecting to have a harder go of it, given that surprise would not be a factor. In fact, Douglas MacArthur received a phone call at 3:40 a.m. Philippines time alerting him to the attack on Pearl Harbor and the need to be prepared. In the nine hours that elapsed between that phone call and the attack on the Philippines, MacArthur did nothing. He left U.S. airplanes lined up and waiting, like the ships had been in Pearl Harbor. The result of the attack on the Philippines was, according to the U.S. military, as devastating as that on Hawaii. The United States lost 18 of 35 B-17s plus 90 other airplanes, and many more damaged.[311] In contrast, in Pearl Harbor, despite the myth that eight battleships were sunk, the reality is that none could be sunk in such a shallow harbor, two were rendered inoperable, and six were repaired and went on to fight in WWII.[312]

On the same day of December 7th / 8th — depending on the position of the International Date Line — Japan attacked the U.S. colonies of the Philippines and Guam, plus the U.S. territories of Hawaii, Midway, and Wake, as well as the British colonies of Malaya, Singapore, Honk Kong, and the independent nation of Thailand. While the attack on Hawaii was a one-off attack and retreat, in other locations, Japan attacked repeatedly, and in some cases invaded and conquered. Falling under Japanese control in the coming weeks would be the Philippines, Guam, Wake, Malaya, Singapore, Hong Kong, and the western tip of Alaska. In the Philippines, 16 million U.S. citizens fell under a brutal Japanese occupation. Before they did, the U.S. occupation interned people of Japanese origin, just as was done in the United States.[313]

Immediately after the attacks, the U.S. media didn't know it was supposed to refer to them all with the shorthand of "Pearl Harbor," and instead used a variety of names and descriptions. In a draft of his "day of infamy" speech, Roosevelt referred to both Hawaii and the Philippines. In his 2019 *How to Hide an Empire*, Daniel Immerwahr argues that Roosevelt made every effort to depict the attacks as attacks on the United States. While the people of the Philippines and Guam actually were citizens of the U.S. empire, they were the wrong sort of people. The Philippines was generally viewed as insufficiently white for statehood and on a track to possible independence. Hawaii was whiter, and also closer, and a possible candidate for future statehood. Roosevelt ultimately chose to omit the Philippines from that part of his speech, relegating it to one item in a later list that included the British colonies, and to describe the attacks as having happened on "The American Island of Oahu" — an island whose Americanness is, of course, disputed to this day by many native Hawaiians. The focus has been kept on Pearl Harbor ever since, even by those intrigued by the blundering or plotting behind the attacks.[314]

FURTHER INTO THE PAST

It's not hard to think of things that could have been done differently in the years and months leading up to U.S. entry into WWII, or even leading up to the first sparks of war in Asia or Europe. It's even easier to describe things that could have been done differently if one goes back a little further into the past. Things could have been done differently by every government and military involved, and each is responsible for its atrocities. But I want to mention some things that the U.S. government could have done differently, because I'm trying to counter the idea that the U.S. government was forced reluctantly into a war that was exclusively of others' choosing.

The United States could have elected William Jennings Bryan president over William McKinley who was succeeded by his vice president, Teddy Roosevelt. Bryan campaigned against empire, McKinley in favor of it. To many, other issues seemed more important at the time; it's not clear that they should have.

Teddy Roosevelt didn't do anything halfway. That went for war, imperialism, and his previously noted belief in theories about the Aryan "race." TR supported the abuse and even killing of Native Americans, Chinese immigrants, Cubans, Filipinos, and Asians and Central Americans of nearly every variety. He believed only whites capable of self-rule (which was bad news for the Cubans when their U.S. liberators discovered some of them to be black). He created a display of Filipinos for the St. Louis World's Fair depicting them as savages who could be tamed by white men.[315] He worked to keep Chinese immigrants out of the United States.

James Bradley's 2009 book, *The Imperial Cruise: A Secret History of Empire and War*, tells the following story.[316] I'm leaving out portions of the book that have had doubts raised about them.

In 1614 Japan had cut itself off from the West, resulting in centuries of peace and prosperity and the blossoming of Japanese art and culture. In 1853 the U.S. Navy had forced Japan open to U.S. merchants, missionaries, and militarism. U.S. histories call Commodore Matthew Perry's trips to Japan "diplomatic" although they used armed war ships to compel Japan to agree to relations it adamantly opposed. In the years that followed, the Japanese studied the Americans' racism and adopted a strategy to deal with it. They sought to westernize themselves and present themselves as a separate race superior to the rest of the Asians. They became honorary Aryans. Lacking a single god or a god of conquest, they invented a divine emperor, borrowing heavily from Christian tradition. They dressed and dined like Americans and sent their students to study in the United States. The Japanese were often referred to in the United States as the "Yankees of the Far East." In 1872 the U.S. military began training the Japanese in how to conquer other nations, with an eye on Taiwan.

Charles LeGendre, an American general training the Japanese in the ways of war, proposed that they adopt a Monroe Doctrine for Asia, that is a policy of dominating Asia in the way that the United States dominated its hemisphere. Japan established a Bureau of Savage Affairs and invented new words like *koronii* (colony). Talk in Japan began to focus on the responsibility of the Japanese to civilize the savages. In 1873, Japan invaded Taiwan with U.S. military advisors. Korea was next.

Korea and Japan had known peace for centuries. When the Japanese arrived with U.S. ships, wearing U.S. clothing, talking about their divine emperor, and proposing a treaty of "friendship," the Koreans thought the Japanese had lost their minds, and told them to get lost, knowing that China was there at Korea's back. But the Japanese talked China into allowing Korea to sign the treaty, without explaining to either the Chinese or Koreans what the treaty meant in its English translation.

In 1894 Japan declared war on China, a war in which U.S. weapons, on the Japanese side, carried the day. China gave up Taiwan and the Liaodong Peninsula, paid a large indemnity, declared Korea independent, and gave Japan the same commercial rights in China that the U.S. and European nations had. Japan was triumphant, until China persuaded Russia, France, and Germany to oppose Japanese ownership of Liaodong. Japan gave it up and Russia grabbed it. Japan felt betrayed by white Christians, and not for the last time.

In 1904, Teddy Roosevelt was very pleased with a Japanese surprise attack on Russian ships. As the Japanese again waged war on Asia as honorary Aryans, Roosevelt secretly and unconstitutionally cut deals with them, approving of a Monroe Doctrine for Japan in Asia. In the 1930s, Japan offered to open up trade to the United States in its imperial sphere if the United States would do the same for Japan in Latin America. The U.S. government said no.

CHINA

Britain was not the only foreign government with a propaganda office in New York City leading up to WWII. China was there too.

How did the U.S. government shift from its alliance and identification with Japan to one with China and against Japan (and then back again the other way after WWII)? The first part of the answer has to do with Chinese propaganda and its use of religion rather than race, and with putting a different Roosevelt into the White House. James Bradley's 2016 book, *The China Mirage: The Hidden History of American Disaster in China* tells this story.[317]

For years leading up to World War II, the China Lobby in the United States persuaded the U.S. public, and many top U.S. officials, that the Chinese people wanted to become Christian, that Chiang Kai-shek was their beloved democratic leader rather than a faltering fascist, that Mao Zedong was an insignificant nobody headed nowhere, and that the United States could fund Chiang Kai-shek and he would use it all to fight the Japanese, as opposed to using it to fight Mao.

The image of the noble and Christian Chinese peasant was driven by people like the Trinity (later Duke) and Vanderbilt educated Charlie Soong, his daughters Ailing, Chingling, and Mayling, and son Tse-ven (T.V.), as well as Mayling's husband Chiang Kai-shek, Henry Luce who started *Time* magazine after being born in a missionary colony in China, and Pearl Buck who wrote *The Good Earth* after the same type of childhood. TV Soong hired retired U.S. Army Air Corps colonel Jack Jouett and by 1932 had access to all the expertise of the U.S. Army Air Corps and had nine instructors, a flight surgeon, four mechanics, and a secretary, all U.S. Air Corps trained but now working for Soong in China. It was just the start of U.S. military assistance to China that made less news in the United States than it did in Japan.

In 1938, with Japan attacking Chinese cities, and Chiang barely fighting back, Chiang instructed his chief propagandist Hollington Tong, a former Columbia University journalism student, to send agents to the United States to recruit U.S. missionaries and give them evidence of Japanese atrocities, to hire Frank Price (Mayling's favorite missionary), and to recruit U.S. reporters and authors to write favorable articles and books. Frank Price and his brother Harry Price had been born in China, without ever encountering the China of the Chinese. The Price brothers set up shop in New York City, where few had any idea they were working for the Soong-Chiang gang. Mayling and Tong assigned them to persuade Americans that the key to peace in China was an embargo on Japan. They created the American Committee for Non-Participation in Japanese Aggression. "The public never knew," writes Bradley, "that the Manhattan missionaries diligently working on East Fortieth Street to save the Noble Peasants were paid China Lobby agents engaged in what were possibly illegal and treasonous acts."

I take Bradley's point to be not that Chinese peasants are not necessarily noble, and not that Japan wasn't guilty of aggression, but that the propaganda campaign convinced most Americans that Japan would not attack the United States if the United States cut off oil and metal to Japan — which was false in the view of informed observers and would be proved false in the course of events.

Former Secretary of State and future Secretary of War Henry Stimson became chair of the American Committee for Non-Participation in Japanese Aggression, which quickly added former heads of Harvard, Union Theological Seminary, the Church Peace Union, the World Alliance for International Friendship, the Federal Council of Churches of Christ in America, the Associate Boards of Christian Colleges in China, etc. Stimson and gang were paid by China to claim Japan would never attack the United States if embargoed, would in fact transform into a democracy in response — a claim dismissed by those in the know in the State Department and White House. By February 1940, Bradley writes, 75% of Americans supported embargoing Japan. And most Americans, of course, did not want war. They had bought the China Lobby's propaganda.

Franklin Roosevelt's maternal grandfather had gotten rich selling opium in China, and Franklin's mother had lived in China as a child. She became honorary chairwoman of both the China Aid Council and the American Committee for Chinese War Orphans. Franklin's wife Eleanor was honorary chairwoman of Pearl Buck's China Emergency Relief Committee. Two thousand U.S. labor unions backed an embargo on Japan. The first economic advisor to a U.S. president, Lauchlin Currie, worked for both the U.S. government and the Bank of China simultaneously. Syndicated columnist and Roosevelt relative Joe Alsop cashed checks from TV Soong as an "advisor" even while performing his service as a journalist. "No British, Russian, French, or Japanese diplomat," writes Bradley, "would have believed that Chiang could become a New Deal liberal." But Franklin Roosevelt may have believed it. He communicated with Chiang and Mayling secretly, going around his own State Department.

Yet Franklin Roosevelt believed that if embargoed, Japan would attack the Dutch East Indies (Indonesia) with the possible result of a wider world war. Morgenthau, in Bradley's telling, repeatedly tried to slip through a total embargo on petroleum to Japan, while Roosevelt resisted for a time. Roosevelt did impose a partial embargo on aviation-fuel and scrap. He did loan money to Chiang. He did supply airplanes, trainers, and pilots. When Roosevelt asked his advisor Tommy Corcoran to check out the leader of this new air force, former U.S. Air Corps captain Claire Chennault, he may have been unaware that he was asking someone in the pay of TV Soong to advise him on someone else in the pay of TV Soong.

Whether the British or Chinese propagandists working in New York moved the U.S. government anywhere it didn't already want to go is an open question.

12. *WWII does not prove that violence is needed for defense*

Suppose the argument for the justifiability of WWII is not a Holocaust that wasn't opposed until after the war (see Chapter 2), and not a surprise attack on an innocent peaceful government that wasn't innocent, peaceful, or surprised (see Chapter 11), but the need to defend against military aggression. And suppose we're forbidden to wind back the clock a single day or month or year to propose wiser behavior that could have prevented the war (see Chapters 3 through 10). The attack is underway! What do you do?

Military aggression against whom? The weakest answer available is: the United States. The Nazis did not have the ability to occupy even half of the Soviet Union. Some of the nations they occupied in Europe, as we will see below, effectively challenged their rule. Nonviolent resistance in Germany itself, as we will also see below, showed great potential. Nonviolent resistance to tyranny around the world, as we will see, in the past 75 years has proven itself more effective than armed struggle. The idea that Nazism could have lasted and grown to eventually include an attack on the United States is more fantasy than history. The idea that either Germany, Italy, and/or Japan could have occupied the United States is almost delusional. There are books and movies about such a scenario, but it's important to stress that they are fiction, entertainment, and propaganda with roots in the sort of propaganda found in Franklin Roosevelt's speech quoted in Chapter 11 of this book.

Military aggression against whom? A stronger answer is: Europe, or China. If, for the moment, before addressing it directly, we assume that answer to be strong enough, then an argument can be attempted to justify U.S. participation in the war along the following lines. The United States needed to act as a good global citizen. Others were in danger. Getting imperial forces in Hawaii attacked and selling it as an assault on the United States itself merely resulted in moving a self-centered populace to support the noble and generous intentions of the wise (if antidemocratic) U.S. government whose extended global military presence ever since has perhaps been similarly motivated by altruistic (if paternalistic and widely resented) identification with all of humanity.

Of course, there are some weaknesses in that argument, beginning with centuries of national governments' actions virtually never being driven by such motivations. But if the U.S. government did the right thing for some other set of reasons, we could still claim it was a just war. There are, however, complications in such arguments. Even most "just war" academics who praise U.S. entry into WWII condemn much of how the United States conducted itself during the war.[318] The United States helped to escalate the targeting of civilians; insisted on total, unconditional surrenders that lengthened the war; refused to take any steps to save victims of the Holocaust; and developed and used nuclear weapons that, as we will see in Chapter 14, did not shorten the war but have done tremendous damage and threaten human existence. This is a trickier argument to make than, I think, most of its adherents recognize. If U.S. actions that were not justified took huge numbers of lives, established practices that took many more lives in the decades to follow, and have right up to this day threatened all of human existence, then the U.S. entry into the war has to have done enough good to outweigh all of that harm — a calculation beyond the ability of any universally accepted mathematics to prove or disprove.

I think we have to turn to a more straightforward, but even more difficult question. What about military aggression against England or France or China or another nation attacked? Forget the United States. Were these other nations justified in fighting back? To make this question as difficult as possible, we have to avoid winding back the clock. We have to ignore England's having acted counterproductively, rather than defensively, right up through yesterday (see, in particular, Chapter 8), and ask: What do we do now that it is under attack today?

But, of course, England and France are not nations that work for this question any more than the United States. They were not attacked by Germany either. They declared war on Germany when Germany attacked Poland. Germany had not attacked England or France.

This was the series of events. In September of 1939, Germany attacked Poland. Britain and France, and Britain's colonies and commonwealth nations, declared war on Germany. President Roosevelt asked all nations to agree not to bomb civilians; Germany, Britain, and France agreed. Germany had already bombed civilians in Spain and Poland, as had Britain in Iraq, India, South Africa, Afghanistan, Egypt, Yemen, and Somaliland, and as had both sides on a smaller scale in WWI. Germany did torpedo a British passenger ship, and Britain did announce a blockade of Germany. Meanwhile, France briefly invaded Germany on the ground. Then came months of the Phoney War, which did include Britain and Germany occasionally sinking each other's war ships. In October, 1939, Britain and France rejected a peace proposal from Germany. The Phoney War meandered along. On March 16, 1940, German bombs killed one British civilian. On April 12, 1940, Germany blamed Britain for bombing a railroad line in Schleswig-Holstein, far from any war zone; Britain denied it.[319] On April 22, 1940, Britain bombed Oslo, Norway.[320] On April 25, 1940, Britain bombed the German town of Heide. Germany threated to bomb British civilians if British bombings of civilian areas continued.[321] On May 10, 1940, Germany invaded Belgium, France, Luxembourg, and the Netherlands. On May 14, 1940, Germany bombed Dutch civilians in Rotterdam. On May 15, 1940, and during the following days, Britain bombed German civilians in Gelsenkirchen, Hamburg, Bremen, Cologne, Essen, Duisburg, Düsseldorf, and Hanover. Churchill said, "We must expect this country to be hit in return." Also on May 15, Churchill ordered the rounding up and imprisoning behind barbed wire of "enemy aliens and suspect persons," most of whom were recently arrived Jewish refugees.[322] On May 30, 1940, the British cabinet debated whether to continue war or make peace, and decided to continue the war. The bombings of civilians escalated from there, and escalated dramatically after the United States entered the war. The United States and Britain leveled German cities. The United States burned Japanese cities; residents were "scorched and boiled and baked to death" in the words of U.S. General Curtis LeMay.[323]

So, let's switch the argument to another nation: Poland. Can we argue that England or France was justified in entering the war on behalf of Poland? Can we ignore their conduct — and for that matter Poland's — on Czechoslovakia, and begin our moral calculations as though the invasion of Poland was the first day of the world's existence? Could England or France be justified in having entered the war at that moment, regardless of their actual motivations for doing so? Or what about Poland itself? Poland didn't enter the war on behalf of others. In fact, it refused to do so. Poland was attacked. Was it justified in fighting back? Was China? In later decades, was Vietnam or Afghanistan or Iraq? Is any nation that has ever been attacked justified in fighting back?

There are a number of factors that make this a difficult point to address, and other factors that make it undesirable to address. By undesirable I mean that it is arguably inappropriate to tell anybody who's being attacked what they should or shouldn't do. They are the ones being attacked; they get to decide. (Period. Exclamation point. Appropriate cursing.) In cases where a commentator actually lives in the territory of the nation doing the attacking, or who can otherwise somehow be accused of sympathizing with the nation doing the attacking, then we move from inappropriate to scandalous. This undesirability of addressing this question is exacerbated and muddled by concepts like "rights." Suggesting that meeting violence with violence might not be the most effective action is often met with a response along the lines of "What do you mean they didn't have the right to fight back?" But rights aren't things you can actually go out and discover as objects in the world; they're concepts you create. And whether someone "has the right" to do something is simply not the same question as whether doing that thing is — even purely in the interests of that someone — the wisest thing to do. Surely, I have the right to compose the rest of this book in pig Latin, but that hardly means doing so would produce the results I'm after.

This argument is still difficult, even if we overcome its undesirability. It's difficult because no two incidents are identical, because there are no absolute laws in human affairs, because what someone arguably should have done is often something that person probably never would have thought about doing, and because we are raised in a culture of violence. Alternatives to violence are rarely discussed. Successes of nonviolent actions are rarely studied. Death and suffering in the commission of violence is often justified and even glorified. In contrast, death and suffering — even on a smaller scale and achieving a greater success — in the commission of nonviolent action is often lamented as horrific and inexcusable.

Mohandas Gandhi, an indisputably weird and deeply flawed individual, was often a strategic genius, yet his proposal that Germans use nonviolent resistance against Nazism is quickly dismissed as naïve stupidity, without anyone bothering to attempt or approximate any calculation as to whether the deaths and suffering would have outweighed the incredible death and suffering actually created in Europe, and elsewhere, by WWII. It's an impossible calculation to perform with precision. Had the vast majority of Germans skillfully and determinedly refused all cooperation with Nazism, Nazism would surely have perished, though not without suffering. Had a couple of dozen more Germans done so than actually did, they would almost certainly have failed and suffered without success — at least without preventing major suffering in the world, as opposed to protecting the purity of the activists' souls or providing some small measure of inspiration — as provided in Nazi Germany by, for example, the White Rose activists. Had some number in between two dozen and a vast majority acted, I suspect the number needed for success would have been much smaller than would generally be supposed, but of course I have no way to test it.

We do, however, have academic studies of the results of principally violent and principally nonviolent campaigns around the world over the decades, campaigns against foreign occupations and against domestic tyrannies. Both violence and nonviolence often fail, and advocates of one adore pointing out the failures of the other. But the important points, I think, which were documented by Erica Chenoweth and Maria Stefan in 2011 in *Why Civil Resistance Works: The Strategic Logic of Nonviolent Conflict*, is that nonviolence succeeds at over twice as high a rate as violence, those successes are usually far longer lasting — not tending to generate more violence — and those successes come in a huge variety of circumstances. Nonviolence is more likely to succeed both at regime change and at territorial change.[324]

In Algeria in 1961, four French generals staged a coup. "There was even a possibility of an invasion of France," Jørgen Johansen and Brian Martin tell us in their 2019 book, *Social Defence*. "There were far more French troops in Algeria than in mainland France. There was massive popular opposition to the revolt. After a couple of days of indecisiveness, [French President Charles] De Gaulle went on national radio and called for resistance by any possible means. In practice all the resistance was nonviolent. There were huge protests and a general strike. People occupied airstrips to prevent aeroplanes from Algeria landing. The resistance within the French military in Algeria was even more significant. . . . Many of them simply refused to leave their barracks. Another form of noncooperation was deliberate inefficiency, for example losing files and orders, and delaying communications. Many pilots flew their planes out of Algeria and did not return. Others feigned mechanical breakdowns or used their planes to block airfields. The level of noncooperation was so extensive that within a few days the coup collapsed."[325]

In the Soviet Union in 1991, President Mikhail Gorbachev was arrested at his dacha in Crimea. Johansen and Martin recount: "Tanks were sent to Moscow, Leningrad and other cities, and plans were made for mass arrests. Strikes and rallies were banned, liberal newspapers were closed and broadcast media were controlled, so most of the country had no news of resistance. . . . The coup leaders seemed to have all the advantages: backing from the armed forces, the KGB (Soviet secret police), the Communist Party and the police, plus the Soviet people's long acceptance of authority. . . . There was an immediate response, including protests, strikes, and messages of opposition. Across the country, including at major industrial complexes, many workers went on strike or just stayed home. Some civilians stood in the path of tanks, whose drivers then took another route. Rallies were held; when the army did not disperse the crowd, this provided a boost for the demonstrators. . . . Within a few days the coup collapsed, almost entirely due to popular noncooperation."[326]

Stephen Zunes lists a number of similar examples: "During the first Palestinian intifada in the 1980s, much of the subjugated population effectively became self-governing entities through massive noncooperation and the creation of alternative institutions, forcing Israel to allow for the creation of the Palestine Authority and self-governance for most of the urban areas of the West Bank. Nonviolent resistance in the occupied Western Sahara has forced Morocco to offer an autonomy proposal which — while still falling well short of Morocco's obligation to grant the Sahrawis their right of self-determination — at least acknowledges that the territory is not simply another part of Morocco. . . . Lithuania, Latvia, and Estonia freed themselves from Soviet occupation through nonviolent resistance prior to the USSR's collapse. In Lebanon, a nation ravaged by war for decades, thirty years of Syrian domination was ended through a large-scale, nonviolent uprising in 2005. And . . . Mariupol became the largest city to be liberated from control by Russian-backed rebels in Ukraine, not by bombings and artillery strikes by the Ukrainian military, but when thousands of unarmed steelworkers marched peacefully into occupied sections of its downtown area and drove out the armed separatists."

Other cases include, of course, the Gandhian example of booting the British out of India. Cases little known in the United States that should be widely studied include the numerous nonviolent movements that have succeeded around the world against U.S. military bases.[327]

When the Soviet military invaded Czechoslovakia in 1968, "There were huge demonstrations. There was a one-hour general strike on 22 August. Graffiti, posters, and leaflets were used to publicise the resistance. A few individuals sat down in front of tanks. Farmers and shopkeepers refused to provide supplies to the invading troops. Staff at Prague airport cut off central services. The Czechoslovak radio network allowed synchronous broadcasting from many locations across the country. . . The Soviets brought in radio-jamming equipment by train. When this information was broadcast, workers held up the train at a station. Next it was stopped on the main line due to an electricity failure. Finally it was shunted onto a branch line where it was blocked by locomotives at both ends. . . . . Announcers told how to avoid detection, harm and arrest, including details of when particular individuals were being hunted. To make the KGB's job more difficult, citizens removed house numbers and took down or covered over street signs. . . . An effective part of the resistance involved local people talking to the invading soldiers, engaging them in conversation, explaining why they were protesting. Some soldiers had falsely been told there was a capitalist takeover in Czechoslovakia; some of them thought they were in Ukraine or East Germany. . . . For the invading troops, the combination of being met with strong arguments while being refused food and normal social relationships was upsetting, possibly leading some troops to be deliberately inefficient."[328]

Czechoslovakia's Prague Spring lasted a week. "Dubcek, Svoboda, and other Czechoslovak political leaders were arrested and held in Moscow. Under severe pressure and without communication with the resistance back in Czechoslovakia, they made unwise concessions. They didn't realise how widespread and resolute the resistance was. The leaders' concessions deflated the resistance, so its active phase lasted only a week. However, it took another eight months before a puppet government could be installed in Czechoslovakia. The resistance thus failed in its immediate aims. However, it was immensely powerful in its impacts. The use of force against peaceful citizens undermined the credibility of the Soviet Communist Party. At this time, most countries around the world had communist parties, some of them quite strong and most looking to the Soviet party for leadership. The Prague spring changed all this. Many foreign communist parties splintered, with some members quitting or the parties splitting into old guard supporters of the Soviet line and supporters of the reform approach." [329]

Of course, all of the preceding stories are carefully chosen examples that don't include Nazi Germany, because — like it or not — Nazi Germany was uniquely evil and mercilessly violent.

Really? If that were so, we could stop worrying about a new Nazi Germany right now. But it isn't. Here's a sentence I omitted from that quote of Stephen Zunes above: "In the final years of German occupation of Denmark and Norway during WWII, the Nazis effectively no longer controlled the population." Nonviolent action had remarkable success, and showed tremendous potential, against the Nazis and even in Germany prior to the Nazis.

In Germany in 1920, a coup, led by Wolfgang Kapp, overthrew and exiled the government, but on its way out the government called for a general strike. "Workers shut down everything: electricity, water, restaurants, transport, garbage collection, deliveries. . . . Civilians shunned Kapp's troops and officials, who could not get anything done. For example, Kapp issued orders, but printers refused to print them. Kapp went to a bank to obtain funds to pay the troops, but bank officials refused to sign cheques. . . . In less than five days, Kapp gave up and fled from the country."[330] This incident is recounted in detail by Gene Sharp in his 2005 book, *Waging Nonviolent Struggle*, in which he quotes German historian Erich Eych as writing, "The putsch was defeated by two principle forms of resistance: the general strike of the workers and the refusal of the higher civil servants to collaborate with their rebel masters."[331] While hundreds died, thousands and millions did not.

Three years later, in 1923, also in Germany, when French and Belgian troops occupied the Ruhr, "The German government called on its citizens to resist the occupation by what was called, at the time, 'passive resistance,' namely resistance without physical violence. The key resistance tactic was to refuse to obey orders from the French occupiers. This was costly: thousands who ignored orders were arrested and tried by military tribunals, which handed out heavy fines and prison sentences. There were also protests, boycotts, and strikes. The resistance had many facets. The French demanded that owners of coal mines provide them coal and coke. When negotiations broke down, the German negotiators were arrested and court martialed. . . . Civil servants resisted. The German government said they should refuse to obey instructions from the occupiers. Some civil servants were tried for insubordination and given long prison sentences. Others were expelled from the Ruhr; over the course of 1923 nearly 50,000 civil servants were expelled. Transport workers resisted. The French-Belgian occupiers tried to run the railways. Only 400 Germans agreed to work for the new administration, compared to 170,000 who worked in the railways prior to the occupation."[332] People nonviolently turned public opinion in Britain, the U.S., and even in Belgium and France, in favor of the occupied Germans. By international agreement, through the Dawes Commission, the French troops were withdrawn. The Ruhr campaign is recounted in more detail in both the book (also a film), *A Force More Powerful: A Century of Nonviolent Conflict*, by Peter Ackerman and Jack Duvall.

So, after WWI and before the rise of the Nazis, Germany had demonstrated the power of nonviolent action against a German coup and against a foreign invasion. But it's not clear that all the appropriate lessons really sank in, either in Germany or anywhere else. When the Nazis took power, the resistance was far from sufficient. And yet the successes were significant.

When the Nazis took over Germany, Austria, Poland, Italy, France, Holland and other countries, there was resistance to shipping Jews off to be killed, but usually individual, not mass, resistance. In Bulgaria, on the other hand, which aligned with the Nazis without being occupied by them, the people filled the streets and public squares to protest. In March of 1943, they held rallies across Bulgaria to do just what people in the United States imagine the U.S. military was doing at that time, namely to save the Jews.

And they saved them. They persuaded the Bulgarian government to defy Berlin and refuse to send 48,000 Jews off to suffer or die.[333] The same thing would not, of course, have been possible in the exact same way in any other place, because no two places are the same, but it does begin to suggest what was possible. So does what happened in Rose Street in Berlin, also in February and March of 1943. (One is tempted to wonder what actions that same month in a few other places could have added up to.)

On February 27, 1943, the Nazi Gestapo in Berlin began rounding up Jewish men who were married to non-Jewish women, as well as their male children. Totaling about 2,000, the men and boys were held in a building on Rosenstrasse (Rose Street), pending deportation to . . . their families knew not where. In growing numbers composed mainly of wives and mothers, family members gathered daily outside the community center to wage the only major public protest by German citizens throughout the war. Wives of the Jewish detainees chanted, "Give us our husbands back." When Nazi guards aimed machine guns at the crowd, it responded with yells of "Murderer, murderer, murderer . . . ." Fearing that a massacre of hundreds of German women in the middle of Berlin might well cause unrest among broader sections of the German population, Nazi Minister of Propaganda Joseph Goebbels ordered the release of the intermarried male Jews, most of whom subsequently survived the war without going into hiding.[334]

Goebbels, according to his deputy, Leopold Gutterer, "released the Jews in order to eliminate that protest from the world . . . . So that others didn't take a lesson [from the protest], so others didn't begin to do the same, the reason [for the protest] had to be eliminated. There was unrest, and it could have spread from neighborhood to neighborhood . . . . Why should Goebbels have had them [the protestors] all arrested? Then he would have only had even more unrest, from the relatives of these newly arrested persons."[335]

Also according to Gutterer, "In Berlin were also representatives of the international press, who immediately grabbed hold of something like this, to loudly proclaim it. Thus news of the protest would travel from one person to the next." Goebbels did not want the people of Germany to believe anything other than that the people of Germany were united behind the Nazis. Nor did he want to focus attention on what was being done to Jews.[336] Hitler shared Goebbels' concerns and approved his decision, as did Himmler, who believed that using force would just enlarge the protests. For fear of reigniting the protests, the Nazis left these 2,000 Jews alone afterwards, and asked them to cease wearing yellow stars. French Jews married to Gentiles were also saved as a result of the change in policy in Germany.

The Civil Rights movement in the United States would struggle in places like Athens, Georgia, where authorities refused to respond with public violence. Activists had to seek out places like Selma, Alabama, where officials could be counted on to engage in counterproductive brutality. But this required organization, planning, and self-awareness, not just spontaneous — if courageous — demands for the lives of particular loved-ones. What if the protests in Rosenstrasse had been followed by strategic organizing and further courageous protest by a more diverse group of Germans acting on a broader agenda? Could the Nazis have eventually been brought down? Could the world's governments have been compelled to confront the Holocaust two years earlier? There is no way of knowing, and activists / scholars have developed an understanding of nonviolent strategies that can be used now but that didn't exist back then. Yet there is no reason to think that smart, brave, and popular nonviolent struggles against the Nazis, especially if begun years earlier, would not have had a good chance of success. Many hints of what was possible are provided by what was actually done. The story of Rosenstrasse is found in the book, *A Force More Powerful,* together with what happened in Denmark and the Netherlands.[337]

The Nazis had signed a treaty of non-aggression with Denmark that the Danes saw little harm in but that few expected the Nazis to comply with any more than Native Americans expected the U.S. government to comply with treaties. The Nazis did not comply. They invaded and occupied without military resistance from Denmark. But the people of Denmark found their own ways to resist. They refused to cooperate. They sabotaged Nazi equipment. They delayed shipments. They did work slowly. They gathered in large numbers to sing songs about Danish wars against Germany. They began demonstrating in the streets. They created an underground press. They voted for anti-Nazi officials. They went on strike. They ignored curfews. They developed skills and consciousness as they went along.

When the Nazis planned to seize Denmark's 8,000 Jews, Danish officials spread the word, and the non-Jewish people of Denmark immediately hid the Jews. Then they organized to secretly transport Jews on ships to Sweden, successfully transporting 7,220 people. Only 472 were captured.

The Danish resistance prioritized nonviolent activities in order to maximize participation. They created a general strike and mass demonstrations, the success of which was so dramatic that even more efforts were put into them, and less into sabotage or military action. Denmark was only fully freed of the Nazis by the ending of the war, but never succumbed to the Nazis or suffered under them as other nations did. Denmark consequently emerged from the war in better shape. Would the Nazis have been more brutal had the Danes not ranked high in their crazy racist theories? Probably. Would such brutality have succeeded or backfired? That's a harder question to answer. What seems clear is that what worked best and showed the most potential in Denmark was nonviolent action. Ackerman and Duvall conclude: "If the Nazis, the cruelest killing machine in the century's history, could be kept off balance by Danish schoolboys, amateur saboteurs, and underground clergymen, what other regime could ever be thought invulnerable to nonviolent resistance?"[338]

One day after invading Denmark, Nazi troops crossed into the Netherlands. German planes bombed Rotterdam, and the Royal family fled to London. The Dutch military surrendered after five days. Public demonstrations began within weeks, followed by student strikes, and efforts to protect Jews, eventually followed by a general strike and general noncompliance with Nazi orders, as well as the creation of an underground press. Dutch who were relocated to work in the Ruhr escaped and returned. They also engaged in sabotage. Over three-quarters of doctors refused to follow Nazi practices and officially abandoned their medical offices. Nazis shot into crowds of demonstrators, killing hundreds. The Netherland's nonviolent resistance lacked the national leadership and organizing that Denmark's had. The overall failure in the Netherlands, even while impeding the Nazis' plans, suggests that what was needed in Germany was something much more substantial, not just slightly more developed, than what happened at Rosenstrasse. But, of course, had nonviolent activism been even moderately more widespread and strategic in a dozen different countries, the cumulative effect would have been significant. Had enough people in enough different places acted with wisdom and courage, Nazism could have been ended.

Further contributions to resisting the Nazis were made by the Norwegians, and in particular by Norwegian teachers. Military resistance in Norway lasted two months. As elsewhere, without any theory or organization or plan behind it, nonviolent resistance developed. People refused to sign loyalty oaths or turn in their radios. They developed underground newspapers. Then the Nazi-imposed dictatorship of Minister-President Vidkun Quisling announced that the first step in creating a fascist state would be with teachers and youth, creating a new teachers' organization and a new youth organization. A small group of resisters asked teachers to make use of a statement of refusal and to share it with other teachers. Of 12,000 teachers in the country, between 8,000 and 10,000 mailed the statement to the Nazi-imposed government. So, the government closed the schools (just like Virginia would do years later when told it had to let black kids attend them); but tens of thousands of parents wrote to protest too. The government arrested 1,000 male teachers and sent them to concentration camps. But the new fascist institutions were never created, Quisling declared that "You teachers have destroyed everything for me," teachers who had been sent to an Arctic work camp were brought back and released, the whole fascist plan for Norway was abandoned,[339] and "quisling" entered the world's languages as a term for "a person who betrays his or her own country by aiding an invading enemy, often serving later in a puppet government."[340]

If teachers could do that, imagine what a whole society committed to a better path could do. But our schools teach war, war, war — so many wars that the years between them fade and war seems normal to the reader of history texts. And they don't teach peace, they don't inform students of the skills and successes of nonviolent action. It's a reality denied. We might call it nonviolence denial. In so far as it makes violence seem inevitable, it may be as dangerous as climate denial or other avoidance of critical information.

"Would you do nothing?" is the tendentious shorthand in common discourse for "Would you use diplomacy and negotiation and disarmament and aid and economic pressure and the rule of law and criminal prosecution and treaty creation and international organization and creative civil disobedience and grand public gestures and private discussions and the hundreds of tools of nonviolence, as opposed to mass slaughter or, as it's commonly called, "doing something"?

Another term for "doing nothing" that entered the language with WWII is "appeasement." Appeasement is basically the concept that anything other than mass slaughter is shameful, not just cowardly but unwise and doomed to backfire. Leading up to WWII there were not a lot of good arguments available for starting wars. The joy of war that was palatable in Teddy Roosevelt's day had dried up — even for him with his son's death in WWI. But after WWII, and ever since, politicians could either claim the other guy started it (Pearl Harbor, Gulf of Tonkin, 9/11) or argue that war was the path to peace, while the only other option was the doomed mistake of "appeasement" (Afghanistan harboring terrorists, Iraq building WMDs).

As we have seen in Chapter 8, those accused of appeasing Hitler were not seeking peace so much as seeking to direct German war-making against the Soviets. If they had been seeking peace, they would have taken different steps. They would have supported anti-Nazi activism and plots; they would have boycotted, divested, or sanctioned; they would have gotten serious about ceasing to arm and supply Germany; they would have held court proceedings like those that would happen after the war in Nuremberg but could have happened (at least *in absentia*) as soon as any country was attacked; they would have sought to make use of the League of Nations; they would have evacuated the Jews; they would have created a United Nations; they would have dropped the obsession with opposing the Soviet Union at all costs, they would have distributed a guidebook on how to non-cooperate with and completely disable a Nazi occupation.

When Hitler proposed peace in October, 1939, Chamberlain turned him down, claiming that if Britain were to discuss peace with Hitler it would be abandoning its claim that disputes should be settled by discussion and not force. The logic was supposed to be that Britain could not condone the force that had been used against Poland. But the illogic was that in order to uphold the resolution of disputes by discussion rather than force, Britain was going to refuse to discuss anything and commit to using force. If Britain had discussed matters with Hitler or even reached some agreement, would Hitler have been as good as his word? Probably not. But what delay in a war is not desirable? What sliver of a chance of preventing a war is not desirable? And was there not a sliver of a chance, when Germany had been viciously treated at Versailles and shut out of the League of Nations or any nonviolent forum for seeking redress of grievances? The shadow of "appeasement" should not be allowed to obscure the obvious desirability of avoiding tens of millions of deaths and massive, widespread destruction.[341]

Ted Grimsrud, in his 2014 book *The Good War That Wasn't and Why It Matters*, suggests nine things the U.S. government might have done differently[342]:

- Don't enter WWI
- Work for better postwar relationships
- Cultivate a positive relationship with Japan
- Overtly work to aid threatened Jews in Germany
- Don't move the Pacific fleet to Pearl Harbor

- Don't begin the Manhattan Project and don't build the Pentagon
- Respond positively to Japanese initiative just prior to Pearl Harbor
- Don't insist on unconditional surrender

I hope at this point in the current book you can think of additional items to add to that list. While it's popular to distinguish between the decision to join in a war and decisions of exactly how to wage that war, both decisions to join WWII and decisions to wage it brutally are opposed in similar ways to what ought to have been done.

In the real world, you are allowed to "roll back the clock," that is, to refrain from taking steps likely to result in WWIII, and to actively take steps likely to create lasting peace. Many such steps have already been taken, making the appearance of a "new Hitler" highly unlikely. We'll look at those steps in Chapter 17. Other steps could be taken — in fact must be taken if we are to survive. We'll consider those in Chapter 18.

13. WWII was the worst thing humanity has done to itself and the earth in any short period of time

In recorded human history, there's no worse catastrophe than WWII. There's nothing else that did as much immediate and lasting damage in the space of less than a decade. WWII killed 70 to 85 million human beings.[343] In most wars prior to WWII, including WWI, the majority of deaths were of participants in the wars. With WWII and most wars that have followed it, the majority of deaths have been civilians. WWII injured, traumatized, rendered homeless, and displaced millions of people on an unmatched scale.[344] This unprecedented assault on *homo sapiens* by *homo sapiens* was in part the result of people creating new kinds of weapons, and in part the result of governments deciding to engage in new kinds of atrocities — establishing new deadly practices that have lasted.

WWII destroyed more property, required greater financial expense (shortchanging alternatives, such as saving lives from starvation or disease), and created more lasting environmental damage than any other single disaster. It also established new disastrous policies that have lasted. The earth-attacking practices of extraction and consumption that grew out of WWII may yet doom us all, if not undone and corrected, as of course may the climate impact of the wars and the fuels they're fought over, and as of course may the nuclear weapons. People employed making weapons during WWII benefitted from the jobs, but people could have been employed making something useful and benefitted even more.[345]

WWII brought us total war that targets everyone and everything without limit, and total war that consumes the vast resources of the societies waging it. It brought us air war in a major way, the bombing of civilians and infrastructure and crops and hospitals. WWII was largely aerial genocide by multiple parties, or what prior to WWII would have been called horrific unimaginable murder but ever since WWII has simply been called war — or, sometimes, humanitarian war, liberation, or "doing something." WWII developed and created lasting legacies of chemical and biological war. It created permanent militarism from that day to this, and the nuclear arms race from that day to this — as well as the "But what about Hitler?" justification for these apocalyptic outrages.

The practice of bombing civilians as a supposed means of winning wars began, in a smaller way, in WWI. The British claimed before, during, and after major air strikes on German civilians in WWI that such a practice had a dramatic impact on the morale of the enemy. No postwar surveys found any evidence to support that claim. Following WWI, the British bombed Afghanistan, Egypt, India, Yemen, Somaliland, South Africa, and Iraq.[346]

The scale of the first bombings of Iraq (in what would become a century of bombings) can be understood from a few examples. On July 10, 1922, 19 planes were used to attack Rowanduz. They dropped 400 gallons of gasoline followed by incendiary and delayed bombs. Planes attacked for three more days. Over four days they dropped five tons of bombs on the town. On November 30 – December 1, 1923, British planes bombed Samawah. Forty planes dropped 25 tons of bombs plus 8,600 incendiary bombs and 15,000 rounds of ammunition. The town was completely destroyed. Reportedly 9,000 people were killed in the first 9 months of 10 years of bombing.[347] Had this horror been widely recognized as such, had Iraqis been valued like "white" people, had there been a work of art like *Guernica* or *Massacre in Korea*, who knows what might have been prevented.

In 1935 – 1936, Italy bombed Ethiopia with conventional bombs, fire bombs, and chemical bombs. Winston Churchill had advocated using chemical bombs on Iraqis but been overruled. "I am strongly in favour of using poisoned gas against uncivilised tribes," he wrote in a memo.[348] Which were the civilized tribes is not very clear. Churchill used chemical weapons against the Russians in 1919.[349] He raised the idea of using them against the Germans during WWII, writing in a June 7, 1944, memo, "I quite agree that it may be several weeks or even months before I shall ask you to drench Germany with poison gas, and if we do it, let us do it one hundred per cent. In the meanwhile, I want the matter studied in cold blood by sensible people and not by that particular set of psalm-singing uniformed defeatists which one runs across now here now there. Pray address yourself to this. It is a big thing and can only be discarded for a big reason. I shall of course have to square Uncle Joe and the President; but you need not bring this into your calculations at the present time. Just try to find out what it is like on its merits."[350]

Churchill didn't get to gas Germans, but he sure did get to bomb them. Germany had bombed Guernica in 1937. Japan had bombed China beginning in 1938, using chemical bombs, and delayed bombs that did damage similar to today's cluster bombs. But WWII saw dramatically new levels of aerial attacks on civilians, including massive U.S. and British bombing and fire-bombing of Germany, and U.S. fire-bombing of Japan, as well as the first two uses of nuclear bombs on cities.

The mythical belief that brutal air strikes on civilians can cause a government so indifferent to its citizens as to be engaged in a war to halt that war predates the development of airplanes and may last as long as our species. In 1941 President Franklin Roosevelt urged Britain to bomb German towns to "break German morale." Officials planning urban bombings in World War II expected civilians to react with the sort of trauma experienced by soldiers. They predicted that herds of "gibbering lunatics" would emerge from the rubble. But bombing victims do not endure the hardship of having to kill. Nor do they endure the "wind of hate," the hardship of having to face individuals who want to kill them specifically at close range. Bombing victims can be traumatized, but they can also be strengthened in their resolve against the enemy. Their government can also remain completely indifferent to their suffering or their opposition to continuing a war.

"The way to lick Hitler," Roosevelt told Henry Morgenthau in August of

1941, "is the way I have been telling the English, but they won't listen to me." Roosevelt's idea was to bomb smaller towns that were imagined to be safe. "There must be some kind of factory in every town. That is the only way to break German morale."[351] There is no evidence that the years of such bombing that followed ever broke German morale. But we do know that German officials used the bombings as justifications for rounding up Jews and seizing their houses. "The bombing offensive," according to historian Shlomo Aaronson, "fed Hitler's wrath, in direct connection with his concept of the 'Jew's war' against him, and helped him unite his nation behind him and justify further Nazi atrocities against the remaining Jews."[352]

In 1996, Harlan Ullman and James P. Wade coined the phrase "shock and awe." They believed that bombing the morale out of a nation had failed to work for decades because the bombing and other destruction hadn't been intense enough. The theory was tested on Iraq in 2003 and, predictably, failed miserably.

During WWII, the U.S. military dumped huge quantities of chemical weapons into the Atlantic and Pacific oceans. In 1943 German bombs sank a U.S. ship at Bari, Italy, that was secretly carrying a million pounds of mustard gas. Many of the U.S. sailors died from the poison, which the United States said it was using as a deterrent, though I don't think it ever explained how something deters while kept secret. That ship is expected to keep leaking the gas into the sea for centuries. Meanwhile the United States and Japan left over 1,000 ships on the floor of the Pacific, including fuel tankers. In 2013, the U.S. government identified 87 oil tankers on the ocean floor in U.S. waters in danger of leaking. Fifty-three of them were put there by WWII.[353] Efforts to extract oil from tankers sunk during WWII are ongoing all over the world.[354]

The Nazi Army flooded 17% of the Netherlands' farms with saltwater. Allied bombers breached two dams in Germany's Ruhr Valley, destroying 7,500 acres of German farmland. In Norway, the Nazis intentionally destroyed crops, forests, water supplies, and wildlife, including half of the reindeer.[355] To this day, WWII bombs are exploding or being discovered and removed before they can explode in France and Germany. Millions of acres remain off-limits, and victims are still claimed by explosions.

If a bombing occurs when bombs that have been dropped from U.S. airplanes explode, then the United States has been bombing Germany every year for over 75 years. There are still over 100,000 yet-to-explode U.S. and British bombs from World War II lying hidden in the ground in Germany. The *Smithsonian Magazine* noted in 2016:

"Before any construction project begins in Germany, from the extension of a home to track-laying by the national railroad authority, the ground must be certified as cleared of unexploded ordnance. Still, last May, some 20,000 people were cleared from an area of Cologne while authorities removed a one-ton bomb that had been discovered during construction work. In November 2013, another 20,000 people in Dortmund were evacuated while experts defused a 4,000-pound 'Blockbuster' bomb that could destroy most of a city block. In 2011, 45,000 people — the largest evacuation in Germany since World War II — were forced to leave their homes when a drought revealed a similar device lying on the bed of the Rhine in the middle of Koblenz. Although the country has been at peace for three generations, German bomb-disposal squads are among the busiest in the world. Eleven bomb technicians have been killed in Germany since 2000, including three who died in a single explosion while trying to defuse a 1,000-pound bomb on the site of a popular flea market in Göttingen in 2010."[356]

A 2015 film called *The Bomb Hunters* focuses on the town of Oranienburg, where a huge concentration of bombs keeps up a constant menace. In particular the film focuses on one man whose house blew up in 2013. He lost everything. Oranienburg, now known as the city of bombs, was a center of (not very advanced) nuclear research, that had been abandoned in 1942, but that the U.S. government did not want the advancing Soviets to acquire. At least that's one reason offered for the massive bombing of Oranienburg. Rather than possibly speed up the Soviet acquisition of nukes by a handful of years, Oranienburg had to be rained on with blankets of enormous bombs — to explode for decades to come.[357]

They weren't just bombs. They were delayed-fuse bombs, all of them. Delayed-fuse bombs were usually included along with non-delaying bombs in order to terrorize a population further and hinder humanitarian rescue operations after a bombing, similar to how cluster bombs have been used in recent U.S. wars to extend the terrorizing of a population by blowing up children for months to come, and similar to "double taps" in the business of drone murder — the first missile or "tap" to kill, the second to kill any rescuer bringing aid. Delayed-fuse bombs go off some hours or days after landing, but only if they land the right way up. Otherwise they can go off some hours or days or weeks or months or years or decades or who-knows-when later. Presumably this was understood at the time and intended.

A bomb or two goes off every year, but the greatest concentration is in Oranienburg where thousands and thousands of bombs were dropped. The town has been making a concerted effort to find and eliminate the bombs. Hundreds may remain. When bombs are found, neighborhoods are evacuated. The bomb is disabled, or it is detonated. Even during the search for bombs, the government must damage houses as it drills test holes into the ground at evenly spaced intervals. Sometimes the government even tears down a house in order to conduct the search for bombs beneath it.

A U.S. pilot involved in this madness way back when says in the film that he thought about those under the bombs, but believed the war to be for the salvation of humanity, thus justifying anything. Now, he says, he can see no justification for war.

Also in the film, a U.S. veteran writes to the Mayor of Oranienburg and sends $100 to apologize. But the Mayor says there's nothing to be sorry for, that the United States was only doing what it had to. Well, thanks for the codependency, Mr. Mayor. I'd love to get you on a talk show with Kurt Vonnegut's ghost. Germany's guilt is immensely admirable and worthy of emulation in the United States, which imagines itself forever sinless. But these two extremes build on each other in a toxic relationship.

When imagining that you've justified a war involves imagining that you've thereby justified any and every atrocity in that war, the results are things like nuclear bombings and bombings so intense that a country remains covered with unexploded bombs at a time when almost nobody involved in the war is still alive.

"WWII's most destructive event," writes Gar Smith, "involved the detonation of two nuclear bombs over the Japanese cities of Hiroshima and Nagasaki. The fireballs were followed by a 'black rain' that pelted survivors for days, leaving behind an invisible mist of radiation that seeped into the water and air, leaving a chilling legacy of cancers and mutations in plants, animals, and newborn children. Before the Nuclear Test Ban Treaty was signed in 1963, the U.S. and USSR had unleashed 1,352 underground nuclear blasts, 520 atmospheric detonations, and eight sub-sea explosions — equal to the force of 36,400 Hiroshima-sized bombs. In 2002, the National Cancer Institute warned that everyone on Earth had been exposed to fallout levels that had caused tens of thousands of cancer deaths."[358]

In *Baseless*, a 2020 book by Nicholson Baker, the author provides evidence that the U.S. military spread a horribly effective disease to the rice crop in Japan in 1945 — possibly including with flights that happened five and six days after the bombing of Nagasaki.[359]

The destruction of WWII stretched into regions of the globe that took no part in it, such as Latin America. People of German and Japanese ancestry were hauled from some countries north to the United States to prison camps, or to forced labor in Panama. Mexican oil fueled the Nazis — just as U.S. oil did. Brazil's forests were sacrificed for U.S. rubber. The two sides of WWII spied on each other in Latin America, sank each other's ships off the coast, and left their traces behind. Brazilians fought with the Allies in Italy, and veterans of that fighting established a U.S.-backed military dictatorship in Brazil from 1964 to 1985 — a tradition Brazil has not yet completely left behind. Argentina set up its own form of fascism under Juan Peron, and rat lines to Argentina became the Catholic Church's retirement plan for Nazis not tried at Nuremberg and not included in Operation Paperclip — rat lines also used by Allen Dulles and U.S. "intelligence" types to protect Nazis.[360]

While only the tiniest fraction of the environmental damage of WWII was done in the United States, that damage was enormous. U.S. forests were hit hard by WWII clearcutting.[361]

Huge new bases were created or expanded at Fort Bragg, Fort Knox, and Fort Hood. After WWII, the U.S. military owned 20 times the U.S. land that it had before the war.[362] Farmers massively ramped up production with government subsidies. A land of family farms until WWII exited WWII as an area of industrialized farming by vast conglomerates profiting a narrow slice of the population but unloading the environmental costs of factory farming on everyone.[363]

"In 1938," write Thomas Robertson and Richard P. Tucker, "before massive wartime spending began, most Americans lived in small towns, farms, or small urban areas; traveled by rail; and had never heard of penicillin, DDT, or atomic bombs. By 1945, the scales had tipped decidedly toward military-industrial urban areas, the Sunbelt, machine and chemical agriculture, air travel, oil-based materials, such as nylon, and a Keynesian "growth" economy stressing government-sponsored consumption."[364] WWII consumed unprecedented quantities of oil and gas, guns, tanks, and planes. While there were no propaganda posters asking you to save the Jews, there were plenty asking you to produce metals and other materials needed for the war.[365]

WWII created atomic weapons; new chemical weapons; new biological weapons; chemical fertilizers; synthetics, such as plastic and nylon; new metal alloys; drugs like penicillin; sonar; new jet engines; DDT; insecticides; herbicides; bulldozers; assembly-line housing; processed foods; dehydrated foods; canned and frozen foods; and much more, all with reckless disregard for the earth. Tons of pollutants went into the atmosphere and waterways. By 1945 cities like Pittsburgh had to have street lights on at noon. In Los Angeles WWII created the problem called smog. In Niagara, N.Y., in 1941, the Hooker Chemical Company began dumping toxic waste in Love Canal. Residents didn't notice the horrible health impacts until the 1970s. When they did, it helped start the Superfund program to clean up the worst environmental disaster sites, most of which have military and WWII origins.[366]

Even the damage of U.S. resource production and supply provision for WWII impacted much of the globe, with major construction in Alaska, Hawaii, the Panama Canal zone, and in numerous nations. Of 136 raw materials that the U.S. government deemed strategic and critical 48 came from outside the United States and its colonies and territories. During WWII, the U.S. military became the world's top consumer of petroleum; it still is.[367]

During WWII, the U.S. government subsidized and promoted to the U.S. military and domestically the heavy use of cigarettes. We know how that worked out.[368]

Many WWII-era U.S. military bases have never been closed, across the United States and the world. The United States still keeps huge numbers of troops in Germany and Japan. The Military Industrial Complex has never shut down. And the wartime thinking that accompanies these programs has never disappeared.

Much of the thinking in U.S. culture about WWII is about the glory of the U.S. troops who fought in it. So, it's an inconvenient fact that most of them only pretended to fight. Lacking intense modern training and psychological conditioning to prepare soldiers to engage in the unnatural act of murder, some 80% of U.S. and other troops in WWII did not fire their weapons at "the enemy."[369] According to the analysis of police-murder-instigator Dave Grossman, who now gives domestic U.S. police "warrior training," the reason that only a minority of soldiers attempted to kill in WWII and earlier wars was a general aversion to committing murder. And the reason that the vast majority of U.S. soldiers (and marines, sailors, etc.) have attempted to kill in recent decades is "classical conditioning." A fireman rushes into a fire without thinking, if he or she has been conditioned through drill repetition to do so. Soldiers kill without thinking, if they have been trained to do so through the repetition of the realistic simulation of killing.[370] The same problem — the difficulty that most people have in committing murder — was addressed by the Nazis with the institution of gas chambers as replacements for firing squads.

Veterans of WWII were not immune to the problem recent war veterans call post-traumatic stress disorder (and sometimes moral injury) but earlier veterans called shell shock or combat stress reaction. Whether conditioned to mindlessly kill or not, recovering from the experience of having faced those trying to kill you or the experience of having killed is not usually an easy one. Neither is living one's life with serious physical injuries.

The fact that U.S. veterans of WWII in some ways and in some cases (especially white Veterans) were treated better after the war than other soldiers before or since, was largely the result of the pressure created by the Bonus Army after the previous war. That veterans were given free college, healthcare, and pensions was not due to the merits of the war or in some way a result of the war. Without the war, everyone in the United States could have been given free college for many years — no combat stress reaction or missing limbs required.

In recent years, a movement called "Me Too" has exposed sexual assault and harassment in a variety of industries. I keep waiting for WWII to have its Me Too moment. WWII and its victorious liberation aftermath were massive extravaganzas of brutal rapes and gang rapes on possibly a world-record scale.

Here's the opening of a 2013 book review in the *New York Times:*

"The soldiers who landed in Normandy on D-Day were greeted as liberators, but by the time American G.I.'s were headed back home in late 1945, many French citizens viewed them in a very different light. In the port city of Le Havre, the mayor was bombarded with letters from angry residents complaining about drunkenness, jeep accidents, sexual assault — 'a regime of terror,' as one put it, imposed by bandits in uniform.' This isn't the 'greatest generation' as it has come to be depicted in popular histories. But in *What Soldiers Do: Sex and the American G.I. in World War II France*, the historian Mary Louise Roberts draws on French archives, American military records, wartime propaganda and other sources to advance a provocative argument: The liberation of France was 'sold' to soldiers not as a battle for freedom but as an erotic adventure among oversexed Frenchwomen, stirring up a 'tsunami of male lust' that a battered and mistrustful population often saw as a second assault on its sovereignty and dignity."[371]

Alice Kaplan, an historian at Yale, has written that the U.S. military tolerated rape of German women even more than of French — which is really saying something. Meanwhile J. Robert Lilly, author of *Taken by Force: Rape and American GIs in Europe in World War II*, estimates that U.S. soldiers committed 14,000 rapes in France, Germany, and the United Kingdom between 1942 and 1945. Other estimates, some of which are little more than guesses, extrapolating nationally from local data, go as high as 190,000 rapes, just in Germany, just by U.S. troops. Soviet and French troops seem to have been just as bad or worse.[372]

Rape has been a part of U.S. wars — and many other nations' wars — from the days of slaughtering Native American families, right up through the days of slaughtering Middle Eastern families. In recent years, it's even been a major part of life within the U.S. military, with rapist and victim employed by the same institution.

WWII was a horror, full of horrors — the worst combination of atrocities ever seen. The only way to justify such a thing is with false beliefs so strong that they need to be called myths.

14. WWII in western culture is a dangerous set of myths

In 2015, Alice Sabatini was an 18-year-old contestant in the Miss Italia contest in Italy. She was asked what epoch of the past she would have liked to live in. She replied: WWII. Her explanation was that her text books go on and on about it, so she'd like to actually see it, and she wouldn't have to fight in it, because only men did that. This led to a great deal of mockery. Did she want to be bombed or starved or sent to a concentration camp? What was she, stupid? Somebody photoshopped her into a picture with Mussolini and Hitler. Somebody made an image of a sunbather viewing troops rushing onto a beach.[373]

But could an 18-year-old in 2015 be expected to know that most of the victims of WWII were civilians — men and women and children alike? Who would have told her that? Certainly not her text books. Most definitely not the endless saturation of her culture with WWII-themed entertainment. What answer did anyone think such a contestant would be more likely to give to the question she'd been asked, than WWII? In U.S. culture as well, which heavily influences Italian, a top focus for drama and tragedy and comedy and heroism and historical fiction is WWII. Pick 100 average viewers of Netflix or Amazon and I'm convinced a large percentage of them would give the same answer as Alice Sabatini, who, by the way, was declared the winner of the competition, fit to represent all of Italy or whatever it is Miss Italia does.

WWII is often called "the good war," and sometimes this is thought of as principally or originally a contrast between WWII, the good war, and WWI, the bad war. However, it was not popular to call WWII "the good war" during or immediately after it happened, when the comparison with WWI would have been easiest. Various factors may have contributed to the growth in popularity of that phrase over the decades, including increased understanding of the Holocaust (and misunderstanding of the war's relationship to it),[374] plus, of course, the fact that the United States, unlike all the other major participants, wasn't itself bombed or invaded (but that's also true for dozens of other U.S. wars). I think a major factor was actually the War on Vietnam. As that war became less and less popular, and as opinions were deeply divided by a generation gap, by a division between those who had lived through WWII and those who had not, many sought to distinguish WWII from the war on Vietnam. Using the word "good," rather than "justified," or "necessary," was probably made easier by distance in time from WWII, and by WWII propaganda, most of which had been created (and is still being created) after the conclusion of WWII. Because opposing all wars is considered radical and vaguely treasonous, critics of the war on Vietnam could refer to WWII as "the good war" and establish their balanced seriousness and objectivity. It was in 1970 that just war theorist Michael Walzer wrote his paper, "World War II: Why Was This War Different?" seeking to defend the idea of a just war against the unpopularity of the war on Vietnam. I'll offer a rebuttal to that paper in Chapter 17 of this book. We saw a similar phenomenon in the years 2002 to 2010 or so, with countless critics of the war on Iraq emphasizing their support for the war on Afghanistan and distorting the facts to improve the image of that newer "good war." I'm not sure many, if anyone, would have called Afghanistan a good war without the war on Iraq or called WWII a good war without the war on Vietnam.

In July 2020, U.S. President Donald Trump — in arguing that U.S. military bases named for Confederates should not have their names changed — proclaimed that these bases had been part of "beautiful world wars." "We won two world wars," he said, "two world wars, beautiful world wars that were vicious and horrible."[375] Where did Trump get the idea that the world wars were beautiful, and that their beauty consisted of viciousness and horribleness? Probably the same place Alice Sabatini did: Hollywood. It was the film *Saving Private Ryan* that led Mickey Z in 1999 to write his book, *There Is No Good War: The Myths of World War II*, originally with the title *Saving Private Power: The Hidden History of the "Good War."*

Before rushing back in a time machine to experience the glory of WWII, I'd recommend picking up a copy of Studs Terkel's 1984 book, *The Good War: An Oral History of World War II*.[376] This is first-person accounts from veterans of WWII telling their memories 40 years later. They were young. They were put into a non-competitive brotherhood and asked to do great things and see great places. It was tremendous. There was smoking, and swearing, and alcohol so you could bring yourself to shoot at people, and vicious violence with the simple goal of survival, and stacks of dead bodies in trenches, and ever-watchful vigilance, and deep wrenching moral guilt, and fear, and trauma, and virtually no sense of having made a moral calculation that participation was justified — just pure dumb obedience to be questioned and regretted later. And there was the stupid patriotism of the people who didn't see the real war. And there were all the people who didn't want to see the horrifically disfigured survivors. "What kind of war do civilians suppose we fought anyway?" asked one veteran, quoted in Chapter 5 of this book.

The myths that make up most of what most people think they know about WWII don't resemble the reality, but do endanger our real world. Some of the myths we've already examined in this book: the war was to save the Jews; the United States was an innocent bystander hit with a surprise attack; the war was inevitable or of wholly foreign origin, not contributed to by U.S. eugenics or segregation or funding or supplies or genocide; there were no alternatives but to fight or "do nothing"; the primary enemy was Germany (or Italy or Japan) and not the Soviet Union; the chief victor in the war was the United States; the war ended with no lasting side-effects; the war was good for "the economy," as military spending always is. This package of falsehoods creates acceptance of war, even of nuclear war, even of imperialist war.

Then there's the myth that by participating in WWII, the United States did the world such a favor that the United States now owns the world. In

2013, Hillary Clinton gave a speech to bankers at Goldman Sachs in which
she claimed that she had told China that it had no right to call the South
China Sea the South China Sea, that the United States could in fact claim
to own the entire Pacific by virtue of having "liberated" it in WWII, and
having "discovered" Japan, and having "bought" Hawaii.[377] I'm not sure
how best to debunk that. Perhaps I can advise asking some people in Japan
or Hawaii what they think. But it's worth noting that there was no flood
of mockery for Hillary Clinton of the sort experienced by Alice Sabatini.
There was no noticeable public outrage over this reference to WWII when
it became public in 2016.

Perhaps the strangest myths, though, are those about nuclear weapons,
especially the idea that by murdering huge numbers of people with them a
far greater number of lives, or at least the right kind of lives, were spared.
The nukes did not save lives. They took lives, possibly 200,000 of them.
They were not intended to save lives or to end the war. And they didn't
end the war. The Russian invasion did that. But the war was going to end
anyway, without either of those things. The United States Strategic Bombing
Survey concluded that, "… certainly prior to 31 December, 1945, and in all
probability prior to 1 November, 1945, Japan would have surrendered even
if the atomic bombs had not been dropped, even if Russia had not entered
the war, and even if no invasion had been planned or contemplated."[378]

One dissenter who had expressed this same view to the Secretary of
War and, by his own account, to President Truman, prior to the bombings
was General Dwight Eisenhower.[379] Under Secretary of the Navy Ralph
Bard, prior to the bombings, urged that Japan be given a warning.[380] Lewis
Strauss, Advisor to the Secretary of the Navy, also prior to the bombings,
recommended blowing up a forest rather than a city.[381] General George
Marshall apparently agreed with that idea.[382] Atomic scientist Leo Szilard
organized scientists to petition the president against using the bomb.[383]
Atomic scientist James Franck organized scientists who advocated treating
atomic weapons as a civilian policy issue, not just a military decision.[384]
Another scientist, Joseph Rotblat, demanded an end to the Manhattan

Project, and resigned when it was not ended.[385] A poll of the U.S. scientists who had developed the bombs, taken prior to their use, found that 83% wanted a nuclear bomb publicly demonstrated prior to dropping one on Japan. The U.S. military kept that poll secret.[386] General Douglas MacArthur held a press conference on August 6, 1945, prior to the bombing of Hiroshima, to announce that Japan was already beaten.[387]

The Chairman of the Joint Chiefs of Staff Admiral William D. Leahy said angrily in 1949 that Truman had assured him only military targets would be nuked, not civilians. "The use of this barbarous weapon at Hiroshima and Nagasaki was of no material assistance in our war against Japan. The Japanese were already defeated and ready to surrender," Leahy said.[388] Top military officials who said just after the war that the Japanese would have quickly surrendered without the nuclear bombings included General Douglas MacArthur, General Henry "Hap" Arnold, General Curtis LeMay, General Carl "Tooey" Spaatz, Admiral Ernest King, Admiral Chester Nimitz, Admiral William "Bull" Halsey, and Brigadier General Carter Clarke. As Oliver Stone and Peter Kuznick summarize, seven of the United States' eight five-star officers who received their final star in World War II or just after — Generals MacArthur, Eisenhower, and Arnold, and Admirals Leahy, King, Nimitz, and Halsey — in 1945 rejected the idea that the atomic bombs were needed to end the war. "Sadly, though, there is little evidence that they pressed their case with Truman before the fact."[389]

On August 6, 1945, President Truman lied on the radio that a nuclear bomb had been dropped on an army base, rather than on a city. And he justified it, not as speeding the end of the war, but as revenge against Japanese offenses. "Mr. Truman was jubilant," wrote Dorothy Day. Weeks before the first bomb was dropped, on July 13, 1945, Japan had sent a telegram to the Soviet Union expressing its desire to surrender and end the war. The United States had broken Japan's codes and read the telegram. Truman referred in his diary to "the telegram from Jap Emperor asking for peace." President Truman had been informed through Swiss and Portuguese channels of Japanese peace overtures as early as three months before Hiroshima. Japan objected only to surrendering unconditionally and giving up its emperor, but the United States insisted on those terms until after the bombs fell, at which point it allowed Japan to keep its emperor. So, the desire to drop the bombs may have lengthened the war. The bombs did not shorten the war.[390]

Presidential advisor James Byrnes had told Truman that dropping the bombs would allow the United States to "dictate the terms of ending the war." Secretary of the Navy James Forrestal wrote in his diary that Byrnes was "most anxious to get the Japanese affair over with before the Russians got in." Truman wrote in his diary that the Soviets were preparing to march against Japan and "Fini Japs when that comes about." The Soviet invasion was planned prior to the bombs, not decided by them. The United States had no plans to invade for months, and no plans on the scale to risk the numbers of lives that U.S. school teachers will tell you were saved.[391] The idea that a massive U.S. invasion was imminent and the only alternative to nuking cities, so that nuking cities saved huge numbers of U.S. lives, is a myth. Historians know this, just as they know that George Washington didn't have wooden teeth or always tell the truth, and Paul Revere didn't ride alone, and slave-owning Patrick Henry's speech about liberty was written decades after he died, and Molly Pitcher didn't exist.[392] But the myths have their own power. Lives, by the way, are not the unique property of U.S. soldiers. Japanese people also had lives.

Truman ordered the bombs dropped, one on Hiroshima on August 6th and another type of bomb, a plutonium bomb, which the military also wanted to test and demonstrate, on Nagasaki on August 9th. The Nagasaki bombing was moved up from the 11th to the 9th to decrease the likelihood of Japan surrendering first.[393] Also on August 9th, the Soviets attacked the Japanese. During the next two weeks, the Soviets killed 84,000 Japanese while losing 12,000 of their own soldiers, and the United States continued bombing Japan with non-nuclear weapons — burning Japanese cities, as it had done to so much of Japan prior to August 6th that, when it came time to pick two cities to nuke, there hadn't been many left to choose from. Then the Japanese surrendered.

That there was cause to use nuclear weapons is a myth. That there could again be cause to use nuclear weapons is a myth. That we can survive significant further use of nuclear weapons is a myth. That there is cause to produce nuclear weapons even though you'll never use them is too stupid even to be a myth. And that we can forever survive possessing and proliferating nuclear weapons without someone intentionally or accidentally using them is pure insanity.[394]

Why do U.S. history teachers in U.S. elementary schools today — in 2020! — tell children that nuclear bombs were dropped on Japan to save lives — or rather "the bomb" (singular) to avoid mentioning Nagasaki? Researchers and professors have poured over the evidence for 75 years. They know that Truman knew that the war was over, that Japan wanted to surrender, that the Soviet Union was about to invade. They've documented all the resistance to the bombing within the U.S. military and government and scientific community, as well as the motivation to test bombs that so much work and expense had gone into, as well as the motivation to intimidate the world and in particular the Soviets, as well as the open and shameless placing of zero value on Japanese lives. How were such powerful myths generated that the facts are treated like skunks at a picnic?

In Greg Mitchell's 2020 book, *The Beginning or the End: How Hollywood — and America — Learned to Stop Worrying and Love the Bomb*, we have an account of the making of the 1947 MGM film, *The Beginning or the End*, which was carefully shaped by the U.S. government to promote falsehoods.[395] The film bombed. It lost money. The ideal for a member of the U.S. public was clearly not to watch a really bad and boring pseudo-documentary with actors playing the scientists and warmongers who had produced a new form of mass-murder. The ideal action was to avoid any thought of the matter. But those who couldn't avoid it were handed a glossy big-screen myth. You can watch it online for free, and as Mark Twain would have said, it's worth every penny.[396]

The film opens with what Mitchell describes as giving credit to the UK and Canada for their roles in producing the death machine — supposedly a cynical if falsified means of appealing to a larger market for the movie. But it really appears to be more blaming than crediting. This is an effort to spread the guilt. The film jumps quickly to blaming Germany for an imminent threat of nuking the world if the United States didn't nuke it first. (You can actually have difficulty today getting young people to believe that Germany had surrendered prior to Hiroshima, or that the U.S. government knew in 1944 that Germany had abandoned atomic bomb research in 1942.[397]) Then an actor doing a bad Einstein impression blames a long list of scientists from all over the world. Then some other personage suggests that the good guys are losing the war and had better hurry up and invent new bombs if they want to win it.

Over and over we're told that bigger bombs will bring peace and end war. A Franklin Roosevelt impersonator even puts on a Woodrow Wilson act, claiming the atom bomb might end all war (something a surprising number of people actually believe it did, even in the face of the past 75 years of wars, which some U.S. professors describe as the Great Peace). We're told and shown completely fabricated nonsense, such as that the U.S. dropped leaflets on Hiroshima to warn people (and for 10 days — "That's 10 days more warning than they gave us at Pearl Harbor," a character pronounces) and that the Japanese fired at the plane as it approached its target. In reality, the U.S. never dropped a single leaflet on Hiroshima but did — in good SNAFU fashion — drop tons of leaflets on Nagasaki the day after Nagasaki was bombed. Also, the hero of the movie dies from an accident while fiddling with the bomb to get it ready for use — a brave sacrifice for humanity on behalf of the war's real victims — the members of the U.S. military. The film also claims that the people bombed "will never know what hit them," despite the film makers knowing of the agonizing suffering of those who died slowly.

One communication from the movie makers to their consultant and editor, General Leslie Groves, included these words: "Any implication tending to make the Army look foolish will be eliminated."[398]

The main reason the movie is deadly boring, I think, is not that movies have sped up their action sequences every year for 75 years, added color, and devised all kinds of shock devices, but simply that the reason anybody should think the bomb that the characters all talk about for the entire length of the film is a big deal is left out. We don't see what it does, not from the ground, only from the sky.

Mitchell's book is a bit like watching sausage made, but also a bit like reading the transcripts from a committee that cobbled together some section of the Bible. This is an origin myth of the Global Policeman in the making. And it's ugly. It's even tragic. The very idea for the film came from a scientist who wanted people to understand the danger, not glorify the destruction. This scientist wrote to Donna Reed, that nice lady who gets married to Jimmy Stewart in *It's a Wonderful Life*, and she got the ball rolling. Then it rolled around an oozing wound for 15 months and voilà, a cinematic turd emerged.

There was never any question of telling the truth. It's a movie. You make stuff up. And you make it all up in one direction. The script for this movie contained at times all sorts of nonsense that didn't last, such as the Nazis giving the Japanese the atomic bomb — and the Japanese setting up a laboratory for Nazi scientists, exactly as back in the real world at this very time the U.S. military was setting up laboratories for Nazi scientists (not to mention making use of Japanese scientists). None of this is more ludicrous than *The Man in the High Castle,* to take a recent example of 75 years of this stuff, but this was early, this was seminal. Nonsense that didn't make it into this film, everybody didn't end up believing and teaching to students for decades, but easily could have. The movie makers gave final editing control to the U.S. military and the White House, and not to the scientists who had qualms. Many good bits as well as crazy bits were temporarily in the script, but excised for the sake of proper propaganda.

If it's any consolation, it could have been worse. Paramount was in a nuclear arms film race with MGM and employed Ayn Rand to draft the hyper-patriotic-capitalist script. Her closing line was "Man can harness the universe — but nobody can harness man." Fortunately for all of us, it didn't work out. Unfortunately, despite John Hersey's *A Bell for Adano* being a better movie than *The Beginning or the End*, his best-selling book on Hiroshima didn't appeal to any studios as a good story for movie production. Unfortunately, *Dr. Strangelove* would not appear until 1964, by which point many were ready to question future use of "the bomb" but not past use, making all questioning of future use rather weak. This relationship to nuclear weapons parallels that to wars in general. The U.S. public can question all future wars, and even those wars it's heard of from the past 75 years, but not WWII, rendering all questioning of future wars weak. In fact, recent polling finds horrific willingness to support future nuclear war by the U.S. public.

At the time *The Beginning or the End* was being scripted and filmed, the U.S. government was seizing and hiding away every scrap it could find of actual photographic or filmed documentation of the bomb sites. Henry Stimson was having his Colin Powell moment, being pushed forward to publicly make the case in writing for having dropped the bombs. More bombs were rapidly being built and developed, and whole populations evicted from their island homes, lied to, and used as props for newsreels in which they are depicted as happy participants in their destruction.

Mitchell writes that one reason Hollywood deferred to the military was in order to use its airplanes, etc., in the production, as well as in order to use the real names of characters in the story. I find it very hard to believe these factors were terribly important. With the unlimited budget it was dumping into this thing — including paying the people it was giving veto power to — MGM could have created its own quite unimpressive props and its own mushroom cloud. It's fun to fantasize that someday those who oppose mass murder could take over something like the unique building of the U.S. Institute of "Peace" and require that Hollywood meet peace movement standards in order to film there. But of course the peace movement has no money, Hollywood has no interest, and any building can be simulated elsewhere. Hiroshima could have been simulated elsewhere, and in the movie wasn't shown at all. The main problem here was ideology and habits of subservience.

There were reasons to fear the government. The FBI was spying on people involved, including wishy-washy scientists like J. Robert Oppenheimer who kept consulting on the film, lamenting its awfulness, but never daring to oppose it. A new Red Scare was just kicking in. The powerful were exercising their power through the usual variety of means.

As the production of *The Beginning or the End* winds toward completion, it builds the same momentum the bomb did. After so many scripts and bills and revisions, and so much work and ass-kissing, there was no way the studio wouldn't release it. When it finally came out, the audiences were small and the reviews mixed. The New York daily *PM* found the film "reassuring," which I think was the basic point. Mission accomplished.

Mitchell's conclusion is that the Hiroshima bomb was a "first strike," and that the United States should abolish its first-strike policy. But of course it was no such thing. It was an only strike, a first-and-last strike. There were no other nuclear bombs that would come flying back as a "second strike." Now, today, the danger is of accidental as much as intentional use, whether first, second, or third, and the need is to at long last join the bulk of the world's governments that are seeking to abolish nuclear weapons all together — which, of course, sounds crazy to anyone who has internalized the mythology of WWII.

There are far better works of art than *The Beginning or the End* that we could turn to for myth busting. For example, *The Golden Age*, a novel published by Gore Vidal in 2000 with glowing endorsements by the *Washington Post,* and *New York Times Book Review,* has never been made into a movie, but tells a story much closer to the truth.[399] In *The Golden Age,* we follow along behind all the closed doors, as the British push for U.S. involvement in World War II, as President Roosevelt makes a commitment to Prime Minister Churchill, as the warmongers manipulate the Republican convention to make sure that both parties nominate candidates in 1940 ready to campaign on peace while planning war, as Roosevelt longs to run for an unprecedented third term as a wartime president but must content himself with beginning a draft and campaigning as a drafttime president in a time of supposed national danger, and as Roosevelt works to provoke Japan into attacking on his desired schedule.

Then there's historian and WWII veteran Howard Zinn's 2010 book, *The Bomb*.[400] Zinn describes the U.S. military making its first use of napalm by dropping it all over a French town, burning anyone and anything it touched. Zinn was in one of the planes, taking part in this horrendous crime. In mid-April 1945, the war in Europe was essentially over. Everyone knew it was ending. There was no military reason (if that's not an oxymoron) to attack the Germans stationed near Royan, France, much less to burn the French men, women, and children in the town to death. The British had already destroyed the town in January, similarly bombing it because of its vicinity to German troops, in what was widely called a tragic mistake. This tragic mistake was rationalized as an inevitable part of war, just as were the horrific firebombings that successfully reached German targets, just as was the later bombing of Royan with napalm. Zinn blames the Supreme Allied Command for seeking to add a "victory" in the final weeks of a war already won. He blames the local military commanders' ambitions. He blames the American Air Force's desire to test a new weapon. And he blames everyone involved — which must include himself — for "the most powerful motive of all: the habit of obedience, the universal teaching of all cultures, not to get out of line, not even to think about that which one has not been assigned to think about, the negative motive of not having either a reason or a will to intercede."

When Zinn returned from the war in Europe, he expected to be sent to the war in the Pacific, until he saw and rejoiced at seeing the news of the atomic bomb dropped on Hiroshima. Only years later did Zinn come to understand the inexcusable crime of enormous proportions that was the dropping of nuclear bombs in Japan, actions similar in some ways to the final bombing of Royan. The war with Japan was already over, the Japanese seeking peace and willing to surrender. Japan asked only that it be permitted to keep its emperor, a request that was later granted. But, like napalm, the nuclear bombs were weapons that needed testing.

Zinn also goes back to dismantle the mythical reasons the United States was in the war to begin with. The United States, England, and France were imperial powers supporting each other's international aggressions in places like the Philippines. They opposed the same from Germany and Japan, but not aggression itself. Most of America's tin and rubber came from the Southwest Pacific. The United States made clear for years its lack of concern for the Jews being attacked in Germany. It also demonstrated its lack of opposition to racism through its treatment of African Americans and Japanese Americans. Franklin Roosevelt described fascist bombing campaigns over civilian areas as "inhuman barbarity" but then did the same on a much larger scale to German cities, which was followed up by the destruction on an unprecedented scale of Hiroshima and Nagasaki — actions that came after years of dehumanizing the Japanese. Aware that the war could end without any more bombing, and aware that U.S. prisoners of war would be killed by the bomb dropped on Nagasaki, the U.S. military went ahead and dropped the bombs.

Uniting and strengthening all of the WWII myths is the overarching myth that Ted Grimsrud, following Walter Wink, calls "the myth of redemptive violence," or "the quasi-religious belief that we may gain 'salvation' through violence." As a result of this myth, writes Grimsrud, "People in the modern world (as in the ancient world), and not least people in the United States of America, put tremendous faith in instruments of violence to provide security and the possibility of victory over their enemies. The amount of trust people put in such instruments may be seen perhaps most clearly in the amount of resources they devote to preparation for war."[401]

People aren't consciously choosing to believe in the myths of WWII and violence. Grimsrud explains: "Part of the effectiveness of this myth stems from its invisibility as a myth. We tend to assume that violence is simply part of the nature of things; we see acceptance of violence to be factual, not based on belief. So we are not self-aware about the faith-dimension of our acceptance of violence. We think we *know* as a simple fact that violence works, that violence is necessary, that violence is inevitable. We don't realize that instead, we operate in the realm of belief, of mythology, of religion, in relation to the acceptance of violence."[402]

It takes an effort to escape the myth of redemptive violence, because it's been there since childhood: "Children hear a simple story in cartoons, video games, movies, and books: we are good, our enemies are evil, the only way to deal with evil is to defeat it with violence, let's roll.

The myth of redemptive violence links directly with the centrality of the nation-state. The welfare of the nation, as defined by its leaders, stands as the highest value for life here on earth. There can be no gods before the nation. This myth not only established a patriotic religion at the heart of the state, but also gives the nation's imperialistic imperative divine sanction. . . . World War II and its direct aftermath greatly accelerated the evolution of the United States into a militarized society and . . . this militarization relies on the myth of redemptive violence for its sustenance. Americans continue to embrace the myth of redemptive violence even in face of mounting evidence that its resulting militarization has corrupted American democracy and is destroying the country's economy and physical environment. . . . As recently as the late 1930s, American military spending was minimal and powerful political forces opposed involvement in 'foreign entanglements.'"[403]

Prior to WWII, Grimsrud notes, "when America engaged in military conflict . . . at the end of the conflict the nation demobilized . . . . Since World War II, there has been no full demobilization because we have moved directly from World War II to the Cold War to the War on Terrorism. That is, we have moved into a situation where 'all times are times of war.' . . . Why would non-elites, who bear terrible costs by living in a permanent war society, submit to this arrangement, even in many cases offering intense support? . . . The answer is quite simple: the promise of salvation."[404]

15. There was resistance to WWII in the United States

The U.S. public was against entering WWII right up until December 7, 1941. The U.S. Congress passed its last ever declarations of war (all the wars since have been declaration-free) on December 8th (Japan), 11th (Germany and Italy), 12th (Romania), and 13th (Bulgaria and Hungary). A poll on the 12th to 17th showed widespread support.

In May, 1940, 93% of Americans opposed declaring war on Germany. Gallup was careful never to ask that question again, switching instead to a question of which was more important, staying out of the war or "helping England." In July 1940, 61% said it was more important to keep out than to help England at the risk of getting in; in September that dropped to 44%, by November to 40%, and by March, 1941, to 33%, where it stayed in July, before dropping to 30% in September.[405] But in a Gallup poll from December 12th to 17th, 1941, just after the Japanese attacks and the declarations of war, 97% of Americans approved the United States having entered the war against Japan,[406] and 91% thought Roosevelt should have declared war on Germany too (as Congress had, by this point, in fact done).[407] There have been other wars that were popular at first, if not quite this popular. What is most unusual about WWII is its popularity long after being over.[408]

But for a war to be more popular than other wars, and to do well in polling at its start and even 75 years later, should not suggest that there was no opposition, much less that the support was completely uncoerced. Some 100,000 draftable young men in the United States declared themselves conscientious objectors to WWII, half of whom were not drafted due to holding important civilian jobs or having physical disabilities or other reasons. Those who were drafted and could succeed in achieving conscientious objector status from the U.S. military (which required claiming religious motivation) had the option to take non-combat military jobs (30,000 did so), or to join the Civilian Public Service (12,000 did so), or to go to prison (6,000 did so, of whom 4,500 were Jehovah's Witnesses).[409] Without registering as a conscientious objector, the only option was prison.

Those put to work in the Civilian Public Service (at significant expense to peace churches, as the government wouldn't pay to administer the program) typically worked on fighting forest fires, caring for mental patients, building fences and railroads, or planting trees, but some 500 volunteered (if that's the right word for taking one of a handful of bad choices) to be subjected to dangerous medical experiments, including experiments in starvation, from which some of them died. Many of these "volunteers" stated that they were subjecting themselves to life-threatening experiments in order to show people that they were driven by opposition to war and not by cowardice.[410] The fact that people would do that is an indication of how severe the public condemnations and false accusations were. All the workers in the Civilian Public Service were forbidden to speak publicly against the war.[411]

There were voices raised against war here and there. On October 7, 1939, journalist Milton Mayer wrote in the *Saturday Evening Post* that a war to defeat Hitler would only guarantee the victory of Hitlerism, regardless of who won the war: "I am trying to keep my eye on the ball in spite of my hatred for a man called Hitler. Who is this Hitler, anyway? A man, like the rest of us, a man capable, like the rest of us, of acting like a man; but a man brutalized, as the rest of us may be, by war and the poverty of war and the animal degradation of war — a man, in short, behaving like an animal. Fascism is animalism. The wolves are Fascists; the bees have the perfect Fascist state. It is not Hitler I must fight, but Fascism. And I know, from philosophy and from science, from the Bible and from Freud, that it is not the sinner I must exorcise, but the sin. If I want to beat Fascism, I cannot beat it at its own game. War is at once the essence and the apotheosis, the beginning and the triumph, of Fascism, and when I go to war I join 'Hitler's' popular front against the man in men. I cannot fight animals their way without turning animal myself. . . . I cannot see how we can have, or save, democratic states without democratic men in whom reason governs. War, like Fascism, teaches men two things: How to be governed by the force of others; and how, the force of others permitting, to be governed by the force within themselves. If the worst thing that can happen to men is to come under the rule of the tooth and the claw, I cannot see why men should come under that rule voluntarily by going to war."[412]

Dorothy Day made a speech in New York on December 8, 1941: "There is now all this patriotic indignation about the Japanese attack on Pearl Harbor and Japanese expansionism in Asia. Yet not a word about American and European colonialism in this same area. We, the British, the French, and others set up spheres of influence . . . control national states — against the expressed will of these states — and represent imperialism . . . . and it has become too late in human history to tolerate wars which none can win. Nor dare we quibble about just wars . . . . All wars are, by their very nature, evil and destructive. It has become too late for civilized people to accept this evil. We must take a stand. We must renounce war as an instrument of policy . . . . Evil enough when the finest of our youth perish in conflict and even the causes of these conflicts were soon lost to memory. Even more horrible today when cities go up in flames and brilliant scientific minds are searching out ultimate weapons. War must cease. There are no victories. The world can bear the burden no longer. Yes, we must make a stand. Even as I speak to you, I may be guilty of what some men call treason. But we must reject war: Yes, we must now make a stand. War is murder, rape, ruin, death; war can end our civilization. I tell you that within a decade we will have weapons capable of ending this world as we have known it."[413]

Jeanette Rankin, who had voted against WWI in Congress as the first woman ever in Congress, began thinking in 1939 of running for Congress again. She sent letters to all the high school principals in Montana, telling them that she would be speaking at their schools on upcoming dates. She provided no return address or means of declining the self-invitation. She showed up at each school and spoke against war, and then asked every student to write a letter to President Roosevelt after discussing it with their parents. Rankin was elected to Congress again in 1940, and on December 8, 1941, cast the only vote against WWII. On December 8, 1942, she put into the Congressional Record her case against the war.[414] While Dorothy Day may be declared a saint someday by the Catholic Church, and while the current Pope praised her in a speech at the U.S. Congress in 2015[415], war supporters have tended to use quite different labels for Jeanette Rankin.

In October 1940, eight students at Union Theological Seminary refused to register for the draft, even as conscientious objectors (or to accept the exemption offered to theology students). Their reasoning was as follows: "War consists of mass murder, deliberate starvation, vandalism, and similar evils. Physical destruction and moral disintegration are the inevitable result. The war method perpetuates and compounds the evils it purports to overcome." This was said not through a magical ability to see the future of Korea or Vietnam or dozens of other places, but through simple observation of past wars. "It seems to us," said these theology students, precursors of many students who would oppose the war on Vietnam, "that one of the reasons the government has granted exemptions to ministers and theological students is to gain a religious sanction for its diabolical war. Where actual support could not be gained, it hoped to soothe their consciences so that they could provide no real opposition."[416]

These students did not believe they would prevent U.S. warmaking, but neither were they acting without concern for the consequences of their actions. They believed they were near the beginning of a long struggle to build a movement that could prevent wars. "We do not contend," they said, "that the American people maliciously choose the vicious instrument of war. In a very perplexing situation, they lack the imagination, the religious faith, and the precedents to respond in a different manner. This makes it all the more urgent to build in this country and throughout the world a group trained in the techniques of non-violent opposition to the encroachments of militarism and fascism. Until we build such a movement, it will be impossible to stall the war machine at home. When we do build such a movement, we will have forged the only weapon which can ever give effective answer to foreign invasion. Thus in learning to fight American Hitlerism we will show an increasing group of war-disillusioned Americans how to resist foreign Hitlers as well."[417]

David Dellinger, one of the eight students who made the statement above, worked against poverty during the Great Depression, went to prison rather than fight in WWII, worked for civil rights, and was one of the Chicago 7 arrested during the Democratic National Convention in 1968. When the WWII student draft resisters were locked up in Federal prison in Danbury, Connecticut, Dellinger, who was white, happened to walk into the first Saturday night movie with a black friend. They were ordered to sit in segregated sections, but Dellinger sat with his friend — an offense that landed him in solitary confinement. The war objectors then organized, inside the prison, and later in other prisons, at significant risk to their lives, protests against racial segregation. They won the integration of the dining hall of Danbury Federal Prison, an early victory for what would grow into a national civil rights movement.

Jim Peck, who spent the war years in prison as a draft resister and was also at Danbury, said: "The most effective way for an individual to start outlawing war is simply to refuse to take part in it." He would not fight against Hitler, not due to a lack of a sense of responsibility to stop Hitler, but rather due to a stronger sense of responsibility to stop war, as Grimsrud summarizes.[418] Dellinger and Peck would apply lessons from civil rights actions in prison to civil rights actions out of prison after the war. So would Bayard Rustin, the future organizer of the 1963 March on Washington for Jobs and Freedom, who was also imprisoned for draft resistance during WWII. Dellinger and Rustin were both imprisoned in Lewisburg Federal Penitentiary, where they organized protests against racial segregation. Rustin did the same at Ashland Prison as well.

In 1940, A.J. Muste, who also refused to register for the WWII draft when it was extended to his age group, hired Rustin, James Farmer, and other new staffers for a campaign of the antiwar group, the Fellowship of Reconciliation, to apply Gandhian tactics to the struggle against Jim Crow. When Rustin was later a close advisor to Martin Luther King, Jr., he said he never gave King advice without checking it with Muste.

In April of 1947, eight black and eight white men embarked from Richmond, Va., on a two-week trip called the Journey of Reconciliation. In

1946, the U.S. Supreme Court had overturned state bans on interstate travel by integrated groups. During the Journey of Reconciliation, the men attempted to board 26 buses and trains. Twelve of them were arrested, and three of them served 22 days on a chain gang in North Carolina. James Peck was among those brutally beaten. He was the only participant to also participate in the Freedom Rides of 1961, where he was again brutally beaten.[419]

Eight participants in the Journey of Reconciliation, including Peck and Rustin, were formerly imprisoned conscientious objectors to WWII. One of them, Wally Nelson, had done three-and-a-half years in federal prisons during WWII, where he had engaged in a 107-day hunger strike against racial segregation and been force fed for the last 87 days he spent behind bars.[420] Another of them, George Houser, had been locked up at Danbury. These men took a terrible punishment for refusal to participate in the most terrible disaster ever, and turned it into something that actually advanced freedom and democracy, namely a newly energized and creative movement to end systemic racism.

Resistance also resulted from WWII disasters in the United States. David Wright recounts: "An ammunition plant in Ellwood, Illinois, blew up in 1942, killing 49 people . . . in Cleveland, Ohio, [in 1944], a liquid gas tank explosion killed 135 workers . . . The worst wartime rail disaster took place near Philadelphia on September 6, 1943, when seventy-nine passengers died in a massive derailment . . . in a famous non-combat crash, a U.S. B-25 bomber ran into the Empire State Building in New York City on July 28, 1945, killing fourteen."[421]

In 1944 there was a town in Northern California called Port Chicago. There, African American sailors, relegated to dangerous manual labor by a racist government, unloaded munitions from trains and put them onto ships. The officers in charge were all white, the sailors ordered to ignore basic safety precautions were all black. On July 17, 1944, explosions killed 320 men. Two hundred and fifty-eight survivors refused to return to work as what they called "munitions fodder." Fifty were tried for mutiny by all-white judges and sentenced to 8-15 years in prison, while 208 were court-martialed and dishonorably discharged.[422]

16. WWII created taxes

I'm not for or against taxes in general, but I am for progressive taxes and against regressive taxes, and I'm against spending funds raised through taxes on wars or environmental destruction or mass incarceration.

The reason I single out taxes for attention here is that many people in the United States simply cannot stand them. Little is more resented than taxes. I think this is in part because people in the United States, in comparison with, for example, Scandinavian countries, get so little (other than wars) in return for paying their taxes. I think it is also in part because taxes are often regressive and unfair. Office assistants who pay taxes at a higher rate than top executives know it and do not like it. But I think there may be another reason, as well, that taxes are so resented in the United States. Taxes on ordinary people were created for what was supposed to be a temporary purpose. They were supposed to go away again. But they never did. That feels like we got scammed. It feels that way even if we're only dimly aware of what happened, even if we don't clearly recall that the purpose for which taxes on most ordinary Americans were created was WWII.

If you hate taxes but dutifully cheer for wars, it's advisable to also oppose school funding sufficient to produce historical literacy, because taxes are a byproduct of wars. Were it not for wars and war propaganda, the United States might never have begun paying taxes. Now taxes are deeply resented but considered as inevitable as death. In reality, they could be ended for ordinary working people, but that would probably require ending wars.

War and Taxes is a 2008 book by tax historians Steven Bank, Kirk Stark, and Joseph Thorndike. They lay out the history of U.S. taxation, the debates, the votes, the legislation, the compliance and evasion. Here are all the details in clear chronological order. It turns out that "war and taxes" have a lot more in common than "death and taxes." War and taxes are both optional and are joined at the hip. Or, as these authors put it: "War has been the most important catalyst for long-term, structural change in the nation's fiscal system. Indeed, the history of America's tax system can be written largely as a history of America's wars."[423]

Alexander Hamilton argued in Federalist No. 30, as he and his allies argued elsewhere, for the federal power to tax precisely because the federal government might need to fight wars. Between 1789 and 1815, tariffs produced 90 percent of government revenue. But taxes were needed for wars, including wars against protests of the taxes — such as President George Washington's quashing of the Whiskey Rebellion. A property tax was put in place in 1789 in order to build up a Navy (some people in what is now Libya allegedly needed killing for the good of humanity, oddly enough). More taxes were needed in 1798 because of the troublesome French. But taxation really got going with the War of 1812.[424]

Remember, this was to be an easy cakewalk kind of war with Canadians welcoming U.S. invaders as liberators. But mistakes were made, as they say, and the bill grew hefty (and Washington got burned). Congress passed a tax program in 1812 that included a direct tax on land, and excise taxes on retailers, stills, auction sales, sugar, bank notes, and carriages. In 1815, Congress added a new direct tax and restored that controversial whiskey tax as well, plus taxes on all kinds of items, luxurious and otherwise. The idea of an income tax was raised but rejected.

The income tax was first created by the U.S. Civil War. The North began an income tax in 1862, and the Confederacy in 1863. This was after the routine promises of a cheap and easy war had worn out their welcome. Both sides were forcing men to leave their homes to kill and risk death, but effectively excusing the wealthy from that duty. Thus arose popular pressure to compel the rich to "sacrifice" financially. Both sides enacted progressive, graduated income taxes, and other taxes as well. The North taxed everything in sight, including inheritances and especially corporations. The financial cost of the Civil War was astronomical, and the veterans' pension program was the first major social welfare program in the United States. It required massive funding.

But with the end of war came the end of support for taxes, and the income tax and the inheritance tax lapsed temporarily in 1872. Taxation returned to forms that were often more regressive than a progressive graduated income tax, taxing various forms of consumption. Advocacy was strong in the country, its newspapers, and in Congress in the following years to restore the income and inheritance taxes. Major change would not come, however, until World War I and its army of patriotic propagandists:

"The transition from an almost exclusive reliance on customs duties to a substantial reliance on internal revenues, such as the income tax, the estate tax, and excise taxes, could not have occurred without the demand for fiscal sacrifice that accompanied wartime politics."[425]

What a bargain: we stop taxing foreign goods in order to tax ourselves, and we do that in order to go kill the people who make the foreign goods — unless they kill us first. What's not to like?

"But this process did not flow naturally from the public mood in support of the war. Rather, for the first time, the notion of wartime fiscal sacrifice was cultivated, marketed, and sold to the American public."[426]

New taxes were created in 1914, 1916, 1917, and 1918. The income tax was now back in a big way, along with the estate tax, a munitions tax, an excess profits tax, and other heavy taxes on corporations. The munitions and profits taxes were results of an ongoing debate through most of U.S. history over how to tax war profiteering. Until relatively recently, profiting financially from war was widely considered unacceptable. The draft again served as an argument for taxing the wealthy. Even the U.S. Chamber of Commerce claimed to be "undismayed at the prospect of great taxes," and pledged "its full and unqualified support in the prosecution of the war." The 1917 legislation drew 74% of its revenue from taxing the wealthy and another 13% from taxing luxuries.

Following World War I, various taxes were no longer needed. In 1921 and 1924 Congress repealed the excess profits tax but left the income tax in place, rather than adopting a sales tax favored by business groups. The top rate of taxation on income was reduced from 77% to 25%, but that was still more than double where it had been before the war. Meanwhile, the estate tax remained in place, and corporate taxes were actually increased during the 1920s. Taxation and progressive taxation survived the outbreak of peace.

Then came the most glorious war of all, and with it massive taxation for all. WWII spending, taxation, and — of course — the draft, were off and running long before Pearl Harbor. And by the end of this worst catastrophe in human history, government funding had been transformed:

"The personal income tax, long confined to the upper strata of American society, became mainstream. Between 1939 and 1945, Congress lowered exemptions repeatedly, converting what had long been a 'class tax' into a full-fledged 'mass tax.' . . . [B]y 1945, more than 90 percent of American workers were filing income tax returns. At the same time, lawmakers significantly increased tax rates, with marginal tax rates peaking at 94%. . . . By the war's end, the tax was raising 40% of total federal revenue, making it the largest source of federal funds."[427]

Corporate taxes were increased as well, with a top statutory rate of 95%, and generating almost a third of wartime revenue. An excess profits tax came within a month of the draft. A shift to the sales tax was still successfully resisted. But a relatively progressive tax system was still a tax system, with many Americans forced to pay up for the first time. This required a new round of sweet smelling Donald Duck droppings, otherwise known as propaganda. Taxes were renamed "the Victory Tax." In a Disney cartoon, the narrator warned Donald Duck that "It takes taxes to beat the Axis!" An Irving Berlin song was titled "I Paid My Income Tax Today." Among the lyrics:

"You see those bombers in the sky?

"Rockefeller helped to build them,

"So did I!"

If you pay taxes in the United States today, you should go back and watch these cartoons and listen to these songs, because they're the main reason why.

In 1943 Congress overrode a presidential veto to shift the tax burden more heavily onto working people. Corporations would never again to this day shoulder the share of public funding that they had in the early years of World War II.

Taxes were reduced again after the war. But again, they were not returned to pre-war levels. The 1948 reduction was the only time taxes have been cut by overriding a presidential veto. President Truman was envisioning a permanent military state while millions of other Americans were hoping war had ended at least for a while.

But in 1950 and 1951, Congress passed new tax bills, including an excess profits tax, to pay for war in Korea, and to return the tax system to roughly what it had been during World War II. There was support for "sacrifice" in the air at the start of the Korean War that later fizzled.

The Vietnam War was a different story. In the earlier years of its major escalation, President Lyndon Johnson avoided raising taxes, apparently largely out of fear that talking about the financial strain of the war would lead to cuts in domestic programs. Or, as LBJ delicately put it:

"I knew from the start that I was bound to be crucified either way I moved. If I left the woman I really loved — the Great Society — in order to get involved with that bitch of a war on the other side of the world, then I would lose everything at home. All my programs. All my hopes to feed the hungry and the homeless. All my dreams."[428]

Of course, he would also kill huge numbers of human beings, most of them Vietnamese, and destroy any dreams held by anyone in that country. And he did so. But the war grew unpopular at home, as did the idea of sacrificing financially to pay for it. Nonetheless, the tax bill that was passed in 1968 was the largest single-year increase since World War II. On March 25, 1969, just days after secretly beginning to bomb Cambodia, President Nixon began lobbying Congress for more taxes.

And then came George W. Bush. War as a joint sacrifice was out the window. Wars would be fought by the poor and the privatized. Mercenaries and contractors would outnumber troops. Massive spending would be dedicated to recruitment. Those recruited would meet lower standards and be held for longer periods of "service." Everyone else would benefit from war. There would be patriotism, entertaining news coverage, and major tax cuts, instead of increases. Out as well was progressive taxation, the notion that the wealthy should pay at a greater rate than those who actually needed their money. So, something new arose on the horizon of U.S. history: major and repeated regressive tax cuts during an immensely expensive series of wars.

This pattern has essentially continued to this day. Military spending continues to increase, while taxes continue to decrease, at least for wealthy people. The result has been a huge budget deficit. And the impact of these and related policies on the economy has been disastrous, leading to an even huger budget deficit. A lot of ideas have been proposed to solve this problem: cut back or eliminate self-funding programs that are doing fine financially, such as Social Security or Medicare; or cut back or eliminate basic goods provided through the government, such as schools or healthcare or environmental protection. A lot of those cuts have now gone through.

The fact that over half of the U.S. income tax goes to the military and wars[429], and that a majority want those wars ended[430] and that military reduced[431] — such obvious solutions are not often discussed in respectable company. The conversation is further constrained by the fact that most people no longer remember that the taxes were created for the wars, in particular for WWII.

17. *The world has changed: Hitler is not coming to get us*

There are authoritarian leaders around the world (and the United States!) who draw comparisons to Hitler. They promote racist and ethnic hatred, corporate-oligarchic power, and the glorification of war and violence. But do any of those leaders actually constitute a threat of global conquest? Are any of them not armed and supported by the same nations that warn of their danger? Are any of them operating in a world that resembles the 1930s in relevant ways so that they reasonably raise the specter of a "new Hitler"? Do any of them justify dumping our great grandchildren's unearned pay into multi-billion dollar weapons systems?

Nobody goes back 75 years to find the model for any sort of educational enterprise or social program or medicine or science or fashion or race relations or sexual relations or just about anything. Certainly, nobody goes back 75 years to find the last successful justification for any ongoing project. If the Environmental Protection Agency had to plead its case for funding to the U.S. Congress based on 75 years of counterproductive disasters preceded by one occasion when it had cleaned something up, there would be no funding for the EPA. If the Department of Education couldn't prove it had educated anyone other than a group of kids 75 years ago, there would be no Department of Education. So, why, for the single biggest expense, bigger than all the rest of the discretionary budget put together, does the U.S. government accept the justification that the U.S. military defeated Hitler?

Well, it's paid to do that.[432] But why should we accept it? Never mind that the Soviet Union mostly defeated Hitler, what does WWII have to do with today? I suspect the acceptance of this nonsense has a lot to do with the frequency with which we've heard the second coming of Hitler announced.

In August, 1989, U.S. Deputy Secretary of State Lawrence Eagleburger told the Organization of American States, describing drug dealing by estranged CIA asset and President of Panama Manuel Noriega: "That is aggression as surely as Adolf Hitler's invasion of Poland 50 years ago was aggression. It is aggression against us all, and some day it must be brought to an end."[433]

In November, 1990, U.S. President George H.W. Bush said that Iraqi President Saddam Hussein was holding Americans "in direct contravention of international law. Many of them reportedly staked out as human shields near possible military targets, brutality that I don't believe Adolf Hitler ever participated in anything of that nature." The resulting headlines informed us that Hussein was worse than Hitler.[434]

In January 1999 the *Boston Globe* called the President of Serbia Slobodan Milosevic "the closest thing to Hitler Europe has confronted in the last half century." Not to be left out, at the same time, Serbs were calling the U.S. President "Bill Hitler."[435]

In August 2002, U.S. Secretary of "Defense" Donald Rumsfeld warned that not attacking Saddam Hussein (again) would be just like "appeasing" Hitler.[436]

In October 2002, Jonah Goldberg wrote in the *National Review* that warmongers were calling Hussein Hitler again, while peace activists were pointing out again that he wasn't as bad as Hitler. Goldberg conceded the peace activists' point but still favored war because of the imaginary weapons people were, in those days, supposed to pretend Hussein had. In the process, Goldberg accidentally admitted that nonviolent noncooperation could have stopped Hitler: "What made Hitler dangerous wasn't that he was a meanie. Nor was it that he wanted to invade other countries or rule an Aryan empire — as we speak, there are people restocking the shelves of video stores and driving school buses who have similar ambitions. What made Hitler so destructive was the fact that he had the power of a whole nation at his beck and call. If the *Wehrmacht* and the German people generally had been unwilling to follow his orders, Hitler wouldn't have been much of a threat to anybody. What's different about Saddam Hussein is the fact he's a threat even though the people *aren't* on his side. This is a key difference between Hussein and Hitler — two mustachioed murderers everyone feels compelled to discuss together. Hitler lived in the age when conventional weapons — tanks, bombs, planes, the unabridged works of Heidegger, and the manpower necessary to use them effectively — were the only reliable weapons of mass destruction. Saddam is ruling in an age when mass destruction — whether in the form of a disease or a nuclear bomb — can be delivered by a small handful of men. So while Hitler needed lots of men to be loyal to him and the Fatherland in order to be dangerous, Saddam really doesn't."[437]

The straight-faced comparisons, circa 2006, of Iranian President Mahmoud Ahmadinejad to Hitler are endless and came from U.S. politicians like Newt Gingrich[438] and Mitt Romney[439], U.S. diplomats[440], *Washington Post* columnist Charles Krauthammer[441], Israeli Prime Minister Ehud Olmert[442], the Simon Wiesenthal Center[443], Germany's Central Council of Jews[444], and many others.

In March 2011, any former Libyan who would compare Muammar Gaddafi to Hitler was newsworthy.[445] Also newsworthy, even after the three of them were dead: stories comparing the affection of Hitler, Hussein, and Gaddafi for bunkers[446] or golden guns[447].

In September 2013, U.S. Secretary of State John Kerry likened Syrian President Bashar al Assad to Hitler.[448]

In March 2014, U.S. Secretary of State Hillary Clinton likened Russian President Vladimir Putin to Hitler.[449]

Not only is Hitler coming back, but he's already come back repeatedly, and the appeasers have been overcome, and our brave troops have stamped out evil before it could take away our freedoms, but there are more Hitlers popping up every time we turn around! We must be eternally vigilant (and Lockheed Martin needs more money)!

When I tell a class full of students that we should abolish war, and they say "But what about Hitler?" this is what they mean. He's come back repeatedly, or at least he's come once, and there's nothing like faith in a second coming to create a passionate belief system.

But none of the new Hitlers who have been overthrown and killed have had powerful militaries. None of them have attacked wealthy nations. None of them have conquered large areas of territory. None of them were interested in or capable of conquering the United States, not even a United States without a trillion-dollar-a-year military. The Hitler comparisons are achieved through a focus on something evil (Noriega's drug use and prostitutes and red pajamas, a mistranslation of a comment Ahmadinejad made about Israel450, the weapons that the United States had once helped Hussein acquire, etc.). In fact, the big wealthy countries of the world have not gone to war with each other in 75 years, with or without any participation by a new Hitler. They've waged proxy wars and imperial wars — wars on poor little places accused of being Hitler. It's much easier to sell a war against one demonized individual than against all the thousands of men, women, and children who will suffer and die in the war. And there's no better way to demonize an individual than calling him "Hitler." But Hitler is not coming to get us.

One reason that some of the biggest war-making nations have not gone to war with each other in 75 years is probably that a war with nuclear weapons on both sides would likely end life on earth. But there are many other reasons — so many, I think, that we have no reason to expect that the elimination of nuclear weapons would make wars more likely (though, if it did, at least they wouldn't include nuclear apocalypse). Only one other nation on earth spends even a third of what the United States does on militarism. That country, China, has not been fighting any wars. In 2019, former U.S. President Jimmy Carter, who normalized relations with China in 1979, told U.S. President Donald Trump that China was doing well economically because, in contrast to the endless warmaking of the United States, it had waged no wars from 1979 to 2019.451 Why not? Why hadn't it? Clearly it found no rational motives or irrational cultural motivations to wage any wars, preferring increases in prosperity. Apart from North Korea, the other nuclear-armed nations (United States, Russia, United Kingdom, France, India, Pakistan, and Israel) have all waged wars in recent decades — India and Pakistan against each other. Yet, none of these many wars, or anybody else's wars, have been Hitlerian.

One reason for that is that international law and relations changed radically after WWII. Trials were held that for the first time prosecuted the crime of war, using the 1928 Kellogg-Briand Pact (albeit, twisted from a ban on war into a ban on aggressive war, and perverted from blind justice to victor's justice). To some degree and with some level of hypocrisy, war, conquest, pillaging, and looting became — for the first time — unacceptable on the world stage. At the same time, the Geneva conventions forbade a huge variety of types of cruelty. And the United Nations established a global forum for airing, if not always resolving, disputes (even if opening up loopholes for defensive and UN-authorized wars).

Prior to these changes, it was dangerous for a small country to free itself from colonialism. Once free, it could expect to be quickly attacked by some other colonizer. But with legal boundaries fixed, largely in their 1928 positions, conquest has largely been made a thing of the past (with small exceptions for Israel, Morocco, U.S. military bases, etc.). From 1816 to 1928, there was an average of one conquest of territory by war every month. The average state had a 1.33% chance of being the victim of conquest each year, meaning that more likely than not any country would be conquered within any person's lifetime. The average amount of territory conquered was 295,486 square kilometers per year.452

From 1929 to 1948 — that is, including the conquests by the Nazis — there was only an average of one conquest every 10 months. After WWII, conquests fell to an average of one every 4 years, and the size of territory conquered in a year fell to 14,950 square kilometers, or 5% of what it had been in 1927. The average state now had a 0.17% chance of being the victim of conquest each year, meaning that any country could expect to be conquered, not in a lifetime, but once or twice in a millennium. After WWII, not only was territory that had been conquered during WWII restored, but territories conquered between 1928 and the start of WWII were restored as well, as they had not been recognized as legitimate by the world's nations.453

When the United Nations building was designed for New York City, planners included an extra 20 seats in the General Assembly beyond the 51 out of 60 nations in the world that were members. The United Nations now has 193 members, with most of the seats originally meant for an audience now taken up by nations' representatives. There were 75 nations in the world by the end of the 1940s, 107 by the end of the 1950s. When war ceased to be widely accepted, and conquest was met with condemnation and economic sanction, and international trade carried on better in peace than in war, it became possible for small nations to split off of larger ones or free themselves from colonial domination and survive.454 This is the beautiful little secret that renders the fear of Hitler coming ridiculous: colonialism and conquest are over; wars are not waged for territory; they're waged for weapons sales, fossil fuels, lusts for power, and bragging rights. Wars are waged most frequently by the United States, and most often against U.S.-made weapons and against former U.S. allies.

While the world still lacks a democratic and fair and universally respected system for settling disputes, and while wars still rage, killing and harming and displacing people on a massive scale, the structures of a nonviolent system and the culture of a nonviolent system are partway built. For all their flaws and biases, the United Nations, the World Court, and the International Criminal Court exist. Public opposition to war is strong and widespread. And understanding and experience using the tools of nonviolent movements to pressure governments against war and to create desirable changes without war grow dramatically with each passing year. The means of negotiating and verifying disarmament and driving forward a reverse arms race are available, tried, tested, and proven. The steps needed to reform or replace international agreements and systems with better ones are not mysterious.

It's not that there aren't dictators and oppressive governments on earth right now with similarities, even openly claimed similarities, with Hitler.

But their goals are not world domination (which Hitler himself did not plausibly threaten), and virtually all of the most oppressive dictatorships and other governments in the world, as so understood by the U.S. government, are armed and supported by the U.S. government. As I detailed in 20 Dictatorships Currently Supported by the U.S., of the 50 most oppressive governments on earth, in the view of the U.S. government, the U.S. government sells or gives weapons to 82% of them, gives military training to 88% of them, and provides funding to the militaries of 66% of them, supporting in at least one of these three ways 96% of them, while also propping a number of them up with U.S. bases in their countries.455 These policies, just like promoting eugenics and racism and Nazism and militarism in the 1930s, are optional. They can be changed. And if they are changed, it will become that much more ridiculous to fear that Hitler is coming back to get us.

In 1936, Churchill said the solution was more weapons and more "ruthlessness."456 What politician in the United States of 2020 disagrees? Certainly not the vast majority in Congress who voted against moving 10% out of the Pentagon budget, and not the president who opposed any such move. But what if Churchill had said the solution lay in nonviolence, the rule of law, aid and cooperation? What if he had taken on the U.S. and British CEOs and bankers who were boosting the Nazis? What if he had condemned racism and quack science and antisemitism? What if he had announced the liberation of the British empire? What if he had demanded uncompromising total investment in saving the Jews, assisting ordinary Germans, righting Britain's past wrongs, and sanctioning Italians responsible for invading Ethiopia? (Walter Riddell, Canadian advisory officer to the League of Nations, had proposed sanctions against Italy and later wrote that he believed such a precedent would have prevented WWII.)457 What if he had asked Britain and the world to learn from Gandhi?

Yes, I know, and what if pigs flew? But we are not in the identical situation; we're in a much easier one. We are now capable of widespread understanding of past mistakes. Things that I've written about in this book that sound scandalous — like U.S. companies arming Nazis — are now understood to be the norm. It's no secret that U.S. weapons companies arm the world, that the places with most of the wars (the Middle East, North Africa, Central Asia) manufacture almost no weapons. It's widely known, if not often focused on, that wars are no longer fought for territory, that anything a war can be fought for, other than weapons sales, can be achieved by other means.

No matter what you think of the U.S. Civil War, or of those parts of the world that ended slavery and serfdom without civil wars, nobody advocates ending mass incarceration by picking out some fields, slaughtering huge numbers of young people, and then passing legislation to end mass incarceration. It doesn't even make enough sense for my rejection of the idea to sound worthwhile. It seems too obvious that the proper thing to do would be to jump straight to passing the legislation.

No matter what you think of the first 16 chapters of this book, and no matter what you think of WWII, if you can reject WWII as an argument for militarism going forward, because the world has changed in relevant ways in the past 75 years, then all other arguments for militarism will be at risk of falling like a house of cards, and you'll be at least open to considering an argument for getting rid of war entirely.

In 1970, a U.S. professor worried that the idea of getting rid of war entirely was being talked about on U.S. college campuses. Michael Walzer wrote in 1970 and revised in 1971 a paper called "World War II: Why This War Was Different," explicitly to counter "a new way of talking about war, pervasive especially at our universities."[458] Walzer did not seek to paint the war on Vietnam as exceptional, but rather World War II. He proposed the nearly strict adherence to rules that would forbid war, but to "single out World War II as a case where a wager against the rules might be morally required."

Walzer suggested that such situations, in which critical moral rules would need to be violated, might arise again. But he was clear that they would be extreme exceptions, that they should establish no precedents, that they would go against important basic human values, and that he could not say how one would recognize them. "I realize," he wrote, "that I have not suggested criteria by which they might be recognized; that still needs to be done." The reason that Walzer provided no means of recognizing the next Hitler, the next WWII, the next situation in which war-making would again be justified was clearly not to intentionally leave the door open to cynical politicians who would do that for us over and over and over again. Rather, Walzer professed his inability to succeed in a project that he himself defined as irrational: the identification of "immeasurable evil." Walzer wrote that "while it will obviously not be difficult to offer a formal description of immeasurability, the substance of evil is much harder to grasp and explain, at least for secular minds like my own." When Walzer published his book, *Just and Unjust Wars: A Moral Argument With Historical Illustrations* in 1977 there were, despite the title, no just wars or any recipe for creating a just war anywhere in the book.

Walzer's account of the justness of WWII is one of accident. That is, he did not believe that the British government, on which he focuses as the moral decision maker, had recognized the "immeasurable evil" of Nazism and determined to oppose it for Walzer's just-war reasons. Rather, he believed that Britain had opposed German expansion out of its own somewhat similar interests, but that by moral good luck Britain's actions had turned out to be justified by the evils of Nazism — even if various members of the British government to various degrees sympathized with some of those evils. So, not only do we have no way to spot a future just war, but one may never have been spotted in the past except after the fact. (And, of course, just war professors for many decades now have exhibited no particular skill at spotting all the unjust wars any faster than anybody else.)

That Walzer's argument is intentionally irrational becomes clear when he maintains that the "immeasurable evil" of Nazism would have accidentally justified the British bombing of German cities (except when they overdid it toward the end) even if it had done more harm than good — even if it did do more harm than good. Nazism, Walzer writes, despite his "secular mind," was "evil objectified in the world, and in a form so potent and apparent that there could never have been anything to do but fight against it." This is explicitly an argument against consequentialism. Even if the consequences of war caused greater suffering, there simply could never have been anything else to do. Just because.

"Suppose," writes Walzer, "that Nazism had triumphed unresisted in Europe and that its 'rule of violence' had resulted in twenty million deaths before an internal coup had produced a 'moderate' military regime and ended the reign of terror. But thirty million people (including some but not all of the first twenty million) died in the course of World War II. Foreknowledge of these outcomes would still not provide a sufficient reason for avoiding the war, because the human losses involved in a Nazi victory are not losses of life alone, and the gains of war or peace cannot be measured simply in lives saved. . . . [T]here is human degradation and enslavement on the one side and dignity, courage, and solidarity on the other. . . . One relies on moral intuitions which can be defended and articulated, it seems to me, only in terms of a theory of evil."

"Theory of evil" is of course just an academic way of saying "evil" until something resembling a theory is offered. As a basis for war it is not rational, not usable. Nobody can shape a policy with it, other than the policy of massive preparations for wars in order to be on the safe side. Opposing war to human degradation suggests an incredible ignorance of the nature of war. Requiring war in order to find dignity, courage, and solidarity indicates an immense ignorance of nonviolent activism. Walzer's lengthy 1977 book included a postage-stamp-sized final chapter on the alternative of nonviolent approaches to conflicts in the world — a chapter that had shaped not at all his preceding hundreds of pages on the unjustness of wars, all of which assumed that wars must always be with us, whether we want them or not.

How can I object to calling Nazism "immeasurable evil"? Surely I don't suggest that it wasn't evil? Surely I don't claim to be able to measure it?

Well, I do not claim it wasn't evil. I claim that if the goal was stopping

Nazism, alternatives to WWII included not fighting WWI; not ending WWI in a manner that punished, divided, humiliated, and excluded Germany from formal means of nonviolent recourse; instituting international law; supporting progressive social policies; refraining from funding and arming the Nazis and fueling their ideology; supporting German opposition; negotiating (not merely "appeasing" or declaring war); and utilizing the powerful tools of nonviolent resistance.

Measurability of good and evil is another question. To characterize it as an exact science would be folly. To abandon it is mysticism. Ethics involves the approximation of predicted good and evil, no more and certainly no less. Placing the evil of Nazism beyond the realm of thought is accompanied in Walzer's paper, and in most discourse on this topic, by placing the good of the Allies beyond any mention whatsoever. Is a war against infinite evil the same when waged by a just democratic nation using all volunteer killers, and when waged by a compulsory, racially segregated, and all-male killing crew sent from an imperialist Jim-Crow country with its indigenous people and those of Japanese ancestry in camps? Maybe so, maybe not, but Walzer never touches on the question, preferring to play into a cartoonish conception of light against darkness that crowds ethics right out of consideration.

We cannot accurately say what the death count would have been had Nazism been opposed by all nonviolent means (though we can be sure it would not have been the same as the unresisted triumph of Nazism). We can with some accuracy measure the actual harm done by WWII, which was of course far greater than thirty million lives lost. When we consider those killed, injured, traumatized, and made homeless, no other act of evil compares to WWII. But, I think, we have to go far beyond that. While Walzer may wish his exceptions to moral rules to set no precedents, actions in the world always do. WWII normalized the slaughter of civilians; the destruction of the natural environment on an unprecedented scale; the construction, testing, and threat of weapons of nuclear apocalypse; and the endless dumping of desperately needed resources into a permanent state of war. None of these things can be measured down to the ounce. None of them can be left out of our calculations. All of them are more readily approximated than are such immeasurable criteria of just-war theory as "right intention," "just cause," or "proportionality."

Walzer's argument is, however, even weaker than I have suggested. Like most authors attracted to just-war theory, Walzer distinguishes the decision to fight a war from decisions as to how to fight that war. He declares himself in favor of the British fighting WWII, yet can only bring himself to say that he is "moving uneasily toward" supporting how the British fought WWII, namely by bombing German civilians. Walzer utterly rejects major bombings of German civilians late in the war, but accepts (or moves toward accepting) the bombing of German civilians as necessary earlier in the war. Despite, of course, having no exact measure of how many German civilians were bombed or what sort of suffering resulted in all its details, Walzer identifies that bombing as a "determinate crime," in contrast to the "immeasurable evil" of Nazism. Yet both of those things can only be approximated and generalized about, and unless they are, we have no business trying to engage in a discussion about the ethics of them. Walzer, however, erases the need for ethical calculation entirely by claiming that "there will be no future or no foreseeable future for civilization and its rules unless I accept the burdens of criminality" — this despite his aforementioned consideration of the possible future that included a military coup and twenty million deaths.

Further absent from Walzer's analysis is the reality of the altered world, the fact that major expansionist and colonialist powers are gone. "Let us imagine," Walzer writes, "a state whose government strives to press its boundaries or its sphere of influence outward, a little bit here, a little bit there, continually over a period of time, using force or the threat of force as these appear necessary — a conventional 'great power,' in other words." I disagree. Let us not imagine that. Let us cease imagining that and go out in the world to actually look for it. It isn't there.

It isn't there in Russia or China or North Korea or Iran or the United

States itself. The fascistic tendencies of the U.S. government in 2020, as I write these words, have popularized the idea of opposing fascism, which gives new life to the glorification of WWII, which in turn boosts the U.S. military budget. Opposition to the fascistic Trump government also fuels endless lies and exaggerations about Russia and other foreign menaces, which in turn boosts the U.S. military budget. In September 2020, Donald Trump, who had overseen massive increases in U.S. military spending and in U.S. weapons dealing to the world, was painting himself as an opponent of the military-industrial complex. His earlier demands that NATO nations buy more weapons were widely depicted as opposition to NATO and to good responsible militarism. Reports of his characterizing U.S. war dead as "fools" and "suckers" were being used in support of militarism. But, once again, we were not being offered all the available choices. Support for the same military that seamlessly incorporated large numbers of Nazis through Operation Paperclip is not the only alternative to support for the instigation of racist violence by Donald Trump.

If we were to look beyond words to actions, there would be no doubt that virtually all U.S. politicians have, in effect, taken the Trump/Kissinger view of U.S. troops for as long as there have been U.S. troops.

"Why should I go to that cemetery? It's filled with losers." —Donald Trump, according to Jeffrey Goldberg.[459]

"Military men are just dumb, stupid animals to be used as pawns in foreign policy." —Henry Kissinger, according to Bob Woodward and Carl Bernstein.[460]

It we were to let the non-U.S. 96% of humanity into our vision, it would be even clearer how little value is placed on human life by those who wage U.S. wars in which nearly all the casualties are on the other side.

An article that Jeffrey Goldberg published, to much scandal, in September 2020, about Trump's disrespect for the troops never mentioned, much less objected to, all the senseless wars that Trump had been waging, the war on Afghanistan that he had promised to end four years earlier, the wars in Yemen, Syria, Iraq, Libya, the never-ending death and destruction that

Trump claimed to see no point in but oversaw while fueling more wars made dramatically more likely by his military budgets and hostile actions toward Russia, China, and Iran, his shredding of treaties, his expansion of bases, his nuclear weapons production, or his aggressive weapons dealing to future possible enemies. Trump's government spent a billion dollars a year advertising and recruiting for more of his "losers."

All of that was part of a happy bipartisan consensus, bought by the weapons industry, and supported by the pundits.

Goldberg also never mentioned the possibility of an approach toward troops who died in WWI or any other war, that wasn't either Trump's sociopathic disgust or the weapons dealers' celebration. Trump questioned the justification for WWI and viewed anyone who risked his life in it as a loser or sucker. Goldberg, who had supported the war on Iraq, and seemed a fan of war in general, wanted such questioning to be strictly forbidden by the mandate to worship the troops. There were and are other possibilities. For example, one could admit that a war was an idiotic, senseless waste, but respect and mourn the dead, even apologize to the dead for the propaganda that sold the war, for the prisons that awaited resisters, for the prisons that awaited anyone who spoke against recruitment, for the unfair means of skipping out available only to the wealthy.

Goldberg wants us to believe that failing to celebrate war participation requires failing to comprehend acting generously or making sacrifices for others, but those who acted best for others and made sacrifices most selflessly in past wars were those who publicly refused to participate, spoke out against participation, and suffered the consequences. Trump would consider them losers and suckers too. His respect would go only to those who weaseled out and profited from wars from the safety of their homes. They earn my least respect.

Unfortunately, U.S. politics is dominated by only two choices: be a good war lover who cheers for more militarism and properly honors those duped or pressured into participating, or be a good war lover who ignores all the wars waging on and mocks participants for not having cheated their way out and gotten rich.

Both choices will, sooner rather than later, get us all killed. Another choice is not readily available, and was not to be found in Bernie Sanders, but the fact that Sanders treated Eugene Debs as a hero tells us something about what proved so unacceptable in his 2016 and 2020 candidacies. The existence of Debs and his heroism in WWI renders impossible the limiting to two bad choices that Goldberg seeks to impose on us.

Another U.S. politician who proved unacceptable was John Kennedy, who said, "War will exist until that distant day when the conscientious objector enjoys the same reputation and prestige that the warrior does today."

Or until that distant day when journalists ask sociopathic madmen in high office for their views of conscientious objectors, find out that the answer is "losers" and "suckers," and strive to generate the appropriate outrage over that position.

18. WWII and the case for war abolition

The organization, World BEYOND War, of which I am the executive director, makes a case for ending all war by debunking four myths and then arguing for seven reasons to end the institution of war.[461] The myths are that war is inevitable, necessary, beneficial, or just. The reasons to end war are that war is immoral; war endangers rather than protects; war destroys the natural environment; war erodes liberties; war impoverishes; war promotes bigotry; and the resources spent on war could do incredible good if spent elsewhere — far more good even than the good of preventing wars. I'll review each of these items briefly below, but a longer case and links to resources on each topic can be found at worldbeyondwar.org.

As I reviewed in *War Is Never Just*, just war theorists have developed numerous criteria that could supposedly justify a war that met them.[462] Some of these criteria turn out to not be measurable, to serve purely as rhetoric: "right intention," "just cause," "proportionality." Others are not moral factors at all: "publicly declared," "waged by legitimate authority." And still others are, as I demonstrate in *War Is Never Just*, simply impossible to meet: "last resort," "reasonable prospect of success," "noncombatants immune from attack," "enemy soldiers respected as human beings," "prisoners of war treated as noncombatants." If every immeasurable, amoral, and impossible criterion were met by a miraculously just war, the good done by that war, in order to actually justify it, would have to also outweigh all the harm done by military spending since the last justifiable war (all the lives lost and ruined that could have been saved and transformed), plus all the harm done by all of the patently unjust wars waged during those years, plus all the environmental damage, plus all the damage to civil liberties and self-governance, plus all the promotion of hatred and all the degradation of the culture resulting from maintaining the institution of war, plus the risk of nuclear apocalypse that would be eliminated if wars were. I've never seen anyone attempt an argument that any war since WWII fulfilled these requirements and thereby caused the institution of war to do more good than harm. I've never seen anyone make a persuasive argument that WWII itself or any war before it fulfilled these requirements either — even though the institution of war prior to WWII hardly resembled the permanent military industrial complex that has been with us since WWII.

Let's look briefly at the four myths, beginning with the idea that war is inevitable.

WAR IS NOT INEVITABLE

Any particular war, including WWII as seen above, is clearly not inevitable. Any particular war results from a series of blunders or intentional maneuverings to get it started. Yet, the idea persists that the general idea of war is somehow inevitable.

If war were inevitable, there would be little point in trying to end it (or trying to promote it). If war were inevitable, a moral case might be made for trying to lessen its damage while it continued. And numerous parochial cases could be made for being prepared to win inevitable wars for this side or that side. In fact, governments do just this, but their premise is in error. War is not inevitable.

Even violence on a small scale is not inevitable, but the incredibly difficult task of ending all violence is a million miles past the simpler, if still challenging, task of ending organized mass slaughter. War is not something created by the heat of passion. It takes years of preparation and indoctrination, weapons production, and training.

War is not ubiquitous. Nothing resembling current forms of war existed centuries or even decades ago. War, which has existed in almost completely different forms, has been mostly absent throughout human history and prehistory. While it is very popular to remark that there has always been a war somewhere on earth, there has always been the absence of war a great many somewheres on earth. Societies and even modern nations have gone decades and centuries without war. Anthropologists debate whether anything even resembling war was found in prehistoric hunter-gatherer societies, in which humans evolved for most of our evolution.[463] A number of small nations have abolished their militaries.[464] No other nation on earth is closer to U.S. military spending than to the $0 per year spent by military-free nations.

Developing ways to avoid generating conflicts is part of the answer, but some occurrence of conflict (or major disagreement) is inevitable, which is why we must use more effective and less destructive tools to resolve conflicts and to achieve security.

Institutions that lasted for many years, and which were labeled inevitable, natural, essential, and various other terms of similarly dubious import, have been ended in various societies. These include cannibalism, human sacrifice, trial by ordeal, blood feuds, dueling, polygamy, capital punishment, and slavery. Yes, some of these practices still exist in greatly reduced form, misleading claims are often made about the prevalence of slavery[465], and a single slave is too many. And, yes, war is one of the most troublesome institutions about which to be satisfied with only mostly ending. But war is dependent on major institutions like those that have been fully ended in some of these other cases, and war is not the most effective tool for eliminating smaller scale violence or terrorism. A nuclear arsenal does not deter (and can facilitate) a terrorist attack, but the rule of law, education, aid, and nonviolence are all tools can complete the elimination of war.

What could begin it would be bringing the world's biggest investors in war down to the level of those below them, and ceasing to arm others through global weapons dealing. As things stand, 96% of humanity is ruled by governments that invest radically less in war and proliferate dramatically fewer weapons of war than does the United States. If war is "human nature," it can't be war at the U.S. level. In other words, if you want to use the phrase "human nature," which has never been given any coherent definition, you can't use it for what 4% of humanity happens to do, much less what a relative handful of powerful people among that 4% of humanity happens to do. But scaling the U.S. back to the Chinese level of investing in war, and then the two of them back to the Saudi level, and so forth, would likely create a reverse arms race that would render verbal persuasion of the case for abolishing war much more persuasive if not superfluous.

While the United States spends over $1 trillion a year on militarism, only 19 other nations on earth spend more than $10 billion per year, or 1% of U.S. spending. Seventeen of those nations are U.S. allies and weapons customers.[466]

When military spending is considered per capita, three nations top the United States: Saudi Arabia, Israel, and Singapore (and there are no numbers available for North Korea).[467] Israel only achieves its position by virtue of billions of dollars for military spending that the United States gives to it as a present each year. If such U.S. spending on Israel, Egypt, and other nations were added to the U.S. account, the United States might surpass Singapore as well as Israel in per capita military spending, but nothing any accountant could do would put any nation anywhere near Saudi Arabia. Both Saudi Arabia and Singapore are U.S. allies and weapons customers — Saudi Arabia its largest weapons customer and its partner in the current war on Yemen.

There's also a way in which the per capita comparison makes the U.S. spending appear even larger than a straightforward comparison, namely what a per capita comparison does to the world's second and third biggest overall spenders, China and Russia. On a per capita basis China and Russia drop off the list of top military spenders, leaving only the United States and its chosen allies.

War, as anthropologists like Douglas Fry argue, has likely only been around for the most recent fraction of the existence of our species.[468] We did not evolve with it. But we did evolve with habits of cooperation and altruism. During this most recent 10,000 years, war has been sporadic. Some societies have not known war. Some have known it and then abandoned it.

Just as some of us find it hard to imagine a world without war or murder, some human societies have found it hard to imagine a world with those things. A man in Malaysia, asked why he wouldn't shoot an arrow at slave raiders, replied "Because it would kill them."[469] He was unable to comprehend that anyone could choose to kill. It's easy to suspect him of lacking imagination, but how easy is it for us to imagine a culture in which virtually nobody would ever choose to kill and war would be unknown? Whether easy or hard to imagine, or to create, this is decidedly a matter of culture and not of DNA.

According to myth, war is "natural." Yet a great deal of conditioning is needed to prepare most people to take part in war, and a great deal of mental suffering is common among those who have taken part. In contrast, not a single person is known to have suffered deep moral regret or post-traumatic stress disorder from war deprivation.

In some societies women have been virtually excluded from war-making for centuries and then included. Clearly, this is a question of culture, not of genetic makeup. War is optional, not inevitable, for women and men alike.

War long predates capitalism, and surely Switzerland is a type of capitalist nation just as the United States is. But there is a widespread belief that a culture of capitalism — or of a particular type and degree of greed and destruction and short-sightedness — necessitates war. One answer to this concern is the following: any feature of a society that necessitates war can be changed and is not itself inevitable. The military industrial complex is not an eternal and invincible force. Environmental destructiveness and economic structures based on greed are not immutable.

There is a sense in which this is unimportant; namely, we need to halt environmental destruction and reform corrupt government just as we need to end war, regardless of whether any of these changes depends on the others to succeed. Moreover, by uniting such campaigns into a comprehensive movement for change, strength in numbers will make each more likely to succeed.

But there is another sense in which this is important; namely, we need to understand war as the cultural creation that it is and stop imagining it as something imposed on us by forces beyond our control. In that sense it is important to recognize that no law of physics or sociology requires us to have war because we have some other institution.

War in human history up to this point has not correlated with population density or resource scarcity. The idea that climate change and the resulting catastrophes will inevitably generate wars could be a self-fulfilling prophecy. It is not a prediction based on facts.[470]

The growing and looming climate crisis is a good reason for us to outgrow our culture of war, so that we are prepared to handle crises by other, less destructive means. And redirecting some or all of the vast sums of money and energy that go into war and war preparation to the urgent work of protecting the climate could make a significant difference, both by ending one of our most environmentally destructive activities and by funding a transition to sustainable practices.

In contrast, the mistaken belief that wars must follow climate chaos will encourage investment in military preparedness, thus exacerbating the climate crisis and making more likely the compounding of one type of catastrophe with another.

The idea of eliminating hunger from the globe was once considered ludicrous. Now it is widely understood that hunger could be abolished — and for a tiny fraction of what is spent on war. While nuclear weapons have not all been dismantled and eliminated, there exists a popular movement working to do just that.

Ending all war is an idea that has found great acceptance in various times and places. It was more popular in the United States, for example, in the 1920s and 1930s. Polling is not often done on support for the abolition of war. It was done in Britain in 1934-1935 and found overwhelming support for abolishing war.[471]

In recent decades, the notion has been propagated that war is permanent. That notion is new, radical, and without basis in fact.

WAR IS NOT NECESSARY

Some war proponents have dropped the pretense that it's necessary. Donald Trump openly says he wants troops in Syria for oil[472], John Bolton openly says he wants a coup in Venezuela for oil[473], Mike Pompeo openly says he wants to conquer the arctic for oil (with which to melt more of the arctic into a conquerable state)[474]. But the notion that war is necessary, or that some rare and special wars are necessary, persists. The most popular argument for the necessity of war is WWII, but that has been addressed in the 17 chapters above.

In recent decades, at least pre-Trump, it had become uncommon for most war makers to advertise their wars as desirable, and standard policy to claim that every war is entered into as a last resort. This is progress to be very pleased with and to build on. It is possible to show that the launching of any particular war was not, in fact, the last resort, that superior alternatives existed. So, if war is defensible only as a last resort, war is indefensible.

For any war that occurs, and even many that do not, there can be found people who believe at the time, and after, that each particular war is or was necessary. Some people are unconvinced by claims of necessity for many wars, but insist that one or two wars in the distant past were indeed necessary. And many maintain that some war in the future could conceivably be necessary — at least for one side of the war, thus requiring the permanent maintenance of a military ready to fight.

The U.S. War Department was renamed the Defense Department in 1947, and it is common in many countries to speak of the war departments of one's own and all other nations as "defense." But if the term has any meaning, it cannot be stretched to cover offensive war making or aggressive militarism. If "defense" is to mean something other than "offense," then attacking another nation "so that they can't attack us first" or "to send a message" or to "punish" a crime is not defensive and not necessary.

In 2001, the Taliban government in Afghanistan was willing to turn Osama bin Laden over to a third nation to be tried for crimes the United States was alleging he'd committed.[475] Instead of pursuing legal prosecutions for crimes, the United States and NATO chose an illegal war that did far more damage than the crimes, continued after bin Laden was said to have left the nation, continued after bin Laden's death was announced, and did serious lasting damage to Afghanistan, to Pakistan, to the United States and NATO nations, and to the rule of law.

According to a transcript of a meeting in February 2003 between U.S. President George W. Bush and Prime Minister of Spain Jose Maria Aznar, Bush said that President Saddam Hussein had offered to leave Iraq, and to go into exile, if he could keep $1 billion.[476] A brutal dictator being allowed to flee with $1 billion is not an ideal outcome. But the offer was not revealed to the U.S. public. Instead, Bush's government claimed a war was needed to defend the United States against weapons that did not exist. Rather than losing a billion dollars, the people of Iraq saw the loss of hundreds of thousands of lives, millions made refugees, their nation's infrastructure and education and health systems destroyed, civil liberties lost, vast environmental destruction, and epidemics of disease and birth defects — all of which cost the United States trillions of dollars, not counting additional trillions of dollars in increased fuel costs, future interest payments on war debt, veterans' care, and lost opportunities — not to mention the dead and injured, increased governmental secrecy, eroded civil liberties, damage to the earth and its atmosphere, and the moral damage of public acceptance of kidnapping, torture, and murder.

The same logic that would claim that attacking another nation is "defensive" can be used to try to justify the permanent stationing of troops in another nation. The result, in both cases, is counterproductive, producing threats rather than eliminating them. Of some 196 nations on earth, the United States has troops in at least 177.[477] A handful of other nations also have a much smaller number of troops stationed abroad. This is not a defensive or necessary activity or expense.

A defensive military would consist of a coast guard, a border patrol, anti-aircraft weapons, and other forces able to defend against an attack. The vast majority of military spending, especially by wealthy nations, is offensive. Weapons abroad, on the seas, and in outer space are not defensive. Bombs and missiles targeting other nations are not defensive.

In defining recent wars in Afghanistan and Iraq as non-defensive, have we left out the viewpoint of Afghans and Iraqis? Is it defensive to fight back when attacked? Indeed, it is. That is the definition of defensive. But, let's remember that it is promoters of war who have claimed that defensiveness makes a war justified. Evidence shows that the most effective means of defense is, far more often than not, nonviolent resistance. The mythology of warrior cultures suggests that nonviolent action is weak, passive, and ineffective at solving large-scale social problems. The facts show just the opposite.[478] So it is possible that the wisest decision for Iraq or Afghanistan would have been nonviolent resistance, non-cooperation, and appeal to international justice.

Such a decision is all the more persuasive if we imagine a nation like the United States, with great control over international bodies like the United Nations, responding to an invasion from abroad. Such an invasion is extremely unlikely. Few nations have enough people they could draft, and none have indicated any interest in such a thing. But if it happened, the people of the United States could refuse to recognize the foreign authority. Peace teams from abroad could join the nonviolent non-cooperation with the invading army or country. Unarmed defenders have proven more effective than armed in many cases already. Targeted sanctions and prosecutions could be combined with international diplomatic pressure.

The important question, however, is not how the nation attacked should respond, but how to prevent the aggressive nation from attacking. One way to help do that would be to spread awareness that war making endangers people rather than protecting them, a statement agreed with in numerous particular instances by numerous just-retired U.S. officials.[479]

Denying that war is necessary is not the same as failing to recognize that there is evil in the world. In fact, war needs to be ranked as one of the most evil things in the world. There is nothing more evil that war can be used to prevent. And using war to prevent or punish the making of war has proven a dreadful failure.

War mythology would have us believe that war kills evil people who need to be killed to protect us and our freedoms. In reality, recent wars involving wealthy nations have been one-sided slaughters of children, the elderly, and ordinary residents of the poorer nations attacked. And while "freedom" has served as a justification for the wars, the wars have served as a justification for curtailing actual freedoms.

The idea that you could gain rights by empowering your government to operate in secret and to kill large numbers of people only sounds reasonable if war is our only tool. When all you have is a hammer, every problem looks like a nail. Thus wars are the answer to all foreign conflicts, and disastrous wars that drag on too long can be ended by enlarging them.

Preventable diseases, accidents, suicides, falls, drowning, and hot weather kill many more people in the United States and most other nations than does terrorism. If terrorism makes it necessary to invest $1 trillion a year in war preparations, what does hot weather make it necessary to do?

The myth of a great terrorist threat is wildly inflated by agencies like the FBI that regularly encourage, fund, and entrap people who could never have managed to become terrorist threats on their own.

A study of real motivations for wars makes clear that necessity hardly figures into the decision-making process, other than as propaganda for the public.[480]

Among those who recognize how damaging war is, there exists another mythical justification for this peculiar institution: war is needed for population control. But the planet's capacity to limit human population is beginning to show signs of functioning without war. The results will be horrible. A solution might be to invest some of the vast treasure now dumped into war into the development of sustainable lifestyles instead. The idea of using war to eliminate billions of men, women, and children almost renders the species that could think that thought unworthy of preserving (or at least unworthy of criticizing Nazis); fortunately most people cannot think anything so monstrous.

WAR IS NOT BENEFICIAL

Probably the most common defense of wars is that they are necessary evils. But wars are also — more in recent decades than for WWII —

defended as being in some way beneficial. The reality is that wars do not benefit the people where they are waged, and do not benefit nations that send their militaries abroad to wage wars. Nor do wars help to uphold the rule of law — quite the reverse. Good outcomes caused by wars are dramatically outweighed by the bad and could have been accomplished without war.

Polls in the United States through the 2003-2011 war on Iraq found that a majority in the U.S. believed Iraqis were better off as the result of a war that severely damaged — even *destroyed* — Iraq.[481] A majority of Iraqis, in contrast, believed they were worse off.[482] A majority in the United States believed, at least for a time, that Iraqis were grateful.[483] This is a disagreement over facts, not ideology. But people often choose which facts to become aware of or to accept. Tenacious believers in tales of Iraqi "weapons of mass destruction" tended to believe more, not less, firmly when shown the facts.[484] The facts about Iraq are not pleasant, but they are important.[485]

To believe that the people who live where your nation's government has waged a war are better off for it, despite those people's contention that they are worse off, suggests an extreme sort of arrogance — an arrogance that in many cases has explicitly relied on bigotry of one variety or another: racism, religion, language, culture, or general xenophobia. A poll of people in the United States or any nation involved in occupying Iraq would almost certainly have found opposition to the idea of their own nation being occupied by foreign powers, no matter how benevolent the intentions. This being the case, the idea of humanitarian war is a violation of the most fundamental rule of ethics, the golden rule that requires giving others the same respect you desire. And this is true whether the humanitarian justification of a war is an afterthought once other justifications have collapsed or humanitarianism was the original and primary justification.

There is also a fundamental intellectual error in supposing that a new war is likely to bring benefits to a nation where it is waged, given the dismal record of every war that has occurred heretofore. Scholars at both the Carnegie

Endowment for Peace and the pro-war RAND Corporation have found that wars aimed at nation-building have an extremely low to nonexistent success rate in creating stable democracies.[486] And yet the temptation rises zombie-like to believe that Iraq[487] or Libya[488] or Syria[489] or Iran[490] will finally be the place where war creates its opposite.

Advocates for humanitarian war would be more honest if they totaled the supposed good accomplished by a war and weighed it against the damage done. Instead, the often-quite-dubious good is taken as justifying absolutely any tradeoff. The U.S. didn't count the Iraqi dead. The U.N. Security Council required that the U.N.'s human rights officer report on Libyans killed by NATO only in closed session.

Believers in humanitarian war often distinguish genocide from war. Pre-war demonization of dictators (new Hitlers, often dictators who have been generously funded by their would-be assailants for decades prior) frequently repeats the phrase "killed his own people" (but do not ask who sold him the weapons or provided the satellite views). The implication is that killing "his own people" is significantly worse than killing someone else's people. But if the problem we want to address is mass-killing, then war and genocide are siblings and there is nothing worse than war that war can be used to prevent — even were it the case that war tended to prevent, rather than to fuel, genocide. The opposite was true with WWII and has been before and since.

Wars fought by wealthy nations against poor ones tend to be one-sided slaughters; quite the opposite of beneficial, humanitarian, or philanthropic exercises. In a common mythical view, wars are fought on "a battlefield" — a notion that suggests a sportsmanlike contest between two armies apart from civilian life, an image based on WWI and wars that preceded it. On the contrary, wars are fought in people's towns and homes. These wars are one of the most immoral actions imaginable, which helps explain why governments that wage them lie about them to their own people.

The wars leave lasting damage in the form of brewing hatred and violence, and in the form of a poisoned natural environment, and sow the seeds of future wars. Belief in the humanitarian possibilities for war can be shaken by looking closely at the short- and long-term results of any war. War tends to leave behind danger, not security — in contrast to the more successful record of nonviolent movements for fundamental change.

Violations of human rights can always be found in nations that other nations wish to bomb, just as they can be found in nations whose dictators are being funded and propped up by the very same humanitarian crusaders, and just as they can be found within those warrior nations themselves. But there are two major problems with bombing a nation to expand its respect for human rights. First, it tends not to work. Second, the right not to be killed or injured or traumatized by war ought to be considered a human right worthy of respect as well. Again, a hypocrisy check is useful: How many people would want their own town bombed in the name of expanding human rights?

Wars and militarism and other disastrous policies can generate crises that could benefit from outside assistance, be it in the form of nonviolent peace workers and human shields or in the form of police. But twisting the argument that Rwanda needed police into the argument that Rwanda should have been bombed, or that some other nation should be bombed, is a gross distortion.[491]

Contrary to some mythical views, suffering has not been minimized in recent wars. War cannot be civilized or cleaned up. There's no proper conduct of war that avoids inflicting serious and unnecessary pain. There is no guarantee that any war can be controlled or ended once begun. The damage usually lasts much longer than the war. Wars do not end with victory, which often cannot even be defined.

War can be imagined as a tool for enforcing the rule of law, including laws against war, only by ignoring the hypocrisy and the historical record of failure. War actually violates the most basic principles of law and encourages their further violation. The sovereignty of states and the requirement that diplomacy be conducted without violence fall before the hammer of war. The Kellogg-Briand Pact, the U.N. Charter, and domestic laws on murder and on the decision to go to war are violated when wars are launched and escalated and continued. Violating those laws in order to "enforce" (without actually prosecuting) a law banning a particular type of weapon, for example, does not make nations or groups more likely to be law abiding. This is part of why war, any war, fails to provide security. Organizing a group of nations, such as NATO, to jointly fight a war does not make the war one iota more legal or beneficial; it simply employs a criminal gang.

War and war preparations drain and weaken an economy. The myth that war enriches a nation that wages it, as opposed to enriching a small number of influential profiteers, is, as we will see shortly, not supported by evidence.

A further myth holds that, even if war impoverishes the war making nation, it can nonetheless be enriching it more substantially by facilitating the exploitation of other nations. The leading war-making nation in the world, the United States, has 4% of the world's population but consumes a quarter to a third of various natural resources. According to this myth, only war can allow that supposedly important and desirable imbalance to continue.

There is a reason why this argument is rarely articulated by those in power and plays only a minor role in war propaganda. It is shameful, and most people are ashamed of it. If war serves not as philanthropy but as extortion, admitting as much hardly justifies the crime. Other points help weaken this argument:

- Greater consumption and destruction do not always equal a superior standard of living.
- The benefits of peace and international cooperation would be felt even by those learning to consume less.
- The benefits of local production and sustainable living are immeasurable.
- Reduced consumption is required by the earth's environment regardless of who does the consuming.

- One of the largest ways in which wealthy nations consume the most destructive resources, such as oil, is through the very waging of the wars.

- Green energy and infrastructure would surpass their advocates' wildest fantasies if the funds now invested in war were transferred there.

- War impoverishes (see below).

War provides fewer jobs than alternative spending or tax cuts[492], but war can supposedly provide noble and admirable jobs that teach young people valuable lessons, build character, and train good citizens. In fact, everything good found in war training and participation can be created without war. And war training brings with it much that is far from desirable. War preparation teaches and conditions people for behavior that is normally considered the worst affront to society possible. It also teaches dangerous extremes of obedience. While war can involve courage and sacrifice, pairing these with blind support for ignoble goals sets a bad example indeed. If thoughtless courage and sacrifice is a virtue, then ant warriors (that's not a typo for anti-warriors; I really mean ants) are demonstrably more virtuous than human ones.

Advertisements have credited recent wars with helping to develop brain surgery techniques that have saved lives outside of wars. The internet was developed largely by the U.S. military. But such silver linings could be shining stars if created apart from war. Research and development would be more efficient and accountable and more directly invested in useful ways if separated from the military.

Similarly, humanitarian aid missions could be run better without the military. An aircraft carrier is an overpriced and inefficient means of bringing disaster relief. The use of the wrong tools is compounded by justifiable skepticism from people aware that militaries have frequently used disaster relief as cover for escalating wars or stationing forces permanently in an area.

Wars are marketed as humanitarian, because many people, including many government and military employees, have good intentions. But those at the top deciding to wage war almost certainly do not. In case after case, less than generous motives have been documented.

WAR IS NOT JUST

The idea that wars can sometimes, from at least one side, be deemed "just" is promoted in Western culture by just war theory, a set of ancient and imperialist dogmas that, as mentioned above, do not hold up to scrutiny. Not even the favorite criterion of "last resort" holds up to scrutiny.

It is of course a step in the right direction when a culture moves from Theodore Roosevelt's open desire for a new war for war's sake, to the universal pretense that every war is and must be a last resort. This pretense is so universal now, that the U.S. public simply assumes it without even being told. A scholarly study recently found that the U.S. public believes that whenever the U.S. government proposes a war, it has already exhausted all other possibilities. When a sample group was asked if they supported a particular war, and a second group was asked if they supported that particular war after being told that all alternatives were no good, and a third group was asked if they supported that war even though there were good alternatives, the first two groups registered the same level of support, while support for war dropped off significantly in the third group. This led the researchers to the conclusion that if alternatives are not mentioned, people don't assume they exist — rather, people assume they've already been tried.[493]

There have for years been major efforts in Washington, D.C., to start a war on Iran. Some of the greatest pressure has come in 2007 and 2015. If that war had been started at any point, it would no doubt have been described as a last resort, even though the choice of simply not starting that war has been chosen on numerous occasions. In 2013, the U.S. President told us of the urgent "last resort" need to launch a major bombing campaign on Syria. Then he reversed his decision, largely because of public resistance to it. It turned out the option of *not* bombing Syria was also available.

Imagine an alcoholic who managed every night to consume huge quantities of whiskey and who every morning swore that drinking whiskey had been his very last resort, he'd had no choice at all. Easy to imagine, no doubt. An addict will always justify himself, however nonsensically it has to be done. But imagine a world in which everyone believed him and solemnly said to each other "He really had no other choice. He truly had tried everything else." Not so plausible, is it? Almost unimaginable, in fact. And yet:

It is widely believed that the United States is at war in Syria as a last resort, even though:

The United States spent years sabotaging UN attempts at peace in Syria.[494]

The United States dismissed out of hand a Russian peace proposal for Syria in 2012.[495]

And when the United States claimed a bombing campaign was needed immediately as a "last resort" in 2013 but the U.S. public was wildly opposed, other options were pursued.

In 2015, numerous U.S. Congress Members argued that the nuclear deal with Iran needed to be rejected and Iran attacked as a last resort. No mention was made of Iran's 2003 offer to negotiate away its nuclear program, an offer that had been quickly scorned by the United States.

It is widely believed that the United States is killing people with drones as a last resort, even though in that minority of cases in which the United States knows the names of the people it is aiming for, many (and quite possibly all) of them could have been fairly easily arrested.[496]

It was widely believed that the United States killed Osama bin Laden as a last resort, until those involved admitted that the "kill or capture" policy didn't actually include any capture (arrest) option and that bin Laden had been unarmed when he was killed.[497]

It was widely believed the United States attacked Libya in 2011, overthrew its government, and fueled regional violence as a last resort, even though in March 2011 the African Union had a plan for peace in Libya but was prevented by NATO, through the creation of a "no fly zone" and the initiation of bombing, to travel to Libya to discuss it. In April, the African Union was able to discuss its plan with Libyan leader Muammar Gaddafi, and he expressed his agreement.[498] NATO had obtained UN authorization to protect Libyans alleged to be in danger, but it had no authorization to continue bombing the country or to overthrow the government.

Virtually anyone who works for, and wishes to continue working for, a major U.S. media outlet says the United States attacked Iraq in 2003 as a last resort or sort of meant to, or something, even though:

The U.S. president had been concocting cockamamie schemes to get a war started.[499]

The Iraqi government had approached the CIA's Vincent Cannistraro with an offer to let U.S. troops search the entire country.[500]

The Iraqi government offered to hold internationally monitored elections within two years.[501]

The Iraqi government made an offer to Bush official Richard Perle to open the whole country to inspections, to turn over a suspect in the 1993 World Trade Center bombing, to help fight terrorism, and to favor U.S. oil companies.[502]

The Iraqi president offered, in the account that the president of Spain was given by the U.S. president, to simply leave Iraq if he could keep $1 billion.[503]

The United States always had the option of simply not starting another war.

Most everyone supposes that the United States invaded Afghanistan in 2001 and has stayed there ever since as a series of "last resorts," even though the Taliban repeatedly offered to turn bin Laden over to a third country to stand trial, al Qaeda has had no significant presence in Afghanistan for most of the duration of the war, and withdrawal has been an option at any time.[504]

Many maintain that the United States went to war with Iraq in 1990-1991 as a "last resort," even though the Iraqi government was willing to negotiate withdrawal from Kuwait without war and ultimately offered to simply withdraw from Kuwait within three weeks without conditions. The King of Jordan, the Pope, the President of France, the President of the Soviet Union, and many others urged such a peaceful settlement, but the White House insisted upon its "last resort."[505]

Even setting aside general practices that increase hostility, provide weaponry, and empower militaristic governments, as well as fake negotiations intended to facilitate rather than avoid war, the history of U.S. war making can be traced back through the centuries as a story of an endless series of opportunities for peace carefully avoided at all costs.

Mexico was willing to negotiate the sale of its northern half, but the United States wanted to take it through an act of mass killing. Spain wanted the matter of the *Maine* to go to international arbitration, but the U.S. wanted war and empire. The Soviet Union proposed peace negotiations before the Korean War. The United States sabotaged peace proposals for Vietnam from the Vietnamese, the Soviets, and the French, relentlessly insisting on its "last resort" over any other option, from the day the Gulf of Tonkin incident mandated war despite never having actually occurred.[506]

If you look through enough wars, you'll find nearly identical incidents used on one occasion as the excuse for a war and on another occasion as nothing of the sort. President George W. Bush proposed to U.K. Prime Minister Tony Blair that getting a U2 airplane shot at could get them into a war they wanted.[507] Yet when the Soviet Union shot down a U2 airplane, President Dwight Eisenhower didn't start a war.

Yes, yes, yes, one might reply, hundreds of actual and unjust wars are not last resorts, even though their supporters claim that status for them. But a theoretical Just War would be a last resort. Would it? Would there really be no other option morally equivalent or superior? Just war theorists Mark Allman and Tobias Winright quote Pope John Paul II on the "duty to disarm this aggressor if all other means have proven ineffective."[508] But is "disarm" really the equivalent of "bomb or invade"? We've seen wars launched supposedly to disarm, and the result has been more weapons than ever before. What about *ceasing to arm* as one possible method of disarming? What about an international arms embargo? What about economic and other incentives to disarm?

There was no moment when bombing Rwanda would have been a moral "last resort." There was a moment when armed police might have helped, or cutting off a radio signal being used to provoke killings might have helped. There were many moments when unarmed peace workers would have helped. There was a moment when demanding accountability for the assassination of the president would have helped. There were three years before that when refraining from arming and funding Ugandan killers would have helped.

"Last resort" claims are usually pretty weak when one imagines traveling back in time to the moment of crisis, but dramatically weaker still if one just imagines traveling back a bit further. Many more people try to justify World War II than World War I, even though one of them could never have happened without the other or without the foolish manner of ending it. Of course unjust causes of crises don't render all new decisions unjust, but they suggest that someone with an idea other than more war should intervene in a destructive cycle of self-justifying crisis generation.

Even in the moment of crisis, is it really as urgent a crisis as war supporters claim? Is a clock really ticking here any more than in torture thought experiments? Allman and Winright suggest this list of alternatives to war that must have been exhausted for war to be a last resort: "smart sanctions, diplomatic efforts, third-party negotiations, or an ultimatum."[509] That's it? This list is to the full list of available alternatives what the National Public Radio show "All Things Considered" is to all things. They ought to rename it "Two Percent of Things Considered." Later, Allman and Winright quote a claim that overthrowing governments is kinder than "containing" them. This argument, the authors maintain, challenges "pacifist and contemporary just war theorists alike." It does? Which option were those two types supposedly favoring? "Containment"? That's not a very peaceful approach and certainly not the only alternative to war.

If a nation were actually attacked and chose to fight back in defense, it would not have the time for sanctions and each of the other options listed. It wouldn't even have time for academic support from Just War theorists. It would just find itself fighting back. The area for Just War theory to work in is, therefore, at least in great part, those wars that are something short of defensive, those wars that are "preemptive," "preventive," "protective," etc.

The first step up from actually defensive is a war launched to prevent an imminent attack. The Obama Administration redefined "imminent" to mean theoretically possible someday. They then claimed to be murdering with drones only people who constituted "an imminent and continuing threat to the United States." Of course, if it were imminent under the usual definition, it wouldn't also be continuing. Here is a critical passage from the Department of Justice "White Paper" defining "imminent":

"[T]he condition that an operational leader present an 'imminent' threat of violent attack against the United States does not require the United States to have clear evidence that a specific attack on U.S. persons and interests will take place in the immediate future."[510]

The George W. Bush Administration saw things in a similar way. The 2002 U.S. National Security Strategy states: "We recognize that our best defense is a good offense."[511] Of course, this is false, as offensive wars stir up hostility. But it is also admirably honest.

Once we're talking about non-defensive war proposals, about crises in which one has time for sanctions, diplomacy, and ultimatums, one also has time for all sorts of other things. Possibilities include: nonviolent (unarmed) civilian-based defense: announcing the organization of nonviolent resistance to any attempted occupation, global protests and demonstrations, disarmament proposals, unilateral disarmament declarations, gestures of friendship including aid, taking a dispute to arbitration or court, convening a truth and reconciliation commission, restorative dialogues, leadership by example through joining binding treaties or the International Criminal Court or through democratizing the United Nations, civilian diplomacy, cultural collaborations, and creative nonviolence of endless variety.

But what if we imagine an actually defensive war, either the much feared but ridiculously impossible invasion of the United States, or a U.S. war viewed from the other side? Was it just for the Vietnamese to fight back? Was it just for the Iraqis to fight back? The short answer to that question is that if the aggressor had refrained, no defense would have been needed. Turning resistance to U.S. wars around into justification for further U.S. military spending is too twisted even for a K Street lobbyist. The slightly longer answer is that it's generally not the proper role for someone born and living in the United States to advise people living under U.S. bombs that they should experiment with nonviolent resistance.

But the right answer is the one already discussed in Chapter 12 of this book. Studies like Erica Chenoweth's have established that nonviolent resistance to tyranny is far more likely to succeed, and the success far more likely to be lasting, than with violent resistance.[512] So if we look at something like the nonviolent revolution in Tunisia in 2011, we might find that it meets as many criteria as any other situation for a just war, except that it wasn't a war at all. One wouldn't go back in time and argue for a strategy less likely to succeed but likely to cause a lot more pain and death. Perhaps doing so might constitute a just war argument. Perhaps a just war argument could even be made, anachronistically, for a 2011 U.S. "intervention" to bring democracy to Tunisia (apart from the United States' obvious inability to do such a thing, and the guaranteed catastrophe that would have resulted). But once you've done a revolution without all the killing and dying, it can no longer make sense to propose all the killing and dying — not if a thousand new Geneva Conventions were created, and no matter the imperfections of the nonviolent success.

To be morally right, nonviolent resistance to an actual attack need not appear more likely to succeed than a violent response. It only need appear somewhat close to as likely. Because if it succeeds it will do so with less harm, and its success will be more likely to last. In the absence of an attack, while claims are being made that a war should be launched as a "last resort," nonviolent solutions need only appear reasonably plausible.

Even in that situation, they must be attempted before launching a war can be labeled a "last resort." But because they are infinite in variety and can be tried over and over again, under the same logic, one will never actually reach the point at which attacking another country is a last resort. If you could achieve that, a moral decision would still require that the imagined benefits of your war outweigh all the damage done by maintaining the institution of war.

WAR IS IMMORAL

Militarism is a major public health threat, a significant cause of death, injury, homelessness, and disease, a completely preventable epidemic[513] that consists of the large-scale killing, wounding, impoverishing, making homeless, orphaning, and traumatizing of people.

If the myths about war were true, then we might think of the killing that constitutes war as unlike the smaller scale killings we refer to as murder. Since the myths are not true, we are compelled to agree with Harry Patch, the last British veteran of WWI to die, that "War is organized murder and nothing else."[514]

The victims of wars waged by wealthy nations against poor ones are overwhelmingly on one side[515], and the majority of them civilians by everyone's definition.[516] The top killer of members of the U.S. military is suicide.[517] War victims are disproportionately the elderly and the very young. In many recent wars, violence has directly caused the most deaths and injuries, but wars also still kill huge numbers of people indirectly through destruction of environments and infrastructure resulting in disease epidemics and starvation.[518] The victims of wars are far more numerous than is often imagined.[519]

In the film *The Ultimate Wish: Ending the Nuclear Age*, a survivor of Nagasaki meets a survivor of Auschwitz.[520] It is hard in watching them meeting and speaking together to remember or care which nation committed which horror. War is immoral not because of who commits it but because of what it is. On June 6, 2013, NBC News interviewed a former U.S. drone pilot named Brandon Bryant who was deeply depressed over his role in killing over 1,600 people[521]:

"Brandon Bryant says he was sitting in a chair at a Nevada Air Force base operating the camera when his team fired two missiles from their drone at three men walking down a road halfway around the world in Afghanistan. The missiles hit all three targets, and Bryant says he could see the aftermath on his computer screen—including thermal images of a growing puddle of hot blood. 'The guy that was running forward, he's missing his right leg,' he recalled. 'And I watch this guy bleed out and, I mean, the blood is hot.' As the man died his body grew cold, said Bryant, and his thermal image changed until he became the same color as the ground. 'I can see every little pixel,' said Bryant, who has been diagnosed with post-traumatic stress disorder, 'if I just close my eyes.' 'People say that drone strikes are like mortar attacks,' Bryant said. 'Well, artillery doesn't see this. Artillery doesn't see the results of their actions. It's really more intimate for us, because we see everything.' . . . He's still not certain whether the three men in Afghanistan were really Taliban insurgents or just men with guns in a country where many people carry guns. The men were five miles from American forces arguing with each other when the first missile hit them. . . . He also remembers being convinced that he had seen a child scurry onto his screen during one mission just before a missile struck, despite assurances from others that the figure he'd seen was really a dog. After participating in hundreds of missions over the years, Bryant said he 'lost respect for life' and began to feel like a sociopath. . . . In 2011, as Bryant's career as a drone operator neared its end, he said his commander presented him with what amounted to a scorecard. It showed that he had participated in missions that contributed to the deaths of 1,626 people. 'I would've been happy if they never even showed me the piece of paper,' he said. 'I've seen American soldiers die, innocent people die, and insurgents die. And it's not pretty. It's not something that I want to have — this diploma.' Now that he's out of the Air Force and back home in Montana, Bryant said he doesn't want to think about how many people on that list might've been innocent: 'It's too heartbreaking.' . . . When he told a woman he was seeing that he'd been a drone operator, and contributed to the deaths of a large number of people, she cut him off. 'She looked at me like I was a monster,' he said. 'And she never wanted to touch me again.'"

WAR ENDANGERS AND DOES NOT PROTECT

The U.S. government plays a dominant role in weapons dealing and war.[522] It is responsible for some 80% of international arms dealing[523], 90% of foreign military bases[524], 50% of military spending[525], and it arms, trains, and funds the militaries of 96% of the most oppressive governments on earth.[526] As the world's top war maker — always in the name of "defense" — the United States demonstrates well that war is counterproductive on its own terms. A December 2014 Gallup poll of 65 nations found the United States to be far and away the country considered the largest threat to peace in the world[527], and a Pew poll in 2017 found majorities in most countries polled viewing the United States as a threat[528]. Any other nation hoping to match the United States in these polls would need to wage many more "defensive" wars before it could generate the same levels of fear and resentment.

It's not just the world outside the United States or even outside the U.S. military that is aware of this problem. It has become almost routine for U.S. military commanders, usually just after retiring, to argue that various wars or tactics are creating more new enemies than the enemies they are killing.[529] Here are just a few examples in case you've missed any of them:

—U.S. Lt. General Michael Flynn, who quit as head of the Pentagon's Defense Intelligence Agency (DIA) in August 2014: "The more weapons we give, the more bombs we drop, that just… fuels the conflict."[530]

—Former CIA Bin Laden Unit Chief Michael Scheuer, who says the more the United States fights terrorism the more it creates terrorism.[531]

—The CIA, which finds its own drone program "counterproductive."[532]

—Admiral Dennis Blair, the former director of National Intelligence: While "drone attacks did help reduce the Qaeda leadership in Pakistan," he wrote, "they also increased hatred of America."[533]

—Gen. James E. Cartwright, the former vice chairman of the Joint Chiefs of Staff: "We're seeing that blowback. If you're trying to kill your way to a solution, no matter how precise you are, you're going to upset people even if they're not targeted."[534]

—Sherard Cowper-Coles, Former U.K. Special Representative To Afghanistan: "For every dead Pashtun warrior, there will be 10 pledged to revenge."[535]

—Matthew Hoh, Former Marine Officer (Iraq), Former US Embassy Officer (Iraq and Afghanistan): "I believe it's [the escalation of the war/ military action] only going to fuel the insurgency. It's only going to reinforce claims by our enemies that we are an occupying power, because we are an occupying power. And that will only fuel the insurgency. And that will only cause more people to fight us or those fighting us already to continue to fight us."[536]

—General Stanley McChrystal: "For every innocent person you kill, you create 10 new enemies."[537]

— Lt. Col. John W. Nicholson Jr.: This commander of the war on Afghanistan blurted out his opposition to what he'd been doing on his last day of doing it.[538]

Terrorism predictably increased from 2001 to 2014, principally as a result of the war on terrorism.[539] Almost all (99.5%) of terrorist attacks occur in countries engaged in wars and/or engaged in abuses such as imprisonment without trial, torture, or lawless killing. The highest rates of terrorism are in "liberated" and "democratized" Iraq and Afghanistan. The terrorist groups responsible for the most terrorism (that is, non-state, politically motivated violence) around the world have grown out of U.S. wars against terrorism.

95% of all suicide terrorist attacks are indefensible crimes conducted to encourage foreign occupiers to leave the terrorist's home country.[540]

The wars on Iraq and Afghanistan, and the abuses of prisoners during them, became major recruiting tools for anti-U.S. terrorism. In 2006, U.S. intelligence agencies produced a National Intelligence Estimate that reached just that conclusion. The Associated Press reported: "The war in Iraq has become a cause célèbre for Islamic extremists, breeding deep resentment of the U.S. that probably will get worse before it gets better, federal intelligence analysts conclude in a report at odds with President Bush's contention of a world growing safer. ... [T]he nation's most veteran analysts conclude that despite serious damage to the leadership of al-Qaida, the threat from Islamic extremists has spread both in numbers and in geographic reach."

Veterans of U.S. kill teams in Iraq and Afghanistan interviewed in Jeremy Scahill's book and film *Dirty Wars* said that whenever they worked their way through a list of people to kill, they were handed a larger list; the list grew as a result of working their way through it. An alternative to this vicious cycle is found in Spain. On March 11, 2004, Al Qaeda bombs killed 191 people in Madrid, Spain, just before an election in which one party was campaigning against Spain's participation in the U.S.-led war on Iraq. The people of Spain voted the Socialists into power, and they removed all Spanish troops from Iraq by May.[541] There were no more bombs in Spain. This history stands in strong contrast to that of Britain, the United States, and other nations that have responded to blowback with more war, generally producing more blowback.

The most severe danger produced by the institution of war is probably the nuclear danger. We can either eliminate all nuclear weapons or we can watch them proliferate. There's no middle way. We can either have no nuclear weapons states, or we can have many. This is not a moral or a logical point, but a practical observation backed up by research in books like *Apocalypse Never: Forging the Path to a Nuclear Weapon-Free World* by Tad Daley. As long as some states have nuclear weapons others will desire them, and the more that have them the more easily they will spread to others still. The Doomsday Clock is as close to midnight as it has ever been.[542]

If nuclear weapons continue to exist, there will very likely be a nuclear catastrophe, and the more the weapons have proliferated, the sooner it will come. Hundreds of incidents have nearly destroyed our world through accident, confusion, misunderstanding, and extremely irrational machismo.[543] When you add in the quite real and increasing possibility of non-state terrorists acquiring and using nuclear weapons, the danger grows dramatically — and is only increased by the policies of nuclear states that react to terrorism in ways that seem designed to recruit more terrorists.

Possessing nuclear weapons does absolutely nothing to keep us safe; there is no trade-off involved in eliminating them. They do not deter terrorist attacks by non-state actors in any way. Nor do they add an iota to a dominant military's ability to deter nations from attacking, given the ability of the United States, for example, to destroy anything anywhere at any time with non-nuclear weapons. Nukes also don't win wars, and the United States, the Soviet Union, the United Kingdom, France, and China have all lost wars against non-nuclear powers while possessing nukes. Nor, in the event of global nuclear war, can any outrageous quantity of weaponry protect a nation in any way from apocalypse.

War endangers in additional ways. War abroad increases hatred at home and the militarization of police. While wars are fought in the name of "supporting" those fighting in the wars, veterans are given little assistance in dealing with the deep moral guilt, trauma, brain injury, and other hurdles in the way of adapting to nonviolent society. Those trained in mass killing by the U.S. military, for example, are disproportionately those who become mass shooters in the United States, where such behavior is of course no longer acceptable.[544]

"Speak softly and carry a big stick," said Theodore Roosevelt, who favored building a big military just in case, but of course not actually using it unless forced to. This worked out excellently, with the few minor exceptions of Roosevelt's mobilization of forces to Panama in 1901, Colombia in 1902, Honduras in 1903, the Dominican Republic in 1903, Syria in 1903, Abyssinia in 1903, Panama in 1903, the Dominican Republic in 1904,

Morocco in 1904, Panama in 1904, Korea in 1904, Cuba in 1906, Honduras in 1907, and the Philippines throughout Roosevelt's presidency.

The first people we know of who prepared for war — the Sumerian hero Gilgamesh and his companion Enkido, or the Greeks who fought at Troy — also prepared for the hunting of wild animals. Barbara Ehrenreich theorizes that,

". . . with the decline of wild predator and game populations, there would have been little to occupy the males who had specialized in hunting and anti-predator defense, and no well-trodden route to the status of 'hero.' What saved the hunter-defender male from obsolescence or a life of agricultural toil was the fact that he possessed weapons and the skills to use them. [Lewis] Mumford suggests that the hunter-defender preserved his status by turning to a kind of 'protection racket': pay him (with food and social standing) or be subject to his predations.

"Eventually, the presence of underemployed hunter-defenders in other settlements guaranteed a new and 'foreign' menace to defend against. The hunter-defenders of one band or settlement could justify their upkeep by pointing to the threat posed by their counterparts in other groups, and the danger could always be made more vivid by staging a raid from time to time. As Gwynne Dyer observes in his survey of war, 'pre-civilized warfare . . . was predominantly a rough male sport for underemployed hunters.'"

In other words, war may have begun as a means of achieving heroism, just as it is continued based on the same mythology. It may have begun because people were armed and in need of enemies, since their traditional enemies (lions, bears, wolves) were dying out. Which came first, the wars or the weapons? That riddle may actually have an answer. The answer appears to be the weapons. And those who do not learn from prehistory may be doomed to repeat it.

We like to believe in everyone's good intentions. "Be prepared" is the Boy Scouts' motto, after all. It's simply reasonable, responsible, and safe to be prepared. Not to be prepared would be reckless, right?

The problem with this argument is that it's not completely crazy. On a smaller scale it's not completely crazy for people to want guns in their homes to protect themselves from burglars. In that situation, there are other factors to consider, including the high rate of gun accidents, the use of guns in fits of rage, the ability of criminals to turn home owners' guns against them, the frequent theft of guns, the distraction the gun solution causes from efforts to reduce the causes of crime, etc.

On the larger scale of war and arming a nation for war, similar factors must be considered. Weapon-related accidents, malicious testing on human beings, theft, sales to allies who become enemies, and the distraction from efforts to reduce the causes of terrorism and war must all be taken into account. So, of course, must the tendency to use weapons once you have them. At times, more weapons can't be produced until the existing stock is depleted and new innovations are tested "on the battlefield."

But there are other factors to consider as well. A nation's stockpiling of weapons for war puts pressure on other nations to do the same. Even a nation that intends to fight only in defense, may understand "defense" to be the ability to retaliate against other nations. This makes it necessary to create the weaponry and strategies for aggressive war, and even "preemptive war," keeping legal loopholes open and enlarging them, and encouraging other nations to do the same. When you put a lot of people to work planning something, when that project is in fact your largest public investment and proudest cause, it can be difficult to keep those people from finding opportunities to execute their plans.

WAR DESTROYS THE NATURAL ENVIRONMENT

War and preparations for war are not just the pit into which trillions of dollars that could be used to prevent environmental damage are dumped, but also a major direct cause of that environmental damage.

The U.S. military is one of the biggest polluters on earth. Since 2001, the U.S. military has emitted 1.2 billion metric tons of greenhouse gases, equivalent to the annual emissions of 257 million cars on the road.[545] The U.S. Department of Defense is the largest institutional consumer of oil ($17B/year) in the world, and the largest global landholder with 800 foreign military bases in 80 countries.[546] By one estimate, the U.S. military used 1.2 million barrels of oil in Iraq in just one month of 2008.[547] One military estimate in 2003 was that two-thirds of the U.S. Army's fuel consumption occurred in vehicles that were delivering fuel to the battlefield.[548]

As the environmental crisis worsens, thinking of war as a tool with which to address it threatens us with the ultimate vicious cycle. Declaring that climate change causes war misses the reality that human beings cause war, and that unless we learn to address crises nonviolently we will only make them worse.

A major motivation behind some wars is the desire to control resources that poison the earth, especially oil and gas. In fact, the launching of wars by wealthy nations in poor ones does not correlate with human rights violations or lack of democracy or threats of terrorism, but does strongly correlate with the presence of oil.[549]

War does most of its environmental damage where it happens, but also devastates the natural environment of military bases in foreign and home nations. The U.S. military is the third-largest polluter of U.S. waterways,[550] and a major polluter of the "forever chemicals" known as PFAS.[551]

At least since the Romans sowed salt on Carthaginian fields during the Third Punic War, wars have damaged the earth, both intentionally and — more often — as a reckless side-effect. General Philip Sheridan, having destroyed farmland in Virginia during the Civil War, proceeded to destroy bison herds as a means of restricting Native Americans to reservations. WWI saw European land destroyed with trenches and poison gas. During WWII, the Norwegians started landslides in their valleys, while the Dutch flooded a third of their farmland, the Germans destroyed Czech forests, and the British burned forests in Germany and France.

Wars in recent years have rendered large areas uninhabitable and generated tens of millions of refugees. War "rivals infectious disease as a global cause of morbidity and mortality," according to Jennifer Leaning of Harvard Medical School. Leaning divides war's environmental impact into four areas: "production and testing of nuclear weapons, aerial and naval bombardment of terrain, dispersal and persistence of land mines and buried ordnance, and use or storage of military despoliants, toxins, and waste."

At least 33,480 U.S. nuclear weapons workers who have received compensation for health damage are now dead.[552] Nuclear weapons testing by the United States and the Soviet Union involved at least 423 atmospheric tests between 1945 and 1957 and 1,400 underground tests between 1957 and 1989. The damage from that radiation is still not fully known, but it is still spreading, as is our knowledge of the past. New research in 2009 suggested that Chinese nuclear tests between 1964 and 1996 killed more people directly than the nuclear testing of any other nation. Jun Takada, a Japanese physicist, calculated that up to 1.48 million people were exposed to fallout and 190,000 of them may have died from diseases linked to radiation from those Chinese tests. In the United States, testing in the 1950s led to untold thousands of deaths from cancer in Nevada, Utah, and Arizona, the areas most downwind from the testing.

In 1955, movie star John Wayne, who avoided participating in WWII by opting instead to make movies glorifying war, decided that he had to play Genghis Khan. *The Conqueror* was filmed in Utah, and the conqueror was conquered. Of the 220 people who worked on the film, by the early 1980s, 91 of them had contracted cancer and 46 had died of it, including John Wayne, Susan Hayward, Agnes Moorehead, and director Dick Powell. Statistics suggest that 30 of the 220 might ordinarily have gotten cancer, not 91. In 1953 the military had tested 11 atomic bombs nearby in Nevada, and by the 1980s half the residents of St. George, Utah, where the film was shot, had cancer. You can run from war, but you can't hide.

The military knew its nuclear detonations would impact those downwind, and monitored the results, effectively engaging in human experimentation. In numerous other studies during and in the decades following World War

II, in violation of the Nuremberg Code of 1947, the military and the CIA have subjected veterans, prisoners, the poor, the mentally disabled, and other populations to unwitting human experimentation for the purpose of testing nuclear, chemical, and biological weapons, as well as drugs like LSD, which the United States apparently went so far as to put into the air and food of an entire French village in 1951, with horrific and deadly results.[553]

A report prepared in 1994 for the U.S. Senate Committee on Veterans Affairs begins: "During the last 50 years, hundreds of thousands of military personnel have been involved in human experimentation and other intentional exposures conducted by the Department of Defense (DOD), often without a servicemember's knowledge or consent. In some cases, soldiers who consented to serve as human subjects found themselves participating in experiments quite different from those described at the time they volunteered. For example, thousands of World War II veterans who originally volunteered to 'test summer clothing' in exchange for extra leave time, found themselves in gas chambers testing the effects of mustard gas and lewisite. Additionally, soldiers were sometimes ordered by commanding officers to 'volunteer' to participate in research or face dire consequences. For example, several Persian Gulf War veterans interviewed by Committee staff reported that they were ordered to take experimental vaccines during Operation Desert Shield or face prison." The full report contains numerous complaints about the secrecy of the military and suggests that its findings may be only scraping the surface of what has been hidden.[554]

In 1993, the U.S. Secretary of Energy released records of U.S. testing of plutonium on unwitting U.S. victims immediately following WWII. *Newsweek* commented reassuringly, on December 27, 1993: "The scientists who had conducted those tests so long ago surely had rational reasons: the struggle with the Soviet Union, the fear of imminent nuclear war, the urgent need to unlock all the secrets of the atom, for purposes both military and medical."[555] Oh, well that's all right then.

Perhaps the most deadly weapons left behind by wars are land mines and cluster bombs. Tens of millions of them are estimated to be lying around on the earth, oblivious to any announcements that peace has been declared. Most of their victims are civilians, a large percentage of them children. A 1993 U.S. State Department report called land mines "the most toxic and widespread pollution facing mankind."[556] Land mines damage the environment in four ways, writes Jennifer Leaning: "fear of mines denies access to abundant natural resources and arable land; populations are forced to move preferentially into marginal and fragile environments in order to avoid minefields; this migration speeds depletion of biological diversity; and land-mine explosions disrupt essential soil and water processes."[557]

The amount of the earth's surface impacted is not minor. Millions of hectares in Europe, North Africa, and Asia are under interdiction. One-third of the land in Libya conceals land mines and unexploded WWII munitions. Many of the world's nations have agreed to ban land mines and cluster bombs.

From 1965 to 1971, the United States developed new ways of destroying plant and animal (including human) life; it sprayed 14 percent of South Vietnam's forests with herbicides, burned farm land, and shot livestock. One of the worst chemical herbicides, Agent Orange, still threatens the health of the Vietnamese and has caused some half million birth defects. During the Gulf War, Iraq released 10 million gallons of oil into the Persian Gulf and set 732 oil wells on fire, causing extensive damage to wildlife and poisoning ground water with oil spills. In its wars in Yugoslavia and Iraq, the United States has left behind depleted uranium. A 1994 U.S. Department of Veterans Affairs survey of Gulf War veterans in Mississippi found 67 percent of their children conceived since the war had severe illnesses or birth defects. Wars in Angola eliminated 90 percent of the wildlife between 1975 and 1991. A civil war in Sri Lanka felled five million trees.

The Soviet and U.S. occupations of Afghanistan have destroyed or damaged thousands of villages and sources of water. The Taliban has illegally traded timber to Pakistan, resulting in significant deforestation. U.S. bombs and refugees in need of firewood have added to the damage. Afghanistan's forests are almost gone. Most of the migratory birds that used to pass through Afghanistan no longer do so. Its air and water have been poisoned with explosives and rocket propellants. Ethiopia could have reversed its desertification for $50 million in reforestation, but chose to spend $275 million on its military instead — each year between 1975 and 1985.

WAR ELIMINATES LIBERTIES

We're often told that wars are fought for "freedom." But when a wealthy nation fights a war against a poor (if often resource-rich) nation halfway around the globe, among the goals is not actually to prevent that poor nation from taking over the wealthy one, after which it might restrict people's rights and liberties. The fears used to build support for the wars don't involve such an incredible scenario at all; rather the threat is depicted as one to safety, not liberty.

What happens, predictably and consistently, is just the reverse of wars protecting freedoms. In close proportion to levels of military spending, liberties are restricted in the name of war — including during WWII — even while wars may simultaneously be waged in the name of liberty. Populations try to resist the erosion of liberties, the militarization of the police, the warrantless surveillance, the drones in the skies, the lawless imprisonment, the torture, the assassinations, the denial of a lawyer, the denial of access to information on the government, etc. But these are symptoms. The disease is war and the preparation for war. It is the idea of the enemy that allows government secrecy.

The nature of war, as fought between valued and devalued people, facilitates the erosion of liberties in another way, in addition to the fear for safety. That is, it allows liberties to first be taken away from devalued people. But the programs developed to accomplish that are later predictably expanded to include valued people as well.

Militarism erodes not just particular rights but the very basis of self-governance. It privatizes public goods, it corrupts public servants, it creates momentum for war by making people's careers dependent on it. One way in which war erodes public trust and morals is by its predictable generation of public lies. Also eroded, of course, is the very idea of the rule of law —

replaced with the practice of might-makes-right.

Sometimes we're told that evil people are going to blow us up because they hate our freedoms. But then, that would still mean we were fighting a war for survival, not for freedom — if there were any truth to this absurd propaganda, which there is not. People can be motivated to fight by all kinds of means, including religion, racism, or hatred of a culture, but the underlying motivation for anti-U.S. violence from nations where the U.S. funds and arms dictators or maintains a large troop presence or imposes deadly economic sanctions or bombs houses or occupies towns or buzzes drones overhead . . . is those actions. Many nations equal or surpass the United States in civil liberties without making themselves targets.

War not only shifts power to the government and the few, and away from the people, but it also shifts power to a president or prime minister and away from a legislature or judiciary. James Madison, father of the U.S. Constitution, warned:

"Of all the enemies to public liberty war is, perhaps, the most to be dreaded, because it comprises and develops the germ of every other. War is the parent of armies; from these proceed debts and taxes; and armies, and debts, and taxes are the known instruments for bringing the many under the domination of the few. In war, too, the discretionary power of the Executive is extended; its influence in dealing out offices, honors, and emoluments is multiplied; and all the means of seducing the minds, are added to those of subduing the force, of the people. The same malignant aspect in republicanism may be traced in the inequality of fortunes, and the opportunities of fraud, growing out of a state of war, and in the degeneracy of manners and of morals engendered by both. No nation could preserve its freedom in the midst of continual warfare."[558]

WAR SPREADS BIGOTRY

War and war propaganda have often fueled and been fueled by racism, xenophobia, religious hatred, and other types of bigotry. Historian Kathleen Belew, as quoted in Chapter 5 above, says there has always been a correlation in the United States between the aftermath of war and the rise of white supremacist violence. Dr. Martin Luther King Jr. famously said that we would need to tackle three interlocking problems together: racism, militarism, and extreme materialism. One reason why is that trying to eradicate racism will prove futile while engaged in wars and in the sort of thinking that accompanies wars. As long as it's all right for the U.S. government to bomb a half dozen predominantly Muslim and dark-skinned nations at a time, there will remain an opening to believing there's something wrong with Muslim and dark-skinned people in the United States.

As discussed in Chapters 4, 5, and 6 above, racism was instrumental in fueling WWII. It, or some similar form of hatred, has also been a part of every war before or since. It is much easier for a U.S. soldier to kill a hadji than a human being, just as it was easier for Nazi troops to kill Untermenschen than real people.

Where I live in Charlottesville, Va., there was a fascist rally in 2017 because people were proposing to take down racist war monuments, namely those depicting Confederate generals. While those monuments had been erected for clearly racist reasons in the 1920s, so had a monument depicting and celebrating genocide of Native Americans during the American Revolution. And the other monuments around town to WWI, the war on Vietnam, and other wars were not memorializing a select portion of the victims of non-racist wars. Every war monument is a monument to racism.

WAR IMPOVERISHES

It's common in the United States to hear supporters of war and of military spending, including numerous Congress Members, refer to military spending as a jobs program. How this assertion sounds to victims of the war is worth considering. So is the fact that it is a false assertion on its own terms.

It is common to think that, because many people have jobs in the war industry, spending on war and preparations for war benefits an economy. In reality, spending those same dollars on peaceful industries, on education, on infrastructure, or even on tax cuts for working people would produce more jobs and in most cases better paying jobs — with enough savings to help everyone make the transition from war work to peace work.[559] Rare cuts in certain areas to the U.S. military have not produced the economic damage forecast by the weapons companies. Military spending is worse than nothing economically.

War has a huge direct financial cost, the vast majority of which is in funds spent on the preparation for war — or what's thought of as ordinary, non-war military spending. Very roughly, the world spends $2 trillion every year on militarism, of which the United States spends about half, or $1 trillion. This U.S. spending also accounts for over half of the U.S. government's discretionary budget[560] each year and is distributed through several departments and agencies[561].

Not every well-known measure of military spending accurately conveys the reality. For example, the Global Peace Index (GPI) ranks the United States near the peaceful end of the scale on the factor of military spending.[562] It accomplishes this feat through two tricks. First, the GPI lumps the majority of the world's nations all the way at the extreme peaceful end of the spectrum rather than distributing them evenly.

Second, the GPI treats military spending as a percentage of gross domestic product (GDP) or the size of an economy. This suggests that a rich country with a huge military can be more peaceful than a poor country with a small military. This is not just an academic question, as think tanks in Washington urge spending a higher percentage of GDP on the military, exactly as if one should invest more in warfare whenever possible, without waiting for a defensive need. President Trump has successfully urged NATO nations to spend more on militarism using the same argument.

In contrast to the GPI, the Stockholm International Peace Research Institute (SIPRI) lists the United States as the top military spender in the world, measured in dollars spent.[563] In fact, according to SIPRI, the United States spends as much on war and war preparation as most of the rest of the world combined. The truth may be more dramatic still. SIPRI says U.S. military spending in 2011 was $711 billion. Chris Hellman of the National Priorities Project says it was $1,200 billion, or $1.2 trillion.[564] The difference comes from including military spending found in every department of the government, not just "Defense," but also Homeland Security, State, Energy, the U.S. Agency for International Development, the Central Intelligence Agency, the National Security Agency, the Veterans Administration, interest on war debts, etc. There's no way to do an apples-to-apples comparison to other nations without accurate credible information on each nation's total military spending, but it is extremely safe to assume that no other nation on earth is spending $500 billion more than is listed for it in the SIPRI rankings.

While North Korea almost certainly spends a much higher percentage of its gross domestic product on war preparations than the United States does, it almost certainly spends less than 1 percent what the United States spends.

War and violence cause trillions of dollars' worth of destruction each year.[565] The costs to the aggressor, enormous as they are, can be small in comparison to those of the nation attacked. The financial costs of all the buildings and institutions and homes and schools and hospitals and energy systems destroyed is almost immeasurable.

Wars can cost even an aggressor nation that fights wars far from its shores twice as much in indirect expenses as in direct expenditures. Indirect expenses include future care of veterans, interest on debt, impact on fuel costs, and lost opportunities.

Military spending diverts public funds into increasingly privatized industries through the least accountable public enterprise and one that is hugely profitable for the owners and directors of the corporations involved. As a result, war spending works to concentrate wealth in a small number of hands, from which a portion of it can be used to corrupt government and further increase or maintain military spending.

THE MONEY IS BADLY NEEDED ELSEWHERE

It would cost about $30 billion per year to end starvation and hunger around the world.[566] That sounds like a lot of money to you or me. But if we had $2 trillion it wouldn't. And we do. It would cost about $11 billion per year to provide the world with clean water.[567] Again, that sounds like a lot. Let's round up to $50 billion per year to provide the world with both food and water. Who has that kind of money? We do. Of course, we in the wealthier parts of the world don't share the money, even among ourselves. Those in need of aid are right here as well as far away. Everyone could be given a Basic Income Guarantee for a small fraction of military spending.[568]

About $70 billion per year would help eliminate poverty in the United States. Christian Sorensen writes in *Understanding the War Industry*, "The U.S. Census Bureau indicates that 5.7 million very poor families with children would need, on average, $11,400 more to live above the poverty line (as of 2016). The total money needed . . . would be roughly $69.4 billion/year."

But imagine if one of the wealthy nations, the United States for example, were to put $500 billion into its own education (meaning "college debt" can begin the process of coming to sound as backward as "human sacrifice"), housing (meaning no more people without homes), infrastructure, and sustainable green energy and agricultural practices. What if, instead of leading the destruction of the natural environment, this country was catching up and helping to lead in the other direction?

The potential of green energy would suddenly skyrocket with that sort of unimaginable investment, and the same investment again, year after year. But where would the money come from? $500 billion? Well, if $1 trillion fell from the sky on an annual basis, half of it would still be left. After $50 billion to provide the world with food and water, what if another $450 billion went into providing the world with green energy and infrastructure, topsoil preservation, environmental protection, schools, medicine, programs of cultural exchange, and the study of peace and of nonviolent action?

U.S. foreign aid right now is about $23 Billion a year. Taking it up to $100 billion — never mind $523 billion! — would have a number of interesting impacts, including the saving of a great many lives and the prevention of a tremendous amount of suffering. It would also, if one other factor were added, make the nation that did it the most beloved nation on earth, namely if the money used were taken out of war spending.

FROM SEPTEMBER 11ᵗʰ to CORONAVIRUS

When a few thousand people were murdered on September 11, 2001, I was actually stupid enough — I kid you not — to imagine that the general public would conclude that because massive military forces, nuclear arsenals, and foreign bases had done nothing to prevent and much to provoke those crimes, the U.S. government would need to start scaling back its single biggest expense. By September 12th it was clear that the opposite course would be followed.

Since 2001, we have seen the U.S. government dump over a trillion dollars a year into militarism, and push the rest of the world to expend another trillion dollars a year, much of it on U.S.-made weapons. We've seen the creation of permawars, and the normalization of long-distance, push-button murder with drone wars. All of this has generated more terrorism in the name of fighting it. And it has come at the expense of actual defense.

A government agency aimed at actually defending people from actual dangers would cease activities that are counter-productive, that cause major environmental and climate destruction, and that consume resources that could be put to good use. Militarism meets all of those criteria.

Coronavirus will kill many more than a few thousand people, even just in the United States. The death toll there may fall between 200,000 and 2,200,000. That high figure would be 0.6% of the U.S. population, which compares with 0.3% of the U.S. population killed by World War II, or 5.0% of the Iraqi population killed in the war begun in 2003. The low figure of 200,000 would be 67 times the death count from 9-11. Should we expect to see the U.S. government expending $67 trillion a year on health and wellness? Even one sixty-seventh of that, even a mere trillion a year spent where it's actually useful could work wonders.

The International Campaign to Abolish Nuclear Weapons produced a chart comparing the costs of things. For $35.1 billion, it said, you could have the annual U.S. expenditures on nuclear weapons, or you could have 300,000 beds in intensive care plus 35,000 ventilators, plus 150,000 nurses, plus 75,000 doctors.[569] I adjusted the chart as follows. For $2 trillion, you could have annual global military spending, or you could have 17,100,000 beds in intensive care plus 1,995,000 ventilators, 8,550,000 nurses, 4,275,000 doctors. How is this even a difficult choice?

The microscopic coronavirus, just like the men with boxcutters on airplanes, is simply not addressed by military spending. On the contrary, the environmental destruction of militarism and of the dominant global culture as a whole very likely contributes to the mutation and spread of such viruses. Factory farming and carnivorism likely contribute as well. And at least some diseases, such as Lyme and Anthrax, have been spread by military labs doing openly offensive or supposedly defensive work on bioweapons.

A Department of Actual Defense, as opposed to a Department of War renamed Defense, would be looking very hard at the twin dangers of nuclear and climate apocalypse, and the accompanying spin-offs like coronavirus. I don't mean looking at them with an eye to militarizing borders, getting more oil out of the arctic as the ice melts, demonizing immigrants to sell more weapons, or developing "smaller" and "more usable" nukes. We have all of that sociopathy already. I mean looking at these threats in order to actually defend against them. The biggest dangers include:

- poor health, and poor diets and lifestyles that contribute to poor health,

- diseases and ecosystem destruction that contributes to them,
- poverty and financial insecurity that lead to poor health and to the inability to take necessary steps against a disease like coronavirus,
- suicide, and the unhappy lives and mental illness and access to guns that contribute,
- accidents, and the transportation and workplace policies that contribute,

War is a top cause of death where there are wars. Foreign terrorism is nowhere remotely near a top cause of death in nations that wage distant wars.

The disastrous response that we are seeing from the U.S. and other governments to the current disease pandemic should put to rest once and for all the notion that people will automatically become better and wiser once things get bad enough. But we can put in place preparations to behave more wisely.

A Department of Actual Defense would need to be global, not national, but a national government could do a cheap imitation of parts of it that would be wild improvements over what we're seeing now. Such a department might encompass what's been conceived of as a Department of Peace, an agency aimed at moving from violence to nonviolence. But a Department of Actual Defense would also be dedicated to preventing all major harm.

Imagine if everyone on earth right now had financial security and top medical care. We would all be better off in many ways. That task may sound dreamy or visionary, but it is actually radically smaller than the task of building the militaries that have been built in recent years.

Imagine if climate collapse were being treated like the urgent emergency that coronavirus is now understood to be. Climate collapse should have been treated that way many years ago. The sooner it is, the easier things will be. The later, the harder. Why choose the harder road?

Imagine if the nuclear doomsday clock being closer to midnight than ever before were addressed appropriately, with some hint of interest from human governments in human survival. That's a project that costs nothing and saves billions of dollars and lives.

A Department of Actual Defense would not be a military attacking a different enemy. The problem of disease or illness is one to be addressed as much by improved environment, lifestyle, and diet as by medicine, and by an approach to medicine that attempts all solutions whether or not they resemble "attacking" the "enemy" virus.

A Department of Actual Defense would train pro-environment workers, disaster-relief workers, and suicide-prevention workers in the tasks of protecting the environment, relieving disasters, and preventing suicide, as opposed to training and arming them all to kill large number of people with weapons but then assigning them to other tasks. We don't need a military redirected but disbanded. What humanity needs is not a better militarism, but a better humanity.

In April 2020, the Prime Minister of Norway encapsulated what's wrong with current thinking. She said that since coronavirus had arrived by surprise, more money must be dumped into war preparations.[570] This missed both the fact that governments knew about coronavirus back in November 2019[571] and the fact that we could be far better prepared for health crises if our resources weren't so heavily spent on militarism already.

If you're beginning to be persuaded that not even "What about Hitler?" justifies the ongoing enterprise of war preparations and wars, or at least that we desperately need to scale it back, then I encourage you to visit the website worldbeyondwar.org and begin to get involved by signing the Declaration of Peace found there, which has been signed in almost every country on earth, and which reads:

I understand that wars and militarism make us less safe rather than protect us, that they kill, injure and traumatize adults, children and infants, severely damage the natural environment, erode civil liberties, and drain our economies, siphoning resources from life-affirming activities. I commit to engage in and support nonviolent efforts to end all war and preparations for war and to create a sustainable and just peace.

I also recommend to you the following books, in addition to all of those found in the endnotes:

Human Smoke: The Beginnings of the End of Civilization by Nicholson Baker, 2008.
The Devil's Chessboard: Allen Dulles, the CIA, and the Rise of America's Secret Government, by David Talbot, 2015.
We Who Dared to Say No to War: American Antiwar Writing from 1812 to Now, edited by Murray Polner and Thomas E. Woods, Jr., 2008.
The Untold History of the United States, by Oliver Stone and Peter Kuznick, 2012.
The Internationalists: How a Radical Plan to Outlaw War Remade the World, by Oona Hathaway and Scott J. Shapiro, 2017.
Devil Dog: The Amazing True Story of the Man Who Saved America, by David Talbot, 2010.
There Is No Good War: The Myths of World War II, by Mickey Z, 1999.
Understanding the War Industry by Christian Sorensen, 2020.
No More War by Dan Kovalik, 2020.
Social Defence by Jørgen Johansen and Brian Martin, 2019.
Murder Incorporated: Book Two: America's Favorite Pastime by Mumia Abu Jamal and Stephen Vittoria, 2018.
Waymakers for Peace: Hiroshima and Nagasaki Survivors Speak by Melinda Clarke, 2018.
Preventing War and Promoting Peace: A Guide for Health Professionals edited by William Wiist and Shelley White, 2017.
The Business Plan For Peace: Building a World Without War by Scilla Elworthy, 2017.
War Is Never Just by David Swanson, 2016.
A Global Security System: An Alternative to War by World BEYOND War, 2015, 2016, 2017, 2020.
A Mighty Case Against War: What America Missed in U.S. History Class and What We (All) Can Do Now by Kathy Beckwith, 2015.

War: A Crime Against Humanity by Roberto Vivo, 2014.

Catholic Realism and the Abolition of War by David Carroll Cochran, 2014.

War and Delusion: A Critical Examination by Laurie Calhoun, 2013.

Shift: The Beginning of War, the Ending of War by Judith Hand, 2013.

War No More: The Case for Abolition by David Swanson, 2013.

The End of War by John Horgan, 2012.

Transition to Peace by Russell Faure-Brac, 2012.

From War to Peace: A Guide To the Next Hundred Years by Kent Shifferd, 2011.

War Is A Lie by David Swanson, 2010, 2016.

Beyond War: The Human Potential for Peace by Douglas Fry, 2009.

Living Beyond War by Winslow Myers, 2009.

Enough Blood Shed: 101 Solutions to Violence, Terror, and War by Mary-Wynne Ashford with Guy Dauncey, 2006.

Planet Earth: The Latest Weapon of War by Rosalie Bertell, 2001.

Waging Nonviolent Struggle: 20th century Practice and 21st Century Potential by Gene Sharp, 2005.

Why Civil Resistance Works by Erica Chenoweth and Maria Stephan, 2012.

About the Author

David Swanson is an author, activist, journalist, and radio host. He is executive director of World BEYOND War and campaign coordinator for RootsAction.org. He blogs at DavidSwanson.org and WarIsACrime.org. He hosts Talk Nation Radio at TalkNationRadio.org. He is a Nobel Peace Prize Nominee, and was awarded the 2018 Peace Prize by the U.S. Peace Memorial Foundation.

Acknowledgements

Thank you for helpful comments — whether I listened to them all or not, and with remaining problems being mine alone — to Nicholson Baker, Nicolas Davies, Charlotte Dennett, Mike Ferner, William Geimer, David Hartsough, Jeffrey Kaye, Kathy Kelly, Peter Kuznick, John Reuwer, Gar Smith, Scott Shapiro, Marc Eliot Stein, Wes Swanson, Jason Weixelbaum, and Ann Wright.

Endnotes

1 Here's a PowerPoint I've used for this presentation: https://worldbeyondwar.org/
wp-content/uploads/2020/01/endwar.pptx

2 In the United States, in my experience, the leading contenders are WWII, and in
a distant second and third place, the U.S. Civil War and the American Revolution.
Howard Zinn discussed these in his presentation "Three Holy Wars," https://www.
youtube.com/watch?v=6i39UdpR1F8 My experience roughly matches polling
done in 2019 by YouGov, which found 66% of Americans polled saying that WWII
was completely justified or somewhat justified (whatever that means), compared
to 62% for the American Revolution, 54% for the U.S. Civil War, 52% for WWI,
37% for the Korean War, 36% for the First Gulf War, 35% for the ongoing war
on Afghanistan, and 22% for the Vietnam War. See: Linley Sanders, YouGov,
"America and its allies won D-Day. Could they do it again?" June 3, 2019 https://
today.yougov.com/topics/politics/articles-reports/2019/06/03/american-wars-
dday

3 I've also done debates with a West Point professor on whether war can ever be
justified, with polling of the audience shifting significantly against the idea that
war can ever be justified from before the debate to after. See https://youtu.be/
o88ZnGSRRw0 At events held by the organization World BEYOND War, we use
these forms to survey people on their change in opinion: https://worldbeyondwar.
org/wp-content/uploads/2014/01/PeacePledge_101118_EventVersion1.pdf

4 National Priorities Project, "The Militarized Budget 2020," https://www.
nationalpriorities.org/analysis/2020/militarized-budget-2020 For an explanation
of the discretionary budget and what isn't in it, see https://www.nationalpriorities.
org/budget-basics/federal-budget-101/spending

5 Occasional polls have asked what people thought the military budget was, and
the average answer has been wildly off. A February 2017 poll found a majority
believing military spending was less than it actually was. See Charles Koch Institute,
"New Poll: Americans Crystal Clear: Foreign Policy Status Quo Not Working,"
February 7, 2017, https://www.charleskochinstitute.org/news/americans-clear-
foreign-policy-status-quo-not-working It's also possible to compare surveys in
which people are shown the federal budget and asked how they would change
it (most want big shifts of money out of the military) with polls that simply

ask whether the military budget should be decreased or increased (support for cuts is much lower). For an example of the former, see Ruy Texeira, Center for American Progress, November 7, 2007, https://www.americanprogress.org/issues/democracy/reports/2007/11/07/3634/what-the-public-really-wants-on-budget-priorities For an example of the latter, see Frank Newport, Gallup Polling, "Americans Remain Divided on Defense Spending," February 15, 2011, https://news.gallup.com/poll/146114/americans-remain-divided-defense-spending.aspx

6 Nations' military spending is displayed on a map of the world at https://worldbeyondwar.org/militarism-mapped The data comes from the Stockholm International Peace Research Institute (SIPRI), https://sipri.org U.S. military spending as of 2018 was $718,689, which clearly excludes much of U.S. military spending, which is spread over numerous departments and agencies. For a more comprehensive total of $1.25 trillion in annual spending, see William Hartung and Mandy Smithberger, *TomDispatch*, "Tomgram: Hartung and Smithberger, A Dollar-by-Dollar Tour of the National Security State," May 7, 2019, https://www.tomdispatch.com/blog/176561

7 Nations that import U.S. weapons are displayed on a map of the world at https://worldbeyondwar.org/militarism-mapped The data comes from the Stockholm International Peace Research Institute (SIPRI), http://armstrade.sipri.org/armstrade/page/values.php

8 Data For Progress, "The American People Agree: Cut the Pentagon's Budget," July 20, 2020, https://www.dataforprogress.org/blog/2020/7/20/cut-the-pentagons-budget By 56% to 27% U.S. voters favored moving 10% of the military budget to human needs. If told that some of the money would go to the Centers for Disease Control, the public support was 57% to 25%.

9 In the House, the vote on Pocan of Wisconsin Amendment Number 9, Roll Call 148 on July 21, 2020, was 93 Yeas, 324 Nays, 13 Not Voting, http://clerk.house.gov/cgi-bin/vote.asp?year=2020&rollnumber=148 In the Senate, the vote on Sanders Amendment 1788 on July 22, 2020, was 23 Yeas, 77 Nays, https://www.senate.gov/legislative/LIS/roll_call_lists/roll_call_vote_cfm.cfm?congress=116&session=2&vote=00135

10 Martin Gillens and Benjamin I. Page, "Testing Theories of American Politics: Elites, Interest Groups, and Average Citizens," September 2014, https://www.cambridge.org/core/journals/perspectives-on-politics/article/testing-theories-of-american-politics-elites-interest-groups-and-average-citizens/62327F513959D0A

304D4893B382B992B Cited in BBC, "Study: US Is an Oligarchy, Not a Democracy,"
April 17, 2014, https://www.bbc.com/news/blogs-echochambers-27074746

11 In 2008, the United Nations said that $30 billion per year could end hunger
on earth. See the Food and Agriculture Organization of the United Nations, "The
world only needs 30 billion dollars a year to eradicate the scourge of hunger,"
June 3, 2008, http://www.fao.org/newsroom/en/news/2008/1000853/index.html
This was reported in the *New York Times*, http://www.nytimes.com/2008/06/04/
news/04iht-04food.13446176.html and *Los Angeles Times*, http://articles.latimes.
com/2008/jun/23/opinion/ed-food23 and many other outlets. The Food and
Agriculture Organization of the United Nations has told me that number is still up
to date. As of 2019, the annual Pentagon base budget, plus war budget, plus nuclear
weapons in the Department of Energy, plus the Department of Homeland Security,
and other military spending totaled well over $1 trillion, in fact $1.25 trillion.
See William D. Hartung and Mandy Smithberger, *TomDispatch*, "Boondoggle,
Inc.," May 7, 2019, https://www.tomdispatch.com/blog/176561 Three percent of a
trillion is 30 billion. More on this at https://worldbeyondwar.org/explained

12 According to UNICEF, 291 million children under age 15 died from preventable
causes between 1990 and 2018. See https://www.unicefusa.org/mission/starts-
with-u/health-for-children

13 According to the Stockholm International Peace Research Institute (SIPRI),
U.S. military spending, in constant 2018 dollars, was $718,690 in 2019 and
$449,369 in 1999. See https://sipri.org/databases/milex

14 In fact, the British Ministry of Propaganda made a decision to avoid mentioning
Jews when discussing victims of the Nazis. See Walter Laqueuer, *The Terrible
Secret: Suppression of the Truth about Hitler's "Final Solution."* Boston: Little,
Brown, 1980, p. 91. Cited by Nicholson Baker, *Human Smoke: The Beginnings of
the End of Civilization.* New York: Simon & Schuster, 2008, p. 368.

15 Frank Freidel, *Franklin D. Roosevelt: A Rendezvous With Destiny.* Boston, Little,
Brown, 1990, p. 296. Cited by Nicholson Baker, *Human Smoke: The Beginnings of
the End of Civilization.* New York: Simon & Schuster, 2008, p. 9.

16 Winston Churchill, "Zionism versus Bolshevism," *Illustrated Sunday Herald*,
February 8, 1920. Cited by Nicholson Baker, *Human Smoke: The Beginnings of the
End of Civilization.* New York: Simon & Schuster, 2008, p. 6.

17 Adolf Hitler, *Mein Kampf,* Volume Two - The National Socialist Movement,
Chapter IV: Personality and the Conception of the Folkish State, http://www.hitler.

org/writings/Mein_Kampf/mkv2ch04.html

18   Harry Laughlin testified in 1920 to the House Committee on Immigration and Naturalization in the United States Congress that the immigration of Jews and Italians was damaging the genetic structure of the race. "Our failure to sort immigrants on the basis of natural worth is a very serious national menace," Laughlin warned. Committee Chairman Albert Johnson appointed Laughlin to be the committee's Expert Eugenics Agent. Laughlin supported the Johnson-Reed Immigration Act of 1924, which banned immigration from Asia and curtailed immigration from Southern and Eastern Europe. This law created quotas based on the 1890 U.S. population. Henceforth, immigrants could not just show up at Ellis Island but would have to obtain visas at U.S. consulates abroad. See Rachel Gur-Arie, The Embryo Project Encyclopedia, "Harry Hamilton Laughlin (1880-1943)," December 19, 2014, https://embryo.asu.edu/pages/harry-hamilton-laughlin-1880-1943 Also see Andrew J. Skerritt, Tallahassee Democrat, "'Irresistible Tide' takes unflinching look at America's immigration policy | Book Review," August 1, 2020, https://www.tallahassee.com/story/life/2020/08/01/irresistible-tide-takes-unflinching-look-americas-immigration-policy/5550977002 This story is covered in the PBS film "American Experience: The Eugenics Crusade," October 16, 2018, https://www.pbs.org/wgbh/americanexperience/films/eugenics-crusade For how this influenced the Nazis, see Chapter 4 of this book.

19   United States Holocaust Memorial Museum, Holocaust Encyclopedia, "Immigration to the United States, 1933-41," https://encyclopedia.ushmm.org/content/en/article/immigration-to-the-united-states-1933-41

20   Howard Zinn, *A People's History of the United States* (Harper Perennial, 1995), p 400. Cited by David Swanson, *War Is A Lie: Second Edition* (Charlottesville: Just World Books, 2016), p. 32.

21   United States Holocaust Memorial Museum, Holocaust Encyclopedia, "Evian Conference Fails to Aid Refugees," https://encyclopedia.ushmm.org/content/en/film/evian-conference-fails-to-aid-refugees

22   Holocaust Educational Trust, 70 Voices: Victims, Perpetrators, and Bystanders, "As We Have No Racial Problem," January 27, 2015, http://www.70voices.org.uk/content/day55

23   Lauren Levy, Jewish Virtual Library, a Project of American-Israeli Cooperative Enterprise, "Dominican Republic Provides Sosua as a Haven for Jewish Refugees," https://www.jewishvirtuallibrary.org/dominican-republic-as-haven-for-jewish-

refugees See also Jason Margolis, The World, "The Dominican Republic took in Jewish refugees fleeing Hitler while 31 nations looked away," November 9, 2018, https://www.pri.org/stories/2018-11-09/dominican-republic-took-jewish-refugees-fleeing-hitler-while-31-nations-looked

24 Dennis Ross Laffer, University of South Florida, Scholar Commons, Graduate Theses and Dissertations, Graduate School, "Jewish Trail of Tears II: Children Refugee Bills of 1939 and 1940," March 2018, https://scholarcommons.usf.edu/cgi/viewcontent.cgi?article=8383&context=etd

25 Anne O'Hare McCormick, The New York Times, "The Refugee Question as a Test of Civilization Nation of Free Choice Plight of the Refugee A Way to Rebuke the Reich," July 4, 1938, https://www.nytimes.com/1938/07/04/archives/europe-the-refugee-question-as-a-test-of-civilization-nation-of.html

26 Learning from History, Online Module: The Holocaust and Fundamental Rights, Doc. 11: Comments on the Evian Conference, http://learning-from-history.de/Online-Lernen/content/13338 See whole online course on the Évian conference: http://learning-from-history.de/Online-Lernen/content/13318

27 Ervin Birnbaum, Crethi Plethi, "Evian: The Most Fateful Conference of All Times in Jewish History," http://www.crethiplethi.com/evian-the-most-fateful-conference-of-all-times-in-jewish-history/the-holocaust/2013

28 Ervin Birnbaum, "Evian: The Most Fateful Conference of All Times in Jewish History," Part II, http://www.acpr.org.il/nativ/0902-birnbaum-E2.pdf

29 Crystalizing Public Opinion is available online at http://www.gutenberg.org/files/61364/61364-h/61364-h.htm Regarding Goebbels' use of Bernays' work, see Richard Gunderman, The Conversation, "The manipulation of the American mind: Edward Bernays and the birth of public relations," July 9, 2015, https://theconversation.com/the-manipulation-of-the-american-mind-edward-bernays-and-the-birth-of-public-relations-44393

30 Ronn Torossian, Observer, "Hitler's Nazi Germany Used an American PR Agency," December 22, 2014, https://observer.com/2014/12/hitlers-nazi-germany-used-an-american-pr-agency

31 Zionism and Israel - Encyclopedic Dictionary, "Evian Conference," http://www.zionism-israel.com/dic/Evian_conference.htm

32 Daniel Greene and Frank Newport, Gallup Polling, "American Public Opinion and the Holocaust," April 23, 2018, https://news.gallup.com/opinion/polling-matters/232949/american-public-opinion-holocaust.aspx

33 Jules Archer, *The Plot to Seize the Whitehouse: The Shocking True Story of the Conspiracy to Overthrow FDR* (Skyhorse Publishing, 2007).

34 Cornelius Vanderbilt Jr., *Man of the World: My Life on Five Continents* (New York: Crown Publishers, 1959), p. 264. Cited by David Talbot, *The Devil's Chess Board: Allen Dulles, the CIA, and the Rise of America's Secret Government*, (New York: HarperCollins, 2015), p. 25.

35 Winston Churchill, *Complete Speeches*, vol. 4, pp. 4125-26.

36 Franklin D. Roosevelt, *The Public Papers and Addresses of Franklin D. Roosevelt*, (New York: Russell & Russell, 1938-1950) vol. 7, pp. 597-98. Cited by Nicholson Baker, *Human Smoke: The Beginnings of the End of Civilization*. New York: Simon & Schuster, 2008, p. 101.

37 David S. Wyman, *Paper Walls: America and the Refugee Crisis, 1938-1941* (Amherst: University of Massachusetts Press, 1968), p. 97. Cited by Nicholson Baker, *Human Smoke: The Beginnings of the End of Civilization*. New York: Simon & Schuster, 2008, p. 116.

38 Dennis Ross Laffer, University of South Florida, Scholar Commons, Graduate Theses and Dissertations, Graduate School, "Jewish Trail of Tears II: Children Refugee Bills of 1939 and 1940," March 2018, https://scholarcommons.usf.edu/cgi/viewcontent.cgi?article=8383&context=etd

39 Frank Newport, Gallup Polling, "Historical Review: Americans' Views on Refugees Coming to U.S.," November 19, 2015, https://news.gallup.com/opinion/polling-matters/186716/historical-review-americans-views-refugees-coming.aspx

40 David Talbot, *The Devil's Chess Board: Allen Dulles, the CIA, and the Rise of America's Secret Government*, (New York: HarperCollins, 2015), pp. 42-46.

41 Richard Breitman, *Time*, "The Troubling History of How America's 'Public Charge' Immigration Rule Blocked Jews Fleeing Nazi Germany," October 29, 2019, https://time.com/5712367/wwii-german-immigration-public-charge

42 David Talbot, *The Devil's Chess Board: Allen Dulles, the CIA, and the Rise of America's Secret Government*, (New York: HarperCollins, 2015), p. 45.

43 Elahe Izadi, *Washington Post*, "Anne Frank and her family were also denied entry as refugees to the U.S.," November 24, 2015, https://www.washingtonpost.com/news/worldviews/wp/2015/11/24/anne-frank-and-her-family-were-also-denied-entry-as-refugees-to-the-u-s/?utm_term=.f483423866ac

44 Dick Cheney and Liz Cheney, *Exceptional: Why the World Needs a Powerful*

America (Threshold Editions, 2016).

45   Elahe Izadi, *Washington Post*, "Anne Frank and her family were also denied entry as refugees to the U.S.," November 24, 2015, https://www.washingtonpost.com/news/worldviews/wp/2015/11/24/anne-frank-and-her-family-were-also-denied-entry-as-refugees-to-the-u-s/?utm_term=.f483423866ac

46   Christopher Browning, *The Path to Genocide* (New York: Cambridge University Press, 1992), pp. 18-19. Cited by Nicholson Baker, *Human Smoke: The Beginnings of the End of Civilization*. New York: Simon & Schuster, 2008, p. 233.

47   Nicholson Baker, *Human Smoke: The Beginnings of the End of Civilization*. New York: Simon & Schuster, 2008, p. 257.

48   Nicholson Baker, *Human Smoke: The Beginnings of the End of Civilization*. New York: Simon & Schuster, 2008, pp. 267-268.

49   *Chicago Tribune*, "'Feed Starving War Children,' Hoover Pleads," October 20, 1941. Cited by Nicholson Baker, *Human Smoke: The Beginnings of the End of Civilization*. New York: Simon & Schuster, 2008, p. 411.

50   Walter Laqueuer, *The Terrible Secret: Suppression of the Truth about Hitler's "Final Solution."* Boston: Little, Brown, 1980, p. 91. Cited by Nicholson Baker, *Human Smoke: The Beginnings of the End of Civilization*. New York: Simon & Schuster, 2008, p. 368.

51   Richard Breitman, *Time*, "The Troubling History of How America's 'Public Charge' Immigration Rule Blocked Jews Fleeing Nazi Germany," October 29, 2019, https://time.com/5712367/wwii-german-immigration-public-charge

52   David Talbot, *The Devil's Chess Board: Allen Dulles, the CIA, and the Rise of America's Secret Government*, (New York: HarperCollins, 2015), pp. 50-52. Also, the New York Times reported extensively on this topic 40 years later: Lucy S. Dawidowicz, "American Jews and the Holocaust," New York Times, April 18, 1982, https://www.nytimes.com/1982/04/18/magazine/american-jews-and-the-holocaust.html

53   David Talbot, *The Devil's Chess Board: Allen Dulles, the CIA, and the Rise of America's Secret Government*, (New York: HarperCollins, 2015), pp. 52-55.

54   Mark Horowitz, Commentary Magazine, "Alternate History: Review of 'The Jews Should Keep Quiet' by Rafael Medoff," June 2020, https://www.commentarymagazine.com/articles/mark-horowitz/fdr-jewish-leadership-and-holocaust

55   Lawrence Wittner, *Rebels Against War: The American Peace Movement 1933-1983*, (Temple University Press: Revised Edition, 1984).

56   Lucy S. Dawidowicz, "American Jews and the Holocaust," New York Times, April 18, 1982, https://www.nytimes.com/1982/04/18/magazine/american-jews-and-the-holocaust.html

57   U.S. Department of State, Office of the Historian, "Memorandum of Conversation, by Mr. Harry L. Hopkins, Special Assistant to President Roosevelt 55," March 27, 1943, https://history.state.gov/historicaldocuments/frus1943v03/d23

58   *War No More: Three Centuries of American Antiwar and Peace Writing*, edited by Lawrence Rosendwald (Library of America, 2016).

59   PBS American Experience: "The Bermuda Conference," https://www.pbs.org/wgbh/americanexperience/features/holocaust-bermuda

60   PBS American Experience: "The Bermuda Conference," https://www.pbs.org/wgbh/americanexperience/features/holocaust-bermuda

61   Dr. Rafael Medoff, The David S. Wyman Institute for Holocaust Studies, "The Allies' Refugee Conference–A 'Cruel Mockery," April 2003, http://new.wymaninstitute.org/2003/04/the-allies-refugee-conference-a-cruel-mockery

62   Lucy S. Dawidowicz, "American Jews and the Holocaust," *New York Times*, April 18, 1982, https://www.nytimes.com/1982/04/18/magazine/american-jews-and-the-holocaust.html

63   Charlotte Dennett, *The Crash of Flight 3804: A Lost Spy, a Daughter's Quest, and the Deadly Politics of the Great Game for Oil (Chelsea Green Publishing, 2020), p. 16.*

64   Foreign Relations of the United States, 1944, volume V, Palestine, ed. E.R. Perkins, S.E. Gleason, J.G. Reid, et al. (Washington, DC: US Government Printing Office, 1965), document 705. Cited by Charlotte Dennett, *The Crash of Flight 3804: A Lost Spy, a Daughter's Quest, and the Deadly Politics of the Great Game for Oil (Chelsea Green Publishing, 2020), p. 23 footnote.*

65   Mark Horowitz, *Commentary Magazine*, "Alternate History: Review of 'The Jews Should Keep Quiet' by Rafael Medoff," June 2020, https://www.commentarymagazine.com/articles/mark-horowitz/fdr-jewish-leadership-and-holocaust

66   Frank Newport, Gallup Polling, "Historical Review: Americans' Views on Refugees Coming to U.S.," November 19, 2015, https://news.gallup.com/opinion/polling-matters/186716/historical-review-americans-views-refugees-coming.aspx

67   United States Holocaust Memorial Museum, Holocaust Encyclopedia, "Immigration to the United States, 1933-41," https://encyclopedia.ushmm.org/content/en/article/immigration-to-the-united-states-1933-41

68 Jacques R. Pauwels, *The Myth of the Good War: America in the Second World War* (James Lorimer & Company Ltd. 2015, 2002) p. 36.

69   Independent Lens, "The Political Dr. Seuss," https://www.pbs.org/independentlens/politicaldrseuss/film.html

70 Rob Tannenbaum, *New York Times*, "Billy Joel's Got a Good Job and Hits in His Head," July 25, 2018, https://www.nytimes.com/2018/07/25/arts/music/billy-joel-100-shows-interview.html

71 Wikipedia, "World War II Casualties," https://en.wikipedia.org/wiki/World_War_II_casualties

72 Wikipedia, "World War II Casualties," https://en.wikipedia.org/wiki/World_War_II_casualties

73 Winston Churchill, *The Second World War: The Gathering Storm* (Boston: Houghton Mifflin Company, 1948), p. iv. Cited by Scott Manning, "What Did Churchill Mean by 'Unnecessary War'?" July 17, 2008, https://scottmanning.com/content/what-did-churchill-mean-by-unnecessary-war

74 When the Czar of Russia in 1898 invited all of the world's governments to a peace conference, which would be held in the Hague in 1899, one leading peace advocate wrote to another that now, finally, "the world will not shriek Utopia!" meaning that peace would at last be taken seriously. Sadly, it was not. The major war-making governments shrieked "Utopia" at the top of their lungs. And well-meaning activists were divided between efforts to ban war and efforts to ban particular atrocities, thereby "humanizing" war. Nonetheless, a treaty was produced requiring nations to at least try to settle disputes through arbitration, and a court was created to arbitrate. Key ingredients for avoiding both world wars were placed on the world's shelves and allowed to gather dust. See James Crossland, *War, Law, and Humanity: The Campaign to Control Warfare, 1853-1914* (Bloomsbury Academic, 2019). See also "Convention (I) For The Pacific Settlement Of International Disputes (Hague I) (29 July 1899)" *https://avalon.law.yale.edu/19th_century/hague01.asp*

75 Women's International League for Peace and Freedom, "Versailles Treaty: Reconstructing Patriarchy After WWI," June 28, 2019, https://www.wilpf.org/versaillestreaty

76   The Great Peacemakers, "Jane Addams Biography," https://www. thegreatpeacemakers.com/jane-addams.html

77 Karenna Gore, *New York Times*, "The Remarkable Life of the First Woman on the Harvard Faculty: Alice Hamilton, an expert on public health, foresaw the rise of fascism in Germany," August 29, 2019, https://www.nytimes.com/2019/08/29/ opinion/alice-hamilton-harvard.html

78   Ron Greenslade, *The Guardian,* "First world war: how state and press kept truth off the front page," July 27, 2014, https://www.theguardian.com/media/2014/ jul/27/first-world-war-state-press-reporting

79   "Censorship and propaganda authorities [in Germany] decided to keep bad news quiet from the people at home . . . . During the war German propaganda condemned any behavior endangering the war effort as unpatriotic, helping the enemy, and sabotaging the German military effort. For example, in fall 1918 a caricature showed a German worker resisting the seditious enemy propaganda, symbolized by a satanic creature. After Germany surrendered in 1918 these representations continued and right–wing groups maintained that the valiant German army returned undefeated to the homeland. In this view, the defeat was blamed on the home front that had stabbed the army in the back. Erich Ludendorff alleged that the home front had been hypnotized by enemy propaganda as a rabbit is by a snake. The assumptions that propaganda had been the enemies' decisive weapon and that the German government failed to use propaganda as effectively as the enemy were extremely popular during the 1920s, contributing to the back-stabbing myth." Florian Altenhöner, International Encyclopedia of the First World War, "Press/Journalism (Germany)," October 8, 2014, https://encyclopedia.1914-1918-online.net/article/pressjournalism_germany

80   Cited by Jeffrey Sparks, "Yes, Woodrow Wilson predicted World War II – but so did J. M. Keynes," December 28, 2014, https://sparkscommentary.blogspot. com/2014/12/keynes-wilson-and-wwii.html

81   Thorstein Veblen, "Review of John Maynard Keynes, The Economic Consequences of the Peace," Political Science Quarterly, 35, pp. 467-472, http:// www.adelinotorres.info/economia/THORSTEIN%20VEBLEN-Review%20of%20 John%20Maynard%20Keynes.pdf Cited by Guido Giacomo Preparata, Conjuring Hitler: How Britain and America Made the Third Reich (Pluto Press, 2005), Chapter 2 "The Veblenian Prophecy. From the Councils to Versailles by Way of Russian Fratricide, 1919-20."

82   David Swanson, *When the World Outlawed War* (David Swanson, 2011).

83   Steve Coll, *The New Yorker*, "Woodrow Wilson's Case of the Flu, and How Pandemics Change History," April 17, 2020, https://www.newyorker.com/news/daily-comment/woodrow-wilsons-case-of-the-flu-and-how-pandemics-change-history

84   Michael S. Rosenwald, *The Washington Post*, "In 1918, the Spanish flu infected the White House. Even President Wilson got sick," March 14, 2020, https://www.washingtonpost.com/history/2020/03/14/flu-woodrow-wilson-coronavirus-trump/

85   Bob McGovern and John Kopp, *Philly Voice*, "In 1918, Philadelphia was in 'the grippe' of misery and suffering," September 28, 2018, https://www.phillyvoice.com/1918-philadelphia-was-grippe-misery-and-suffering

86   Margaret MacMillan, *Paris 1919: Six Months That Changed the World*, (New York: Random House, 2001), cited by William Geimer, Canada: The Case for Staying Out of Other People's Wars (iUniverse, 2016), chapter 3.

87   This quotation of Foch has been widely cited, including by Winston Churchill, though there are reasons to doubt that he said it on the date cited, if he said it at all. However, there is strong agreement that it encapsulates his sentiments at the time of the Treaty of Versailles. See Dr. Beachcombing, "Foch and the Twenty Year Armistice: A Myth?" July 11, 2016, http://www.strangehistory.net/2016/07/11/foch-twenty-year-armistice-myth

88   Winston S. Churchill, "Iron Curtain Speech," March 5, 1946, https://weknowourhistory.files.wordpress.com/2012/02/iron-curtain-speech.pdf

89   Scott Manning, "What Did Churchill Mean by 'Unnecessary War'?" July 17, 2008, https://scottmanning.com/content/what-did-churchill-mean-by-unnecessary-war

90   "By the end of the war, psychologists concluded that white and black draftees had an average mental age of 13.15 and 10.1 years old, respectively. In the parlance of the time, anyone with a mental age below 12 was considered a moron (Barbeau and Henri, 1996, 44). Subsequent investigations by historians and psychologists, however, have concluded that the tests more accurately reflected years of schooling and social class rather than intellectual capacity." Jennifer Keene, "A Comparative Study of White and Black American Soldiers during the First World War," Annales de démographie historique 2002/1 (no 103), pp. 71-90, https://www.cairn.info/revue-annales-de-demographie-historique-2002-1-page-71.htm#

91   Pascal Robert, Black Agenda Report, "Black Eugenics: How the Black Mis-leadership Class of the Early 20th Century Supported Sterilization of the Black Poor," September 23, 2015, https://blackagendareport.com/black_eugenics_sterilization_black_poor

92 John Blake, CNN, "When Americans tried to breed a better race: How a genetic fitness 'crusade' marches on," October 18, 2018, https://www.cnn.com/2018/10/16/us/eugenics-craze-america-pbs/index.html

93 Madison Grant, *The Passing of the Great Race*, 1922, https://archive.org/details/passingofgreatra00granuoft Notice the positive recent comments by visitors to the website of this 100-year-old pseudo-scientific, racist, and eliminationist text.

94   Edwin Black, SFGate, "Eugenics and the Nazis — the California connection," November 9, 2003, https://www.sfgate.com/opinion/article/Eugenics-and-the-Nazis-the-California-2549771.php

95   For example, Frank Boas. Also Thomas Hunt Morgan, profiled in this short video:
https://www.pbs.org/wgbh/americanexperience/features/eugenics-thomas-hunt-morgan

96   "Preliminary Report of the American Breeders' Association to Study and to Report on the Best Practical Means for Cutting Off the Defective Germ-Plasm in the Human Population," 1911.

97   Edwin Black, SFGate, "Eugenics and the Nazis — the California connection," November 9, 2003, https://www.sfgate.com/opinion/article/Eugenics-and-the-Nazis-the-California-2549771.php

98   Alex Ross, *The New Yorker,* "How American Racism Influenced Hitler," April 30, 2018, https://www.newyorker.com/magazine/2018/04/30/how-american-racism-influenced-hitler

99   PBS, "American Experience: The Eugenics Crusade," October 16, 2018, https://www.pbs.org/wgbh/americanexperience/films/eugenics-crusade

100   Adolf Hitler, *Mein Kampf,* Volume Two - The National Socialist Movement, Chapter III: Subjects and Citizens, http://www.hitler.org/writings/Mein_Kampf/mkv2ch03.html

101   Edwin Black, SFGate, "Eugenics and the Nazis — the California connection," November 9, 2003, https://www.sfgate.com/opinion/article/Eugenics-and-the-Nazis-the-California-2549771.php

102   John P. Jackson, Nadine M. Weidman, *Race, Racism, and Science: Social*

Impact and Interaction (Rutgers University Press, 2005), p. 123.

103   Stefan Kühl, *The Nazi connection: Eugenics, American racism, and German National Socialism* (New York: Oxford University Press, 1994); Alexandra Stern, *Eugenic nation: faults and frontiers of better breeding in modern America* (Berkeley: University of California Press, 2005); and Wendy Kline, *Building a better race: gender, sexuality, and eugenics from the turn of the century to the baby boom* (Berkeley: University of California Press, 2001), all cited by Wikipedia, "Compulsory Sterilization," https://en.wikipedia.org/wiki/Compulsory_sterilization#cite_note-96

104   Edwin Black, SFGate, "Eugenics and the Nazis — the California connection," November 9, 2003, https://www.sfgate.com/opinion/article/Eugenics-and-the-Nazis-the-California-2549771.php

105   Mickey Z., *There Is No Good War: The Myths of World War II*, (Brooklyn, N.Y.: VoxPopNet, 2000), p. 62. Cited by David Swanson, *War Is A Lie: Second Edition* (Charlottesville: Just World Books, 2016), p. 100.

106   Kevin Begos, *Indy Week*, "The American eugenics movement after World War II (part 1 of 3)," May 18, 2011, https://indyweek.com/news/american-eugenics-movement-world-war-ii-part-1-3

107   Katherine Andrews, Panoramas, University of Pittsburgh, "The Dark History of Forced Sterilization of Latina Women," October 30, 2017, https://www.panoramas.pitt.edu/health-and-society/dark-history-forced-sterilization-latina-women

108   Jean-Jacques Amy and Sam Rowlands, "Legalised non-consensual sterilisation – eugenics put into practice before 1945, and the aftermath. Part 1: USA, Japan, Canada and Mexico," The European Journal of Contraception & Reproductive Health Care, Volume 23, 2018 - Issue 2 , Pages 121-129, April 6, 2018, https://www.tandfonline.com/doi/abs/10.1080/13625187.2018.1450973?journalCode=iejc20

109   Alex Stern and Tony Platt, HuffPost, "Sterilization Abuse in State Prisons: Time to Break With California's Long Eugenic Patterns," September 22, 2013, https://www.huffpost.com/entry/sterilization-california-prisons_b_3631287

110   Stephanie Welch, Paragon Media, Denkmal Film, "A Dangerous Idea: Eugenics, Genetics, and the American Dream," 2016, http://adangerousideafilm.com

111   Allen M. Hornblum, Judith Lynn Newman, and Gregory J. Dober, *Against Their Will: The Secret History of Medical Experimentation on Children in Cold War*

America (St. Martin's Press, 2013).

112 Donald G. McNeil Jr., *The New York Times*, "U.S. Apologizes for Syphilis Tests in Guatemala," October 1, 2010, http://www.nytimes.com/2010/10/02/health/research/02infect.html

113 Allen M. Hornblum, Judith Lynn Newman, and Gregory J. Dober, *Against Their Will: The Secret History of Medical Experimentation on Children in Cold War America* (St. Martin's Press, 2013).

114 Caitlin Dickerson, Morning Edition, National Public Radio, "Secret World War II Chemical Experiments Tested Troops By Race," June 22, 2015, https://www.npr.org/2015/06/22/415194765/u-s-troops-tested-by-race-in-secret-world-war-ii-chemical-experiments

115 Noam Chomsky, "A Just War? Hardly," *Khaleej Times*, May 9, 2006, https://chomsky.info/20060509

116 Allen M. Hornblum, Judith Lynn Newman, and Gregory J. Dober, *Against Their Will: The Secret History of Medical Experimentation on Children in Cold War America* (St. Martin's Press, 2013).

117 Waldemar Kaempffert, *New York Times*, "Meteorites Hitting the Surface of the Moon May Fling Stones to the Earth," April 27, 1947, https://www.nytimes.com/1947/04/27/archives/meteorites-hitting-the-surface-of-the-moon-may-fling-stones-to-the.html

118 Allen M. Hornblum, Judith Lynn Newman, and Gregory J. Dober, *Against Their Will: The Secret History of Medical Experimentation on Children in Cold War America* (St. Martin's Press, 2013).

119 PBS, "American Experience: The Eugenics Crusade," October 16, 2018, https://www.pbs.org/wgbh/americanexperience/films/eugenics-crusade

120 James Q. Whitman, *Hitler's American Model: The United States and the Making of Nazi Race Law (Princeton University Press, 2017).*

121 Douglas Blackmon, *Slavery By Another Name: The Re-Enslavement of Black Americans from the Civil War to World War II (Doubleday, 2008).*

122 Democracy Now, "How America's Perpetual Warfare Abroad Is Fueling an Increase in White Supremacist Violence in U.S.," November 20, 2018, https://www.democracynow.org/2018/11/20/how_americas_perpetual_warfare_abroad_is

123 Barbara Ehrenreich, *Blood Rites: Origins and the History of the Passions of War* (London: Virago Press, 1998), p. 207. Cited By David Swanson, *War Is A Lie: Second Edition* (Charlottesville: Just World Books, 2016), p. 54.

124 Howard Zinn, *The Bomb* (City Lights Books, 2010), p. 42.

125 Here's that image: https://library.ucsd.edu/dc/object/bb71339897

126   Here's that image: https://www.pragmaticmom.com/2016/11/japanese-internment-books-kids

127 Mickey Z., *Dissident Voice*, "Vermin and Souvenirs: How to Justify a Nuclear Attack," August 12, 2005, http://dissidentvoice.org/Aug05/MickeyZ0812.htm

128 Edgar L. Jones, *The Atlantic Monthly*, "One War is Enough," February 1946, https://www.theatlantic.com/past/docs/unbound/bookauth/battle/jones.htm

129 *Korematsu v. United States*, 323 U.S. 214 (1944).

130 Mickey Z., Counterpunch, "Zoot Suit Riots, June 1943," June 18, 2014, https://www.counterpunch.org/2014/06/18/zoot-suit-riots-june-1943

131   Howard Zinn, *A People's History of the United States*, (Harper Perennial Modern Classics; Reissue edition, 2015).

132 Jacques R. Pauwels, *The Myth of the Good War: America in the Second World War* (James Lorimer & Company Ltd. 2015, 2002) p. 34.

133 Daniel Immerwahr, *How to Hide an Empire: A History of the Greater United States,* (Farrar, Straus, and Giroux, 2019), p. 179.

134   Oliver Stone and Peter Kuznick, *The Untold History of the United States* (Simon & Schuster, 2012), p. 153.

135 David Vine, *Base Nation: How U.S. Military Bases Abroad Harm America and the World* (Metropolitan Books, 2015), Chapter 3.

136 David Vine, *Base Nation: How U.S. Military Bases Abroad Harm America and the World* (Metropolitan Books, 2015), Chapter 3.

137 David Vine, *Base Nation: How U.S. Military Bases Abroad Harm America and the World* (Metropolitan Books, 2015), Chapter 3.

138 David Vine, *Island of Shame: The Secret History of the U.S. Military Base on Diego Garcia* (Princeton University Press, Revised edition, 2011).

139 Jacques R. Pauwels, *The Myth of the Good War: America in the Second World War* (James Lorimer & Company Ltd. 2015, 2002) p. 19.

140 Jeffrey Ostler, *Surviving Genocide: Native Nations and the United States from the American Revolution to Bleeding Kansas* (Yale University Press, 2019).

141 Benjamin Madley, *An American Genocide: The United States and the California Indian Catastrophe* (Yale University Press, 2016).

142 Jon Schwarz, *The Intercept*, "As Teddy Roosevelt's Statue Falls, Let's Remember How Truly Dark His History Was," June 22, 2020, https://theintercept.

com/2020/06/22/as-teddy-roosevelts-statue-falls-lets-remember-how-truly-dark-his-history-was

143 Alex Ross, *The New Yorker,* "How American Racism Influenced Hitler," April 30, 2018, https://www.newyorker.com/magazine/2018/04/30/how-american-racism-influenced-hitler

144 Carroll P. Kakel, *The American West and the Nazi East: A Comparative and Interpretive Perspective* (Palgrave Macmillan, 2011).

145 Carroll P. Kakel, The American West and the Nazi East: A Comparative and Interpretive Perspective (Palgrave Macmillan, 2011).

146 Carroll P. Kakel, The American West and the Nazi East: A Comparative and Interpretive Perspective (Palgrave Macmillan, 2011).

147 James Bradley, *The Imperial Cruise: A Secret History of Empire and War* (Back Bay Books, 2010).

148 David Talbot, *Devil Dog: The Amazing True Story of the Man Who Saved America,* (Simon & Schuster, 2010), pp. 120-121.

149 David Talbot, *Devil Dog: The Amazing True Story of the Man Who Saved America,* (Simon & Schuster, 2010), p. 141-142.

150 David Talbot, *Devil Dog: The Amazing True Story of the Man Who Saved America,* (Simon & Schuster, 2010), p. 142.

151 See Chapter 11 of this book.

152 Association for Diplomatic Studies and Training, "Douglas MacArthur, America's Emperor of Japan," July 2, 2015, https://adst.org/2015/07/douglas-macarthur-americas-emperor-of-japan

153 Bruce Cumings, *The Korean War: A History* (Random House, 2010). Cited by David Swanson, *War Is A Lie: Second Edition* (Charlottesville: Just World Books, 2016), p. 62.

154 James Bradley, *The Imperial Cruise: A Secret History of Empire and War* (Back Bay Books, 2010).

155 James Bradley, *The Imperial Cruise: A Secret History of Empire and War* (Back Bay Books, 2010).

156 Sven Lindqvist, *"Exterminate All the Brutes": One Man's Odyssey into the Heart of Darkness and the Origins of European Genocide* (The New Press, 1992).

157 Sven Lindqvist, *"Exterminate All the Brutes": One Man's Odyssey into the Heart of Darkness and the Origins of European Genocide* (The New Press, 1992), p. 157.

158   Alex Ross, *The New Yorker*, "How American Racism Influenced Hitler," April 30, 2018, https://www.newyorker.com/magazine/2018/04/30/how-american-racism-influenced-hitler

159   Carroll P. Kakel, *The American West and the Nazi East: A Comparative and Interpretive Perspective* (Palgrave Macmillan, 2011).

160   Sven Lindqvist, *"Exterminate All the Brutes": One Man's Odyssey into the Heart of Darkness and the Origins of European Genocide* (The New Press, 1992), p. 157.

161   Cited by Nicholson Baker, *Human Smoke: The Beginnings of the End of Civilization*. New York: Simon & Schuster, 2008, p. 156.

162   Andrea Pitzer, *Smithsonian Magazine*, "Concentration Camps Existed Long Before Auschwitz," November 2, 2017, https://www.smithsonianmag.com/history/concentration-camps-existed-long-before-Auschwitz-180967049

163   Jeffrey Ostler, *Surviving Genocide: Native Nations and the United States from the American Revolution to Bleeding Kansas* (Yale University Press, 2019), p. 385.

164   Wikipedia, "World War II Casualties," https://en.wikipedia.org/wiki/World_War_II_casualties

165   Wikipedia, "World War II Casualties," https://en.wikipedia.org/wiki/World_War_II_casualties

166   Wikipedia, "Atrocities in the Congo Free State," https://en.wikipedia.org/wiki/Atrocities_in_the_Congo_Free_State#Population_decline

167   Wikipedia, "Second Congo War," https://en.wikipedia.org/wiki/Second_Congo_War

168   Researchers at Johns Hopkins University found that between March 18, 2003, and June 2006, there were 654,965 excess deaths in Iraq, of which 601,027 were due to violence. Excess deaths means, in this case, deaths exceeding the already high death rate under the preceding sanctions regime. The British based Opinion Research Business found that between March 2003 and August 2007, there were 1,033,000 violent deaths of Iraqis in Iraq. Experts on surveys of this sort have supported the conclusions of Johns Hopkins and of the Opinion Research Business as strenuously as the U.S. corporate media has hypocritically denounced them. A review of this debate is found in Erasing Iraq: The Human Costs of Carnage by Michael Otterman and Richard Hill with Paul Wilson.

169   Wikipedia, "Herero and Namaqua genocide," https://en.wikipedia.org/wiki/Herero_and_Namaqua_genocide

170 Wikipedia, "Dzungar genocide," https://en.wikipedia.org/wiki/Dzungar_genocide

171 See 2008 study by Harvard Medical School and the Institute for Health Metrics and Evaluation at the University of Washington, which estimated 3.8 million violent war deaths, combat and civilian, north and south, during the years of U.S. involvement in Vietnam: Ziad Obermeyer, Christopher J L Murray, and Emmanuela Gakidou, *The BMJ*, "Fifty years of violent war deaths from Vietnam to Bosnia: analysis of data from the world health survey programme," June 28, 2008, 336(7659): 1482–1486, https://www.ncbi.nlm.nih.gov/pmc/articles/PMC2440905 Cited by Nick Turse, *Kill Anything That Moves: The Real American War in Vietnam (Picador, 2013)*. Turse believes the estimate is low. The relevant excerpt of his book is published here: https://billmoyers.com/2013/02/08/excerpt-kill-anything-that-moves/5

172 Wikipedia, "Circassian genocide," https://en.wikipedia.org/wiki/Circassian_genocide

173 Wikipedia, "Greek Genocide," https://en.wikipedia.org/wiki/Greek_genocide

174 Wikipedia, "Armenian Genocide," https://en.wikipedia.org/wiki/Armenian_Genocide

175 Wikipedia, "Cambodian Genocide," https://en.wikipedia.org/wiki/Cambodian_genocide

176 Wikipedia, "Second Italo-Ethiopian War," https://en.wikipedia.org/wiki/Second_Italo-Ethiopian_War

177 UNICEF USA, https://www.unicefusa.org/mission/starts-with-u/health-for-children

178 Alex Ross, *The New Yorker*, "How American Racism Influenced Hitler," April 30, 2018, https://www.newyorker.com/magazine/2018/04/30/how-american-racism-influenced-hitler

179 Roxanne Dunbar-Ortiz, *An Indigenous People's History of the United States (Beacon Press, 2015)*.

180 Edwin Black, *IBM and the Holocaust: The Strategic Alliance Between Nazi Germany and America's Most Powerful Corporation* (Dialog Press, 2001).

181 Edwin Black, *IBM and the Holocaust: The Strategic Alliance Between Nazi Germany and America's Most Powerful Corporation* (Dialog Press, 2001).

182 *New York Times*, "BERLIN HEARS FORD IS BACKING HITLER; Bavarian Anti-Semitic Chief Has American's Portrait and Book in His Office. SPENDS

MONEY LAVISHLY One German Paper Appeals to the United States Ambassador to Make Investigation," December 20, 1922, https://www.nytimes.com/1922/12/20/ archives/berlin-hears-ford-is-backing-hitler-bavarian-antisemitic-chief-has.html Cited by Antony C. Sutton, Wall Street and the Rise of Hitler (GSG & Associates, 2002), pp. 91-92.

183 Jacques R. Pauwels, *The Myth of the Good War: America in the Second World War* (James Lorimer & Company Ltd. 2015, 2002) p. 59.

184   Ken Silverstein, *The Nation,* "Ford and the Führer," January 6, 2000, https:// www.thenation.com/article/archive/ford-and-fuhrer

185   Michael Parenti, *Blackshirts & Reds: Rational Fascism and the Overthrow of Communism* (San Francisco: City Lights, 1997) p. 19. Cited by Mickey Z., *There Is No Good War: The Myths of World War II,* (Brooklyn, N.Y.: VoxPopNet, 2000), p. 13.

186   Richard Billstein, Karola Fings, Anita Kugler, and Nicholas Levis, *Working for the Enemy: Ford, General Motors and Forced Labor in Germany During the Second World War* (Berghahn Books, 2000), p. 98.

187   Jason Weixelbaum, "Debunking Conspiracy: Ford-Werke and the Allied bombing Campaign of Cologne," May 9, 2012, https://jasonweixelbaum.wordpress. com/2012/05/09/debunking-conspiracy-ford-werke-and-the-allied-bombing-campaign-of-cologne

188   Charles Higham, *Trading With the Enemy: An Exposé of the Nazi-American Money Plot 1933-1949* (Dell Publishing Co., 1983) p. 183.

189   Charles Higham, *Trading With the Enemy: An Exposé of the Nazi-American Money Plot 1933-1949* (Dell Publishing Co., 1983) p. 183.

190   Charles Higham, *Trading With the Enemy: An Exposé of the Nazi-American Money Plot 1933-1949* (Dell Publishing Co., 1983) p. 188.

191   Charles Higham, *Trading With the Enemy: An Exposé of the Nazi-American Money Plot 1933-1949* (Dell Publishing Co., 1983) p. 189.

192   Richard Billstein, Karola Fings, Anita Kugler, and Nicholas Levis, *Working for the Enemy: Ford, General Motors and Forced Labor in Germany During the Second World War* (Berghahn Books, 2000), p. 1.

193   Ofer Aderet, *Haaretz,* "U.S. Chemical Corporation DuPont Helped Nazi Germany Because of Ideology, Israeli Researcher Says," February 5, 2019, https:// www.haaretz.com/us-news/.premium-researcher-dupont-helped-nazi-germany-out-of-ideology-1.7186636

194 Jacques R. Pauwels, *The Myth of the Good War: America in the Second World War* (James Lorimer & Company Ltd. 2015, 2002) p. 205.

195 Ken Silverstein, *The Nation*, "Ford and the Führer," January 6, 2000, https://www.thenation.com/article/archive/ford-and-fuhrer

196 Jason Weixelbaum, "How to Save the Jobs of GM Workers," *Washington Post*, December 19, 2018, https://www.washingtonpost.com/outlook/2018/12/19/how-save-jobs-gm-workers

197 Henry Ashby Turner, *German Big Business and the Rise of Hitler* (Oxford University Press, 1985), cited by Jason Weixelbaum, "Digital Conspiracy? Edwin Black, Henry Ashby Turner Jr., and General Motors in Nazi Germany," April 28, 2013, https://jasonweixelbaum.wordpress.com/2013/04/28/digital-conspiracy-edwin-black-henry-ashby-turner-jr-and-general-motors-in-nazi-germany

198 Antony C. Sutton, *Wall Street and the Rise of Hitler* (GSG & Associates, 2002), p. 109.

199 United States Congress. Senate. Hearings before a Subcommittee of the Committee on Military Affairs. *Elimination of German Resources for War.* Report pursuant to S. Res. 107 and 146, July 2, 1945, Part 7. (78th Congress and 79th Congress), (Washington: Government Printing Office, 1945), p. 943. Cited by Antony C. Sutton, *Wall Street and the Rise of Hitler* (GSG & Associates, 2002), p. 35.

200 United States Congress, House of Representatives, Special Committee on Un-American Activities, *Investigation of Nazi Propaganda Activities and Investigation of Certain Other Propaganda Activities.* 73rd Congress, 2nd Session, Hearings No. 73-DC-4. (Washington: Government Printing Office, 1934), Volume VIII, p. 952 and p. 1293. Cited by Antony C. Sutton, *Wall Street and the Rise of Hitler* (GSG & Associates, 2002), p. 39.

201 Mary Jo McConahay, *The Tango War: The Struggle for the Hearts, Minds, and Riches of Latin America During World War II* (St. Martin's Press, 2018).

202 Jason Weixelbaum, "Collaboration in Context: New Historiographical Approaches to Alleged American/Nazi Business Ties," May 17, 2011, https://jasonweixelbaum.wordpress.com/2011/05/17/collaboration-in-context-new-historiographical-approaches-to-alleged-americannazi-business-ties

203 Charles Higham, *Trading With the Enemy: An Exposé of the Nazi-American Money Plot 1933-1949* (Dell Publishing Co., 1983) p. 118.

204 Charles Higham, *Trading With the Enemy: An Exposé of the Nazi-American*

Money Plot 1933-1949 (Dell Publishing Co., 1983) p. 119.

205 David Talbot, *The Devil's Chess Board: Allen Dulles, the CIA, and the Rise of America's Secret Government*, (New York: HarperCollins, 2015), pp. 25-28.

206 Charles Higham, *Trading With the Enemy: An Exposé of the Nazi-American Money Plot 1933-1949* (Dell Publishing Co., 1983) p. 29.

207 Charles Higham, *Trading With the Enemy: An Exposé of the Nazi-American Money Plot 1933-1949* (Dell Publishing Co., 1983) pp. 12, 43.

208 Ken Silverstein, *The Nation*, "Ford and the Führer," January 6, 2000, https://www.thenation.com/article/archive/ford-and-fuhrer

209 David Talbot, *The Devil's Chess Board: Allen Dulles, the CIA, and the Rise of America's Secret Government*, (New York: HarperCollins, 2015). Also: The Brothers

210 Jason Weixelbaum, "Collaboration in Context: New Historiographical Approaches to Alleged American/Nazi Business Ties," May 17, 2011, https://jasonweixelbaum.wordpress.com/2011/05/17/collaboration-in-context-new-historiographical-approaches-to-alleged-americannazi-business-ties

211 Jason Weixelbaum, "Collaboration in Context: New Historiographical Approaches to Alleged American/Nazi Business Ties," May 17, 2011, https://jasonweixelbaum.wordpress.com/2011/05/17/collaboration-in-context-new-historiographical-approaches-to-alleged-americannazi-business-ties

212 Jacques R. Pauwels, *The Myth of the Good War: America in the Second World War* (James Lorimer & Company Ltd. 2015, 2002) p. 32.

213 Edgar B. Nixon, ed., *Franklin D. Roosevelt and Foreign Affairs*, Volume III: September 1935-January 1937, (Cambridge: Belknap Press, 1969) p. 456. Cited by Antony C. Sutton, *Wall Street and the Rise of Hitler* (GSG & Associates, 2002), p. 15.

214 Ofer Aderet, *Haaretz*, "U.S. Chemical Corporation DuPont Helped Nazi Germany Because of Ideology, Israeli Researcher Says," February 5, 2019, https://www.haaretz.com/us-news/.premium-researcher-dupont-helped-nazi-germany-out-of-ideology-1.7186636

215 Thom Hartmann, *The Hidden History of Monopolies: How Big Business Destroyed the American Dream* (Berrett-Koehler Publishers, 2020) pp. 35-37.

216 Thom Hartmann, *The Hidden History of Monopolies: How Big Business Destroyed the American Dream* (Berrett-Koehler Publishers, 2020) p. 38.

217 Ofer Aderet, *Haaretz*, "U.S. Chemical Corporation DuPont Helped Nazi Germany Because of Ideology, Israeli Researcher Says," February 5, 2019, https://

www.haaretz.com/us-news/.premium-researcher-dupont-helped-nazi-germany-out-of-ideology-1.7186636

218 Jacques R. Pauwels, *The Myth of the Good War: America in the Second World War* (James Lorimer & Company Ltd. 2015, 2002) p. 37.

219　H.C. Engelbrecht, "The Problem of the Munitions Industry," *Annals of American Academy of Political and Social Science* (September 1934). Cited by Nicholson Baker, *Human Smoke: The Beginnings of the End of Civilization.* New York: Simon & Schuster, 2008, pp. 48-49.

220　*New York Times*, "Big Orders Tax Plants," June 19, 1938. Also: *New York Times*, "Air Experts in Japan Only Fill Contracts," May 27, 1939. Both cited by Nicholson Baker, *Human Smoke: The Beginnings of the End of Civilization.* New York: Simon & Schuster, 2008, pp. 85, 124.

221 Neil Forbes, *Doing Business with the Nazis: Britain's Economic and Financial Relations with Germany 1931-1939* (London: Frank Cass Publishers, 2000), cited by Jason Weixelbaum, "Collaboration in Context: New Historiographical Approaches to Alleged American/Nazi Business Ties," May 17, 2011, https://jasonweixelbaum. wordpress.com/2011/05/17/collaboration-in-context-new-historiographical-approaches-to-alleged-americannazi-business-ties

222 FRASER, "Full text of Commercial and Financial Chronicle: September 30, 1933, Vol. 137, No. 3562," https://fraser.stlouisfed.org/title/commercial-financial-chronicle-1339/september-30-1933-518572/fulltext

223 Nicholson Baker, *Human Smoke: The Beginnings of the End of Civilization.* New York: Simon & Schuster, 2008, p. 32.

224 Charles Higham, *Trading With the Enemy: An Exposé of the Nazi-American Money Plot 1933-1949* (Dell Publishing Co., 1983) p. 152.

225 Jacques R. Pauwels, *The Myth of the Good War: America in the Second World War* (James Lorimer & Company Ltd. 2015, 2002) p. 45.

226 The *New York Times* has a page about the Appeasement of Nazis with reader comments permanently displayed below it (no further comments allowed) claiming that the lesson was not learned because Vladimir Putin was Appeased in Crimea in 2014. The fact that the people of Crimea voted overwhelmingly to rejoin Russia, in part because they were being threatened by neo-Nazis, is not mentioned anywhere: https://learning.blogs.nytimes.com/2011/09/30/sept-30-1938-hitler-granted-the-sudentenland-by-britain-france-and-italy

227 Wikipedia, "World War II Casualties," https://en.wikipedia.org/wiki/World_

War_II_casualties

228 John Moser, Ashbrook, Ashland University, "Principles Without Program: Senator Robert A. Taft and American Foreign Policy," September 1, 2001, https:// ashbrook.org/publications/dialogue-moser/#12

229 *Time Magazine*, "National Affairs: Anniversary Remembrance," Monday, July 02, 1951, http://content.time.com/time/magazine/article/0,9171,815031,00.html

230 Oliver Stone and Peter Kuznick, *The Untold History of the United States* (Simon & Schuster, 2012), p. 96.

231 Oliver Stone and Peter Kuznick, *The Untold History of the United States* (Simon & Schuster, 2012), pp. 97, 102.

232 Oliver Stone and Peter Kuznick, *The Untold History of the United States* (Simon & Schuster, 2012), p. 102.

233 Oliver Stone and Peter Kuznick, *The Untold History of the United States* (Simon & Schuster, 2012), p. 103.

234 Oliver Stone and Peter Kuznick, *The Untold History of the United States* (Simon & Schuster, 2012), pp. 104-108.

235 Gaetano Salvamini and Giorgio La Piana, *La sorte dell'Italia* (1945).

236 Brett Wilkins, *Common Dreams*, "The Beasts and the Bombings: Reflecting on Dresden, February 1945," February 10, 2020, https://www.commondreams. org/views/2020/02/10/beasts-and-bombings-reflecting-dresden-february-1945

237 See Chapter 14 of this book.

238 Max Hastings, *Daily Mail*, "Operation unthinkable: How Churchill wanted to recruit defeated Nazi troops and drive Russia out of Eastern Europe," August 26,   2009,   https://www.dailymail.co.uk/debate/article-1209041/Operation-unthinkable-How-Churchill-wanted-recruit-defeated-Nazi-troops-drive-Russia-Eastern-Europe.html

239 David Talbot, *The Devil's Chess Board: Allen Dulles, the CIA, and the Rise of America's Secret Government*, (New York: HarperCollins, 2015).

240 Dave Lindorff, "Rethinking Manhattan Project Spies and the Cold War, MAD — and the 75 years of no nuclear war — that their efforts gifted us," August 1, 2020, https://thiscantbehappening.net/rethinking-manhattan-project-spies-and-the-cold-war-mad-and-the-75-years-of-no-nuclear-war-that-their-efforts-gifted-us

241 Erin Blakemore, *Smithsonian Magazine*, "The Rules About How to Address the U.S. Flag Came About Because No One Wanted to Look Like a Nazi," August 12, 2016, https://www.smithsonianmag.com/smart-news/rules-about-

how-to-address-us-flag-came-about-because-no-one-wanted-to-look-like-a-nazi-180960100

242   Jessie Guy-Ryan, Atlas Obscura, "How the Nazi Salute Became the World's Most Offensive Gesture: Hitler invented German roots for the greeting—but its history was already filled with fraud," March 12, 2016, https://www.atlasobscura.com/articles/how-the-nazi-salute-became-the-worlds-most-offensive-gesture

243   *Hitler's Table Talk: 1941-1944* (New York: Enigma Books, 2000), https://www.nationalists.org/pdf/hitler/hitlers-table-talk-roper.pdf page 179

244   Wikipedia, "Deutschlandlied," https://en.wikipedia.org/wiki/Deutschlandlied

245   Wikipedia, "Horst-Wessel-Lied," https://en.wikipedia.org/wiki/Horst-Wessel-Lied

246   The Youth's Companion, 65 (1892): 446–447. Reprinted in Scot M. Guenter, *The American Flag, 1777–1924: Cultural Shifts* (Cranbury, N.J.: Fairleigh Dickinson Press, 1990). Cited By History Matters: The U.S. Survey Course on the Web, George Mason University, "'One Country! One Language! One Flag!' The Invention of an American Tradition," http://historymatters.gmu.edu/d/5762

247   U.S. Code, Title 4, Chapter 1, Section 4, https://uscode.house.gov/view.xhtml?path=/prelim@title4/chapter1&edition=prelim

248   "A list of all the nations where children regularly pledge allegiance to a flag would be pretty short, and not include any wealthy Western countries apart from the United States. While some countries have oaths to nations (Singapore) or dictators (North Korea), I can only find one country other than the United States where anyone claims that children regularly pledge allegiance to a flag: Mexico. And I'm aware of two other countries that have a pledge of allegiance to a flag, although neither seems to use it as regularly as does the United States. Both are nations under heavy U.S. influence, and in both cases the pledge is relatively new. The Philippines has had a pledge of allegiance since 1996 , and South Korea since 1972, but its current pledge since 2007." From David Swanson, *Curing Exceptionalism: What's Wrong With How We Think About the United States? What Can We Do About It?* (David Swanson, 2018).

249   Annie Jacobsen, *Operation Paperclip: The Secret Intelligence Program That Brought Nazi Scientists to America* (Little, Brown, and Company, 2014).

250   Annie Jacobsen, *Operation Paperclip: The Secret Intelligence Program That Brought Nazi Scientists to America* (Little, Brown, and Company, 2014).

251   Annie Jacobsen, *Operation Paperclip: The Secret Intelligence Program That*

Brought Nazi Scientists to America (Little, Brown, and Company, 2014).

252 Dan Beaumont Space Museum, Youtube.com, "Wernher von Braun Project: 'Trip Around the Moon,' Walt Disney (1955)," https://www.youtube.com/watch?v=Zjs3nBfyIwM

253 Annie Jacobsen, *Operation Paperclip: The Secret Intelligence Program That Brought Nazi Scientists to America* (Little, Brown, and Company, 2014).

254 Annie Jacobsen, *Operation Paperclip: The Secret Intelligence Program That Brought Nazi Scientists to America* (Little, Brown, and Company, 2014).

255 Unit 731: Japan's Biological Warfare Project, https://unit731.org/aftermath

256 See the website of the U.S. Space and Rocket Center: https://rocketcenter.com/biergarten

257 Paul Huggins, AL.com, "Wernher von Braun's 1958 Huntsville home for sale; some updates, lots of history, only 2 owners," December 23, 2014, Updated March 6, 2019, https://www.al.com/news/huntsville/2014/12/wernher_von_braun_historic_hom.html

258 Bob Carlton, AL.com, "'Priceless and then some,' 'Antiques Roadshow' expert says of Huntsville's von Braun collection," June 22, 2014, Updated March 6, 2019, https://www.al.com/entertainment/2014/06/priceless_and_then_some_antqit.html

259 Shawn Ryan, *Chattanooga Times Free Press*, "Hidden in plain sight: German influence is everywhere in Huntsville, but you may not know it," December 14th, 2014, https://www.timesfreepress.com/news/life/entertainment/story/2014/dec/14/hidden-plain-sight/277749

260 C-Span, "Newspaper Warning Notice and the Lusitania," April 22, 2015, https://www.c-span.org/video/?c4535149/newspaper-warning-notice-lusitania

261 The Lusitania Resource, "Conspiracy or Foul-Up?" https://www.rmslusitania.info/controversies/conspiracy-or-foul-up

262 William M. Leary, "Wings for China: The Jouett Mission, 1932-35," *The Pacific Historical Review* 38, no. 4 (November 1969). Cited by Nicholson Baker, *Human Smoke: The Beginnings of the End of Civilization*. New York: Simon & Schuster, 2008, p. 32.

263 Associated Press January 17, printed in *New York Times,* "'WAR UTTER FUTILITY,' SAYS MRS. ROOSEVELT; President's Wife Tells Peace Advocates People Should Think of War as Suicide," January 18, 1934, https://www.nytimes.com/1934/01/18/archives/-war-utter-futility-says-mrs-roosevelt-presidents-wife-

tells-peace-.html Cited by Nicholson Baker, *Human Smoke: The Beginnings of the End of Civilization*. New York: Simon & Schuster, 2008, p. 46.

264   *New York Times*, "JAPANESE GENERAL FINDS US 'INSOLENT'; Tanaka Decries Roosevelt's 'Loud' Praise of Our Naval Establishment in Hawaii. DEMANDS ARMS EQUALITY He Says Tokyo Will Not Flinch From Disrupting London Parley if Request Is Denied," August 5, 1934, https://www.nytimes.com/1934/08/05/archives/japanese-general-finds-us-insolent-tanaka-decries-roosevelts-loud.html Cited by Nicholson Baker, *Human Smoke: The Beginnings of the End of Civilization*. New York: Simon & Schuster, 2008, p. 51.

265   George Seldes, *Harper's Magazine*, "The New Propaganda for War, "October 1934, https://harpers.org/archive/1934/10/the-new-propaganda-for-war Cited by Nicholson Baker, *Human Smoke: The Beginnings of the End of Civilization*. New York: Simon & Schuster, 2008, p. 52.

266   David Talbot, *Devil Dog: The Amazing True Story of the Man Who Saved America*, (Simon & Schuster, 2010).

267   Major General Smedley Butler, *War Is a Racket*, https://www.ratical.org/ratville/CAH/warisaracket.html

268   Nicholson Baker, *Human Smoke: The Beginnings of the End of Civilization*. New York: Simon & Schuster, 2008, p. 56.

269   Nicholson Baker, *Human Smoke: The Beginnings of the End of Civilization*. New York: Simon & Schuster, 2008, p. 63.

270   Nicholson Baker, *Human Smoke: The Beginnings of the End of Civilization*. New York: Simon & Schuster, 2008, p. 71.

271   Nicholson Baker, *Human Smoke: The Beginnings of the End of Civilization*. New York: Simon & Schuster, 2008, p. 266.

272   U.S. Navy Department, "Building the Navy's Bases in World War II," Volume I (Part I) Chapter V Procurement and Logistics for Advance Bases, https://www.history.navy.mil/research/library/online-reading-room/title-list-alphabetically/b/building-the-navys-bases/building-the-navys-bases-vol-1.html#1-5

273   Arthur H. McCollum, "Memorandum for the Director: Estimate of the Situation in the Pacific and Recommendations for Action by the United States," October 7, 1940, https://en.wikisource.org/wiki/McCollum_memorandum

274   Conrad Crane, Parameters, U.S. Army War College, "Book Reviews: Day of Deceit," Spring 2001. Cited by Wikipedia, "McCollum memo," https://en.wikipedia.org/wiki/McCollum_memo#cite_note-15

275   Robert B. Stinnett, *Day of Deceit: The Truth About FDR and Pearl Harbor* (Touchstone, 2000) p. 11.

276   Interview for the History Channel Program "Admiral Chester Nimitz, Thunder of the Pacific." Cited by Wikipedia, "McCollum memo," https://en.wikipedia.org/wiki/McCollum_memo#cite_note-13

277   Oliver Stone and Peter Kuznick, *The Untold History of the United States* (Simon & Schuster, 2012), p. 98.

278   Joseph C. Grew, *Ten Years in Japan*, (New York: Simon & Schuster, 1944) p. 568. Cited by Nicholson Baker, *Human Smoke: The Beginnings of the End of Civilization*. New York: Simon & Schuster, 2008, p. 282.

279   *New York Times*, "CHINESE AIR FORCE TO TAKE OFFENSIVE; Bombing of Japanese Cities Is Expected to Result From New View at Chungking," May 24, 1941,   https://www.nytimes.com/1941/05/24/archives/chinese-air-force-to-take-offensive-bombing-of-japanese-cities-is.html Cited by Nicholson Baker, *Human Smoke: The Beginnings of the End of Civilization*. New York: Simon & Schuster, 2008, p. 331.

280   *New York Times*, "AVOIDANCE OF WAR URGED AS U.S. AIM; Speakers at Roundtable Talks at Washington Meetings Ask Revised Foreign Policy," June 1,   1941,   https://www.nytimes.com/1941/06/01/archives/avoidance-of-war-urged-as-us-aim-speakers-at-roundtable-talks-at.html Cited by Nicholson Baker, *Human Smoke: The Beginnings of the End of Civilization*. New York: Simon & Schuster, 2008, p. 333.

281   Nicholson Baker, *Human Smoke: The Beginnings of the End of Civilization*. New York: Simon & Schuster, 2008, p. 365.

282   Mount Holyoke College, "Informal Remarks of President Roosevelt to the Volunteer Participation Committee on Why Oil Exports Continued to Japan, Washington, July 24, 1941," https://www.mtholyoke.edu/acad/intrel/WorldWar2/fdr25.htm

283   Dissentient Judgement of R.B. Pal, Tokyo Tribunal, Part 8, http://www.cwporter.com/pal8.htm

284   Otto D. Tolischus, *New York Times*, "JAPANESE INSIST U.S. AND BRITAIN ERR ON THAILAND; Warnings by Hull and Eden Held 'Difficult to Understand' in View of Tokyo's Policies," August 8, 1941, https://www.nytimes.com/1941/08/08/archives/japanese-insist-us-and-britain-err-on-thailand-warnings-by-hull-and.html Cited by Nicholson Baker, *Human Smoke: The Beginnings of the End of*

Civilization. New York: Simon & Schuster, 2008, p. 375.

285   Oliver Stone and Peter Kuznick, *The Untold History of the United States* (Simon & Schuster, 2012), p. 98.

286   Cited by Congresswoman Jeanette Rankin in Congressional Record, December 7, 1942.

287   Cited by Congresswoman Jeanette Rankin in Congressional Record, December 7, 1942.

288   Cited by Congresswoman Jeanette Rankin in Congressional Record, December 7, 1942.

289   Cited by Congresswoman Jeanette Rankin in Congressional Record, December 7, 1942.

290   Cited by Nicholson Baker, *Human Smoke: The Beginnings of the End of Civilization.* New York: Simon & Schuster, 2008, p. 387

291   Video of a key section of this speech is here: https://archive.org/details/ FranklinD.RooseveltsDeceptiveSpeechOctober271941 Full text of the speech is here: *New York Times,* "President Roosevelt's Navy Day Address on World Affairs," Oct. 28, 1941, https://www.nytimes.com/1941/10/28/archives/president-roosevelts-navy-day-address-on-world-affairs.html

292   William Boyd, *Daily Mail,* "Hitler's amazing map that turned America against the Nazis: A leading novelist's brilliant account of how British spies in the US staged a coup that helped drag Roosevelt to war," June 28, 2014, https://www. dailymail.co.uk/news/article-2673298/Hitlers-amazing-map-turned-America-against-Nazis-A-leading-novelists-brilliant-account-British-spies-US-staged-coup-helped-drag-Roosevelt-war.html

293   Ivar Bryce, *You Only Live Once* (Weidenfeld & Nicolson, 1984).

294   Edgar Ansel Mowrer, *Triumph and Turmoil: A Personal History of Our Time* (New York: Weybright and Talley, 1968), pp. 323, 325. Cited by Nicholson Baker, *Human Smoke: The Beginnings of the End of Civilization.* New York: Simon & Schuster, 2008, p. 415.

295   Joseph C. Grew, *Ten Years in Japan,* (New York: Simon & Schuster, 1944) p. 468, 470. Cited by Nicholson Baker, *Human Smoke: The Beginnings of the End of Civilization.* New York: Simon & Schuster, 2008, p. 425.

296   Wikipedia, "Hull Note," https://en.wikipedia.org/wiki/Hull_note

297   Nicholson Baker, *Human Smoke: The Beginnings of the End of Civilization.* New York: Simon & Schuster, 2008, p. 431.

298   John Toland, *Infamy: Pearl Harbor and Its Aftermath* (Doubleday, 1982), p. 166.

299   Japanese Proposal (Plan B) of 20 November 1941, https://www.ibiblio.org/hyperwar/PTO/Dip/PlanB.html

300   American Counter-Proposal to Japanese Plan B — November 26, 1941, https://www.ibiblio.org/hyperwar/PTO/Dip/PlanB.html

301   Cited by Congresswoman Jeanette Rankin in Congressional Record, December 7, 1942.

302   Lydia Saad, Gallup Polling, "Gallup Vault: A Country Unified After Pearl Harbor," December 5, 2016, https://news.gallup.com/vault/199049/gallup-vault-country-unified-pearl-harbor.aspx

303   Robert B. Stinnett, *Day of Deceit: The Truth About FDR and Pearl Harbor* (Touchstone, 2000) pp. 171-172.

304   Statement of Lieutenant Clarence E. Dickinson, U.S.N., in the *Saturday Evening Post* of October 10, 1942, cited by Congresswoman Jeanette Rankin in Congressional Record, December 7, 1942.

305   Al Hemingway, *Charlotte Sun,* "Early warning of attack on Pearl Harbor documented," Dec 7, 2016, https://www.newsherald.com/news/20161207/early-warning-of-attack-on-pearl-harbor-documented

306   Cited by Congresswoman Jeanette Rankin in Congressional Record, December 7, 1942.

307   Paul Bedard, *US News & World Report,* "Declassified Memo Hinted of 1941 Hawaii Attack: Blockbuster book also reveals FDR scuttled war announcement against axis powers," November 29, 2011, https://www.usnews.com/news/blogs/washington-whispers/2011/11/29/declassified-memo-hinted-of-1941-hawaii-attack-

308   United States Holocaust Memorial Museum, Americans and the Holocaust: "How did Public Opinion About Entering World War II Change Between 1939 and 1941?" https://exhibitions.ushmm.org/americans-and-the-holocaust/us-public-opinion-world-war-II-1939-1941

309   Robert B. Stinnett, *Day of Deceit: The Truth About FDR and Pearl Harbor* (Touchstone, 2000) p. 263.

310   Richard Bernstein, *New York Times,* "'Day of Deceit': On Dec. 7, Did We Know We Knew?" December 15, 1999, https://archive.nytimes.com/www.nytimes.com/books/99/12/12/daily/121599stinnett-book-review.html

311 Daniel Immerwahr, *How to Hide an Empire: A History of the Greater United States,* (Farrar, Straus, and Giroux, 2019).

312   Richard K. Neumann Jr., History News Network, George Washington University, "The Myth That 'Eight Battleships Were Sunk' At Pearl Harbor," https://historynewsnetwork.org/article/32489

313 Daniel Immerwahr, *How to Hide an Empire: A History of the Greater United States,* (Farrar, Straus, and Giroux, 2019).

314 Daniel Immerwahr, *How to Hide an Empire: A History of the Greater United States,* (Farrar, Straus, and Giroux, 2019).

315   "Overview of the Philippine Reservation," https://ds-carbonite.haverford.edu/spectacle-14/exhibits/show/vantagepoints_1904wfphilippine/_overview_

316 James Bradley, *The Imperial Cruise: A Secret History of Empire and War* (Back Bay Books, 2010).

317 James Bradley, *The China Mirage: The Hidden History of American Disaster in Asia* (Little, Brown, and Company, 2015).

318 Mark J. Allman and Tobias L. Winright, *After the Smoke Clears: The Just War Tradition and Post-War Justice* (Maryknoll, N.Y.: Orbis Books, 2010), p. 97. Cited by David Swanson, *War Is Never Just* (Charlottesville: David Swanson, 2016), pp. 95-96.

319   C. Brooks Peters, *New York Times,* "NAZIS WARN BRITISH OF MAJOR AIR RAIDS; NAZI WARSHIPS REPORTED SUNK AT OSLO BY THE NORWEGIANS," April 13, 1940, https://www.nytimes.com/1940/04/13/archives/nazis-warn-british-of-major-air-raids-nazi-warships-reported-sunk.html   Cited by Nicholson Baker, *Human Smoke: The Beginnings of the End of Civilization.* New York: Simon & Schuster, 2008, p. 172.

320 *New York Times,* "Allies Warn Oslo of Approaching Air-Raid," April 24, 1940. Cited by Nicholson Baker, *Human Smoke: The Beginnings of the End of Civilization.* New York: Simon & Schuster, 2008, p. 172.

321 *New York Times,* "Nazis Give British Third Air Warning," April 26, 1940. Cited by Nicholson Baker, *Human Smoke: The Beginnings of the End of Civilization.* New York: Simon & Schuster, 2008, p. 172.

322   Gilbert, *Churchill War Papers* (London: Heinemann, 1993-2000) vol. 2, pp. 40-43. Cited by Nicholson Baker, *Human Smoke: The Beginnings of the End of Civilization.* New York: Simon & Schuster, 2008, pp. 181-182.

323   Oliver Stone and Peter Kuznick, *The Untold History of the United States*

(Simon & Schuster, 2012), p. 158.

324   Erica Chenoweth and Maria J. Stephan, *Why Civil Resistance Works: The Strategic Logic of Nonviolent Conflict* (Columbia University Press, 2011).

325   Jørgen Johansen and Brian Martin, *Social Defence* (Irene Publishing, 2019), https://www.bmartin.cc/pubs/19sd/19sd.pdf

326   Jørgen Johansen and Brian Martin, *Social Defence* (Irene Publishing, 2019), https://www.bmartin.cc/pubs/19sd/19sd.pdf

327   World BEYOND War, "Foreign bases that have been closed," https://worldbeyondwar.org/basesclosed

328   Jørgen Johansen and Brian Martin, *Social Defence* (Irene Publishing, 2019), https://www.bmartin.cc/pubs/19sd/19sd.pdf

329   Jørgen Johansen and Brian Martin, *Social Defence* (Irene Publishing, 2019), https://www.bmartin.cc/pubs/19sd/19sd.pdf

330   Jørgen Johansen and Brian Martin, *Social Defence* (Irene Publishing, 2019), https://www.bmartin.cc/pubs/19sd/19sd.pdf

331   Gene Sharp, *Waging Nonviolent Struggle: 20th Century Practice and 21st Century Potential,* (Porter Sargent Publishers, Inc. 2005), p. 98.

332   Jørgen Johansen and Brian Martin, *Social Defence* (Irene Publishing, 2019), https://www.bmartin.cc/pubs/19sd/19sd.pdf

333   Justin Moyer, *Washington Post,* "How Bulgaria saved its Jews from Nazi concentration camps," May 9, 2013, https://www.washingtonpost.com/lifestyle/style/how-bulgaria-saved-its-jews-from-nazi-concentration-camps/2013/05/08/e866bdda-8cb1-11e2-9838-d62f083ba93f_story.html

334   Gene Sharp, *Waging Nonviolent Struggle: 20th Century Practice and 21st Century Potential,* (Porter Sargent Publishers, Inc. 2005), p. 147

335   Nathan Stolzfus, *Resistance of the Heart* (New York: W.W. Norton, 1996), p. 245. Cited by Wikipedia, "Rosenstrasse Protest," https://en.wikipedia.org/wiki/Rosenstrasse_protest#cite_note-:1-14

336   Nathan Stolzfus, *Resistance of the Heart* (New York: W.W. Norton, 1996), p. 245. Cited by Wikipedia, "Rosenstrasse Protest," https://en.wikipedia.org/wiki/Rosenstrasse_protest#cite_note-:1-14

337   Peter Ackerman and Jack Duvall, *A Force More Powerful: A Century of Nonviolent Conflict* (Palgrave, 2000).

338   Peter Ackerman and Jack Duvall, *A Force More Powerful: A Century of Nonviolent Conflict* (Palgrave, 2000), p. 231.

339   Gene Sharp, *Waging Nonviolent Struggle: 20ᵗʰ Century Practice and 21ˢᵗ Century Potential,* (Porter Sargent Publishers, Inc. 2005), pp. 135-140. See also a booklet on the Norwegian resistance that is available online: Gene Sharp, "Tyranny Could Not Quell Them," https://www.nonviolent-conflict.org/resource/tyranny-not-quell

340   Dictionary.com, "quisling," https://www.dictionary.com/browse/quisling

341   Cyril Joad, *Journey Through the War Mind* (London: Faber, 1940), pp. 89, 93, 99, 118. Cited by Nicholson Baker, *Human Smoke: The Beginnings of the End of Civilization.* New York: Simon & Schuster, 2008, p. 154.

342   Ted Grimsrud, *The Good War That Wasn't and Why It Matters: World War II's Moral Legacy* (Cascade Books, 2014).

343   Wikipedia, "World War II Casualties," https://en.wikipedia.org/wiki/World_War_II_casualties

344   High-end estimates of displaced persons by the combination of all U.S. wars from 2001 through 2020, in a world with a much larger population, rival those for World War II alone. See "Creating Refugees: Displacement Caused by the United States' Post-9/11 Wars," by David Vine, Cala Coffman, Katalina Khoury, Madison Lovasz, Helen Bush, Rachel Leduc, and Jennifer Walkup, September 8, 2020, https://watson.brown.edu/costsofwar/files/cow/imce/papers/2020/Displacement_Vine%20et%20al_Costs%20of%20War%202020%2009%2008.pdf

345   Robert Pollin and Heidi Garrett-Peltier, University of Massachusetts Amherst, "The U.S. Employment Effects of Military and Domestic Spending Priorities: 2011 Update," November 28, 2011, https://www.peri.umass.edu/publication/item/449-the-u-s-employment-effects-of-military-and-domestic-spending-priorities-2011-update

346   *Bombing Civilians,* edited by Yuki Tanaka and Marilyn B. Young, (The New Press, New York, 2009).

347   *Bombing Civilians,* edited by Yuki Tanaka and Marilyn B. Young, (The New Press, New York, 2009).

348   Center for Research on Globalisation, "Winston Churchill's Secret Poison Gas Memo," July 29, 2004, https://archives.globalresearch.ca/articles/CHU407A.html

349   Giles Milton, *The Guardian,* "Winston Churchill's shocking use of chemical weapons," September 1, 2013, https://www.theguardian.com/world/shortcuts/2013/sep/01/winston-churchill-shocking-use-chemical-weapons

350   Center for Research on Globalisation, "Winston Churchill's Secret Poison Gas Memo," July 29, 2004, https://archives.globalresearch.ca/articles/CHU407A. html

351   Conrad C. Crane, *Bombs, Cities, and Civilians: American Airpower Strategy in World War II* (Lawrence, Kansas: University Press of Kansas, 1993), p. 32. Cited by Nicholson Baker, *Human Smoke: The Beginnings of the End of Civilization.* New York: Simon & Schuster, 2008, p. 374.

352   Nicholson Baker, *Human Smoke: The Beginnings of the End of Civilization.* New York: Simon & Schuster, 2008, p. 391.

353   James Burgess, OilPrice.com, "Oil Tankers Sunk Along U.S. Coastline in WWII Pose Environmental Threat," May 21, 2013, https://oilprice.com/Latest-Energy-News/World-News/Oil-Tankers-Sunk-Along-U.S.-Coastline-in-WWII-Pose-Environmental-Threat.html

354   Jóhann Páll Ástvaldsson, Iceland Review, «Sunken WWII Tanker Still Leaking Oil Into Seyðisfjörður Fjord,» July 23, 2020, https://www.icelandreview. com/nature-travel/sunken-wwii-tanker-still-leaking-oil-into-seydisfjordur-fjord

355   Gar Smith, World BEYOND War, "Stones to Drones: A Short History of War on Earth," September 22, 2017, https://worldbeyondwar.org/stones-drones-short-history-war-earth

356   Adam Higginbotham, *Smithsonian Magazine*, "There Are Still Thousands of Tons of Unexploded Bombs in Germany, Left Over From World War II," January 2016, https://www.smithsonianmag.com/history/seventy-years-world-war-two-thousands-tons-unexploded-bombs-germany-180957680

357   Rick Minnich, *The Bomb Hunters* (2015), *https://www.rickfilms.de/film/the-bomb-hunters*

358   Gar Smith, World BEYOND War, "Stones to Drones: A Short History of War on Earth," September 22, 2017, https://worldbeyondwar.org/stones-drones-short-history-war-earth

359   Nicholson Baker, *Baseless: My Search for Secrets in the Ruins of the Freedom of Information Act* (Penguin Press, 2020).

360   Mary Jo McConahay, *The Tango War: The Struggle for the Hearts, Minds, and Riches of Latin America During World War II* (St. Martin's Press, 2018).

361   *Nature at War: American Environments and World War II*, edited by Thomas Robertson, Richard P. Tucker, Nicholas B Breyfogle, and Peter Mansoor (Cambridge University Press, 2020), p. 10.

362   *Nature at War: American Environments and World War II*, edited by Thomas Robertson, Richard P. Tucker, Nicholas B Breyfogle, and Peter Mansoor (Cambridge University Press, 2020), p. 15.

363   *Nature at War: American Environments and World War II*, edited by Thomas Robertson, Richard P. Tucker, Nicholas B Breyfogle, and Peter Mansoor (Cambridge University Press, 2020), p. xx.

364   *Nature at War: American Environments and World War II*, edited by Thomas Robertson, Richard P. Tucker, Nicholas B Breyfogle, and Peter Mansoor (Cambridge University Press, 2020), p. 6.

365   *Nature at War: American Environments and World War II*, edited by Thomas Robertson, Richard P. Tucker, Nicholas B Breyfogle, and Peter Mansoor (Cambridge University Press, 2020), p. 16.

366   *Nature at War: American Environments and World War II*, edited by Thomas Robertson, Richard P. Tucker, Nicholas B Breyfogle, and Peter Mansoor (Cambridge University Press, 2020), p. 12.

367   *Nature at War: American Environments and World War II*, edited by Thomas Robertson, Richard P. Tucker, Nicholas B Breyfogle, and Peter Mansoor (Cambridge University Press, 2020), p. 16.

368   *Nature at War: American Environments and World War II*, edited by Thomas Robertson, Richard P. Tucker, Nicholas B Breyfogle, and Peter Mansoor (Cambridge University Press, 2020), pp. 17-18.

369   Dave Grossman, *On Killing: The Psychological Cost of Learning to Kill in War and Society* (Back Bay Books: 1996).

370   Dave Grossman, *On Killing: The Psychological Cost of Learning to Kill in War and Society* (Back Bay Books: 1996).

371   Jennifer Schuessler, *New York Times*, "The Dark Side of Liberation," May 20, 2013, https://www.nytimes.com/2013/05/21/books/rape-by-american-soldiers-in-world-war-ii-france.html

372   Klaus Wiegrefe, *Der Spiegel*, "Were Americans As Bad as the Soviets?" March 2, 2015, https://www.spiegel.de/international/germany/book-claims-us-soldiers-raped-190-000-german-women-post-wwii-a-1021298.html

373   Sabatini ended up suffering from depression, panic attacks, and bad health. See Luana Rosato, *Il Giornale*, "Miss Italia, Alice Sabatini: 'Dopo la vittoria sono caduta in depressione,'" January 30, 2020, https://www.ilgiornale.it/news/spettacoli/miss-italia-alice-sabatini-vittoria-depressione-1818934.html

374 Geoffrey Wheatcroft, The Guardian, "The Myth of the Good War," December 9, 2014, https://www.theguardian.com/news/2014/dec/09/-sp-myth-of-the-good-war

375   Raw Story, Youtube.com, "Trump mocks renaming Confederate bases by suggesting naming them after Al Sharpton," July 19, 2020, https://www.youtube.com/watch?v=D7Qer5K3pw4&feature=emb_logo

376 Studs Terkel, The Good War: An Oral History of World War II (The New Press, 1997).

377   WikiLeaks, "HRC Paid Speeches," https://wikileaks.org/podesta-emails/emailid/927

378   United States Strategic Bombing Survey: Japan's Struggle to End the War, July 1, 1946, https://www.trumanlibrary.gov/library/research-files/united-states-strategic-bombing-survey-japans-struggle-end-war?documentid=NA&pagenumber=50

379   Oliver Stone and Peter Kuznick, The Untold History of the United States (Simon & Schuster, 2012), p. 164.

380   Bard Memorandum, June 27, 1945, http://www.dannen.com/decision/bardmemo.html

381   Christian Kriticos, The Millions, "An Invitation to Hesitate: John Hersey's 'Hiroshima' at 70," August 31, 2016, https://themillions.com/2016/08/invitation-hesitate-john-herseys-hiroshima.html

382   Christian Kriticos, The Millions, "An Invitation to Hesitate: John Hersey's 'Hiroshima' at 70," August 31, 2016, https://themillions.com/2016/08/invitation-hesitate-john-herseys-hiroshima.html

383   Leo Szilard's Petition to the President, https://www.atomicarchive.com/resources/documents/manhattan-project/szilard-petition.html

384   Report of the Committee on Political and Social Problems, https://www.atomicarchive.com/resources/documents/manhattan-project/franck-report.html

385   Oliver Stone and Peter Kuznick, The Untold History of the United States (Simon & Schuster, 2012), p. 144.

386   Oliver Stone and Peter Kuznick, The Untold History of the United States (Simon & Schuster, 2012), p. 161.

387   Oliver Stone and Peter Kuznick, The Untold History of the United States (Simon & Schuster, 2012), p. 166.

388   Oliver Stone and Peter Kuznick, The Untold History of the United States

(Simon & Schuster, 2012), p. 176.

389   Oliver Stone and Peter Kuznick, *The Untold History of the United States* (Simon & Schuster, 2012), pp. 176-177. The book says six of seven, rather than seven of eight. Kuznick tells me that he did not initially include Halsey because he received his star after the war ended.

390   On the possibility of modifying the surrender terms and ending the war earlier without nuclear bombs, see Oliver Stone and Peter Kuznick, *The Untold History of the United States* (Simon & Schuster, 2012), pp. 146-149.

391   Oliver Stone and Peter Kuznick, *The Untold History of the United States* (Simon & Schuster, 2012), p. 145.

392   Ray Raphael, *Founding Myths: Stories That Hide Our Patriotic Past* (The New Press, 2014).

393   Greg Mitchell, *The Beginning or the End: How Hollywood — and America — Learned to Stop Worrying and Love the Bomb* (The New Press, 2020).

394   Eric Schlosser, *Command and Control: Nuclear Weapons, the Damascus Accident, and the Illusion of Safety* (Penguin Books, 2014).

395   Greg Mitchell, *The Beginning or the End: How Hollywood — and America — Learned to Stop Worrying and Love the Bomb* (The New Press, 2020).

396   "The Beginning Or The End = Classic Film," https://archive.org/details/ TheBeginningOrTheEndClassicFilm

397   Oliver Stone and Peter Kuznick, *The Untold History of the United States* (Simon & Schuster, 2012), p. 144.

398   Greg Mitchell, *The Beginning or the End: How Hollywood — and America — Learned to Stop Worrying and Love the Bomb* (The New Press, 2020).

399   Gore Vidal, *The Golden Age: A Novel* (Vintage, 2001).

400   Howard Zinn, *The Bomb* (City Lights Books, 2010).

401   Ted Grimsrud, *The Good War That Wasn't and Why It Matters: World War II's Moral Legacy* (Cascade Books, 2014), pp. 12-17.

402   Ted Grimsrud, *The Good War That Wasn't and Why It Matters: World War II's Moral Legacy* (Cascade Books, 2014).

403   Ted Grimsrud, *The Good War That Wasn't and Why It Matters: World War II's Moral Legacy* (Cascade Books, 2014).

404   Ted Grimsrud, *The Good War That Wasn't and Why It Matters: World War II's Moral Legacy* (Cascade Books, 2014).

405   United States Holocaust Memorial Museum, Americans and the Holocaust:

"How did Public Opinion About Entering World War II Change Between 1939 and 1941?" https://exhibitions.ushmm.org/americans-and-the-holocaust/us-public-opinion-world-war-II-1939-1941

406   Lydia Saad, Gallup Polling, "Gallup Vault: A Country Unified After Pearl Harbor," December 5, 2016, https://news.gallup.com/vault/199049/gallup-vault-country-unified-pearl-harbor.aspx

407   United States Holocaust Memorial Museum, Americans and the Holocaust: "How did Public Opinion About Entering World War II Change Between 1939 and 1941?" https://exhibitions.ushmm.org/americans-and-the-holocaust/us-public-opinion-world-war-II-1939-1941

408   Linley Sanders, YouGov, "America and its allies won D-Day. Could they do it again?" June 3, 2019 https://today.yougov.com/topics/politics/articles-reports/2019/06/03/american-wars-dday

409   Ted Grimsrud, *The Good War That Wasn't and Why It Matters: World War II's Moral Legacy* (Cascade Books, 2014), p. 191.

410   Darien Cavanaugh, War Is Boring, "America Experimented on Conscientious Objectors During World War II," June 24, 2015, https://medium.com/war-is-boring/america-experimented-on-conscientious-objectors-during-world-war-ii-30494131d25c

411   *We Who Dared to Say No to War: American Antiwar Writing from 1812 to Now*, edited by Murray Polner and Thomas E. Woods, Jr. (Basic Books, 2008), p. 178.

412   *We Who Dared to Say No to War: American Antiwar Writing from 1812 to Now*, edited by Murray Polner and Thomas E. Woods, Jr. (Basic Books, 2008), p. 187-189.

413   Eileen Fleming, OpEdNews.com, "WWDDS? What Would Dorothy Day Say?" June 2, 2008, *https://www.opednews.com/articles/A-Dorothy-Day-Resurrection-by-Eileen-Fleming-080530-499.html*

414   *We Who Dared to Say No to War: American Antiwar Writing from 1812 to Now*, edited by Murray Polner and Thomas E. Woods, Jr. (Basic Books, 2008), pp.162-169.

415   Bill Chappell, NPR, "In Pope Francis' Congress Speech, Praise For Dorothy Day And Thomas Merton," September 24, 2015, https://www.npr.org/sections/thetwo-way/2015/09/24/443126027/in-pope-francis-congress-speech-praise-for-dorothy-day-and-thomas-merton

416　*We Who Dared to Say No to War: American Antiwar Writing from 1812 to Now,* edited by Murray Polner and Thomas E. Woods, Jr. (Basic Books, 2008), pp. 173-175.

417　*We Who Dared to Say No to War: American Antiwar Writing from 1812 to Now,* edited by Murray Polner and Thomas E. Woods, Jr. (Basic Books, 2008), pp. 173-175.

418　Ted Grimsrud, *The Good War That Wasn't and Why It Matters: World War II's Moral Legacy* (Cascade Books, 2014), p. 193.

419　Garrett Felber, *The Boston Review,* "The Struggle to Abolish the Police Is Not New," June 09, 2020, http://bostonreview.net/race/garrett-felber-struggle-abolish-police-not-new

420　Garrett Felber, *The Boston Review,* "The Struggle to Abolish the Police Is Not New," June 09, 2020, http://bostonreview.net/race/garrett-felber-struggle-abolish-police-not-new

421　David K. Wright, *A Multicultural Portrait of World War II* (New York: Marshall Cavendish, 1994) p. 35. Cited by Mickey Z., *There Is No Good War: The Myths of World War II,* 2000, pp. 4-5.

422　A documentary film by the U.S. National Park Service is available at https://www.nps.gov/poch/learn/photosmultimedia/multimedia.htm This incident is described in Mickey Z., *There Is No Good War: The Myths of World War II,* 2000, p. 5.

423　Steven A. Bank, Kirk J. Stark, Joseph J. Thorndike, *War and Taxes* (The Urban Institute Press, 2008).

424　Steven A. Bank, Kirk J. Stark, Joseph J. Thorndike, *War and Taxes* (The Urban Institute Press, 2008).

425　Steven A. Bank, Kirk J. Stark, Joseph J. Thorndike, *War and Taxes* (The Urban Institute Press, 2008).

426　Steven A. Bank, Kirk J. Stark, Joseph J. Thorndike, *War and Taxes* (The Urban Institute Press, 2008).

427　Steven A. Bank, Kirk J. Stark, Joseph J. Thorndike, *War and Taxes* (The Urban Institute Press, 2008).

428　Alpha History, "Quotations: From the Gulf of Tonkin to Tet Offensive," https://alphahistory.com/vietnamwar/quotations-tet-offensive

429　National Priorities Project, "The Militarized Budget 2020," https://www.nationalpriorities.org/analysis/2020/militarized-budget-2020

430   See: Bonnie Kristian, *Washington Examiner*, "Yet another poll shows Americans are done with endless wars," November 25, 2019, https://www. washingtonexaminer.com/opinion/yet-another-poll-shows-americans-are-done-with-endless-wars Also: James Carden, *The Nation*, "Public Is Overwhelmingly Opposed to Endless US Military Interventions," January 9, 2018, https://www. thenation.com/article/archive/new-poll-shows-public-overwhelmingly-opposed-to-endless-us-military-interventions Also: Kevin Baron, *Defense One*, "Do Americans Really Want to End 'Forever Wars?' Survey says...," September 10, 2019, https://www.defenseone.com/policy/2019/09/do-americans-really-want-end-forever-wars-survey-says/159760 Also: Concerned Veterans for America, "POLL: Veterans and military families favor more health care choice for veterans, increasingly support ending 'endless wars,'" April 22, 2020, https://cv4a.org/news-media/poll-veterans-and-military-families-favor-more-health-care-choice-for-veterans-increasingly-support-ending-endless-wars

431   Data For Progress, "The American People Agree: Cut the Pentagon's Budget," July 20, 2020, https://www.dataforprogress.org/blog/2020/7/20/cut-the-pentagons-budget By 56% to 27% U.S. voters favored moving 10% of the military budget to human needs. If told that some of the money would go to the Centers for Disease Control, the public support was 57% to 25%.

432   "Paid," obviously in the sense that Congress Members frequently receive campaign "contributions" from war profiteers, usually have war industry jobs in their districts or states, and find that supporting militarism advances their careers in the corporate media and in their political parties, and their prospects for future careers in war industries, lobbying, think tanks, etc.

433   Deseret News, "U.S. Compares Noriega Regime to Hitler's, Hints It May Act Unilaterally to Topple 'Outlaw,'" Aug 25, 1989, https://www.deseret. com/1989/8/25/18821091/u-s-compares-noriega-regime-to-hitler-s-hints-it-may-act-unilaterally-to-topple-outlaw

434   Tom Raum, Associated Press, "Bush Says Saddam Even Worse Than Hitler," November 1, 1990, https://apnews.com/c456d72625fba6c742d17f1699b18a16

435   Norman Solomon, *War Made Easy: How Presidents and Pundits Keep Spinning Us to Death* (Hoboken, N.J.: John Wiley & Sons, 2005) p. 70. Cited by David Swanson, *War Is A Lie: Second Edition* (Charlottesville: Just World Books, 2016) p. 29.

436   Julian Borger in Washington and Richard Norton-Taylor, *The Guardian*,

"Rumsfeld steps up Iraq war talk," August 21, 2002, https://www.theguardian.com/world/2002/aug/21/iraq.richardnortontaylor

437   Jonah Goldberg, *National Review,* "Hitler Vs. Hussein," October 16, 2002, https://www.nationalreview.com/2002/10/hitler-vs-hussein-jonah-goldberg

438   Patrick Buchanan, "Churchill, Hitler and Newt," February 19, 2006, https://www.realclearpolitics.com/articles/2006/02/_churchill_hitler_and_newt.html

439   *The Jerusalem Post,* "Speaker likens Ahmadinejad to Hitler at Yeshiva U," April 27, 2007, https://www.jpost.com/International/Speaker-likens-Ahmadinejad-to-Hitler-at-Yeshiva-U

440   Maayana Miskin and Elad Benari, *Arutz Sheva,* "WikiLeaks: Ahmadinejad Is Hitler: U.S. criticism of world leaders is revealed as first WikiLeaks files are made public. Ahmadinejad compared to Hitler," November 28, 2010, https://www.israelnationalnews.com/News/News.aspx/140882

441   Charles Krauthammer, *Washington Post,* "Never Again?" May 5, 2006, https://www.washingtonpost.com/wp-dyn/content/article/2006/05/04/AR2006050401458.html?sub=AR

442   AFP, "Olmert compares Ahmadinejad to Hitler," April 29, 2006, https://www.ynetnews.com/articles/0,7340,L-3245121,00.html

443   Rabbi Abraham Cooper, *Huffington Post,* "From Hitler to Ahmadinejad: CEOs You Can Rely On," March 31, 2010, https://www.huffpost.com/entry/from-hitler-to-ahmadineja_b_432739

444   Associated Press, "Ahmadinejad is '2nd Hitler,' Jewish Leader Says," June 8, 2006, https://www.foxnews.com/story/ahmadinejad-is-2nd-hitler-jewish-leader-says

445   ABC News, Australia, "'New Hitler' Gaddafi rounding up opponents," March 2, 2011, https://www.abc.net.au/news/2011-03-03/new-hitler-gaddafi-rounding-up-opponents/1966478

446   Jonathan Glancey, *The Guardian,* "From Hitler to Gaddafi: dictators and their bunkers," August 27, 2011, https://www.theguardian.com/world/2011/aug/27/best-of-the-bunkers-gaddafi-hitler-saddam

447   *National Interest,* "What Do Hitler, Saddam Hussein and Gaddafi Have In Common? They Loved Golden Guns," March 23, 2019, https://nationalinterest.org/blog/buzz/what-do-hitler-saddam-hussein-and-gaddafi-have-common-they-loved-golden-guns-48792

448   Bruce Golding, *New York Post,* "Assad is like Hitler: Kerry," September 2,

2013, https://nypost.com/2013/09/02/assad-is-like-hitler-kerry

449   BBC, "Hillary Clinton's Putin-Hitler analogy," March 6, 2014, https://www.bbc.com/news/blogs-echochambers-26476643

450   Robert Mackey, *New York Times,* "Israeli Minister Agrees Ahmadinejad Never Said Israel 'Must Be Wiped Off the Map,'" April 17, 2012 https://thelede.blogs.nytimes.com/2012/04/17/israeli-minister-agrees-ahmadinejad-never-said-israel-must-be-wiped-off-the-map

451   David Brennan, *Newsweek,* "Jimmy Carter Took Call About China From Concerned Donald Trump: 'China Has Not Wasted a Single Penny on War,'" April 15, 2019, https://www.newsweek.com/donald-trump-jimmy-carter-china-war-infrastructure-economy-trade-war-church-1396086

452   Oona A. Hathaway and Scott J. Shapiro, *The Internationalists: How a Radical Plan to Outlaw War Remade the World* (Simon & Schuster, 2017), pp. 309-335.

453   Oona A. Hathaway and Scott J. Shapiro, *The Internationalists: How a Radical Plan to Outlaw War Remade the World* (Simon & Schuster, 2017), pp. 309-335

454   Oona A. Hathaway and Scott J. Shapiro, *The Internationalists: How a Radical Plan to Outlaw War Remade the World* (Simon & Schuster, 2017), pp. 336-351

455   David Swanson, *20 Dictators Currently Supported by the U.S.* (Charlottesville: David Swanson, 2020).

456   Nicholson Baker, *Human Smoke: The Beginnings of the End of Civilization.* New York: Simon & Schuster, 2008, p. 62.

457   William Geimer, *Canada: The Case for Staying Out of Other People's Wars* (iUniverse, 2016), chapter 4.

458 Michael Walzer, "World War II: Why Was This War Different?" *Philosophy and Public Affairs,* Autumn 1971, Vol 1, No. 1, pp. 3-21, http://jstor.com/stable/2265089

459   Jeffrey Goldberg, "Trump: Americans Who Died in War Are 'Losers' and 'Suckers,'" *The Atlantic,* September 3, 2020, https://www.theatlantic.com/politics/archive/2020/09/trump-americans-who-died-at-war-are-losers-and-suckers/615997

460   Bob Woodward and Carl Bernstein, *The Final Days* (Simon & Schuster; Reissue Edition, 2005).

461   See https://worldbeyondwar.org

462   David Swanson, *War Is Never Just* (Charlottesville: David Swanson, 2016).

463   David Swanson, Talk Nation Radio, "Doug Fry: Humans Have Not Evolved for War," December 14, 2013, https://davidswanson.org/talk-nation-radio-doug-

fry-humans-have-not-evolved-for-war-3

464 Wikipedia, "List of Countries Without Armed Forces," https://en.wikipedia. org/wiki/List_of_countries_without_armed_forces

465   David Swanson, "Slavery Was Abolished," October 25, 2016, https:// davidswanson.org/slavery-was-abolished

466 Nations' military spending is displayed on a map of the world at https:// worldbeyondwar.org/militarism-mapped The data comes from the Stockholm International Peace Research Institute (SIPRI), https://sipri.org U.S. military spending as of 2018 was $718,689, which clearly excludes much of U.S. military spending, which is spread over numerous departments and agencies. For a more comprehensive total of $1.25 trillion in annual spending, see William Hartung and Mandy Smithberger, TomDispatch, "Tomgram: Hartung and Smithberger, A Dollar-by-Dollar Tour of the National Security State," May 7, 2019, https://www. tomdispatch.com/blog/176561 Nations that import U.S. weapons are displayed on a map of the world at https://worldbeyondwar.org/militarism-mapped The data comes from the Stockholm International Peace Research Institute (SIPRI), http:// armstrade.sipri.org/armstrade/page/values.php

467   "List of Countries by Military Expenditure per Capita," *Wikipedia*, https:// en.wikipedia.org/wiki/List_of_countries_by_military_expenditure_per_capita.

468 *War, Peace, and Human Nature: The Convergence of Evolutionary and Cultural Views*, edited by Douglas P. Fry (Oxford University Press, 2015).

469 *War, Peace, and Human Nature: The Convergence of Evolutionary and Cultural Views*, edited by Douglas P. Fry (Oxford University Press, 2015).

470 John Horgan, *The End of War* (McSweeney's Publishing, August 12, 2014).

471 Wikipedia, "Peace Ballot," https://en.wikipedia.org/wiki/Peace_Ballot

472 David Brennan, *Newsweek,* "Trump Says U.S. Troops Stayed in Syria 'Because I Kept the Oil,'" January 15, 2020, https://www.newsweek.com/donald-trump-us-troops-syria-oil-bashar-al-assad-kurds-wisconsin-rally-1482250

473 Andy Rowell, Oil Change International, "John Bolton: 'Big difference' if 'US oil companies invest in & produce oil in Venezuela,' February 4, 2019, http:// priceofoil.org/2019/02/04/john-bolton-big-difference-if-us-oil-companies-invest-in-produce-oil-in-venezuela

474 Tom Porter, *Business Insider,* "Mike Pompeo claims rapidly melting Arctic sea ice could actually be a good thing, as it will create 'new opportunities for trade,'" May 7, 2019, https://www.businessinsider.com/mike-pompeo-melting-sea-ice-

presents-new-trade-opportunities-2019-5?op=1

475 Kathy Gannon, Associated Press, "Bush Rejects Taliban Bin Laden Offer," October 14, 2001, https://www.washingtonpost.com/wp-srv/aponline/20011014/aponline135016_000.htm and Rory McCarthy, *The Guardian*, "New Offer on Bin Laden," October 17, 2001, https://www.theguardian.com/world/2001/oct/17/afghanistan.terrorism11

476 Transcript of the meeting in *El Pais*: https://elpais.com/diario/2007/09/26/espana/1190757601_850215.html

477 World BEYOND War, "Mapping Militarism 2020," https://worldbeyondwar.org/militarism-mapped

478 Erica Chenoweth and Maria J. Stephan, *Why Civil Resistance Works: The Strategic Logic of Nonviolent Conflict* (Columbia University Press, 2012).

479 World BEYOND War, "Even The Warriors Say The Wars Make Us Less Safe," https://worldbeyondwar.org/lesssafe

480 David Swanson, *War Is A Lie: Second Edition* (Charlottesville: Just World Books, 2016).

481 The latest such poll may be Gallup in August 2010: Jeffrey M. Jones, Gallup Polling, "In U.S., Slim Majority Says Iraq War Will Be Judged a Failure," August 20, 2010, https://news.gallup.com/poll/142367/Slim-Majority-Says-Iraq-War-Judged-Failure.aspx

482 The latest such poll may be Zogby in December 2011: Ali Gharib, Think Progress, "POLL: Iraqis Say They're Worse Off After War, View Iran Unfavorably," December 20, 2011, https://thinkprogress.org/poll-iraqis-say-theyre-worse-off-after-war-view-iran-unfavorably-e5696abdee87

483 The latest such poll may be CBS News in August 2010: At that time 41% in the United States thought Iraqis were grateful for the war on Iraq. See Brian Montopoli, CBS News, "Poll: Most Americans Say Iraq War Was a Mistake," https://www.cbsnews.com/news/poll-most-americans-say-iraq-war-was-a-mistake The same position was held by 53% in April 2003, 48% in December 2003, 38% in 2004, and 32% in 2006: https://www.cbsnews.com/htdocs/pdf/031306_poll_iraq.pdf

484 David McRaney, You Are Not So Smart, "The Backfire Effect," June 10, 2011, https://youarenotsosmart.com/2011/06/10/the-backfire-effect

485 David Swanson, "Ever More Shocked, Never Yet Awed," March 18, 2013, https://davidswanson.org/iraq

486 Minxin Pei and Sara Kasper, "Lessons from the Past: The American Record

on Nation Building," Carnegie Endowment for International Peace, 2003. Also: Ben Connable and Martin C. Libicki, "How Insurgencies End," RAND National Defense Research Institute, 2010. Both cited by David Swanson, *War Is A Lie: Second Edition* (Charlottesville: Just World Books, 2016).

487   David Swanson, "Ever More Shocked, Never Yet Awed," March 18, 2013, https://davidswanson.org/iraq

488   World BEYOND War, "The Case of Libya: Excerpt from 'War No More: The Case for Abolition' by David Swanson," https://worldbeyondwar.org/libya

489   World BEYOND War, "The Case of Syria: Excerpt from 'War No More: The Case for Abolition' by David Swanson," https://worldbeyondwar.org/syria

490   David Swanson, "The Case Against Iraqing Iran," December 15, 2017, https://davidswanson.org/iran

491   David Swanson, "Lies About Rwanda Mean More Wars If Not Corrected," March 28, 2014, https://davidswanson.org/lies-about-rwanda-mean-more-wars-if-not-corrected

492   Robert Pollin and Heidi Garrett-Peltier, University of Massachusetts Amherst, "The U.S. Employment Effects of Military and Domestic Spending Priorities: 2011 Update," November 28, 2011, https://www.peri.umass.edu/publication/item/449-the-u-s-employment-effects-of-military-and-domestic-spending-priorities-2011-update

493   David Swanson, "Study Finds People Assume War Is Only Last Resort," http://davidswanson.org/node/4637

494   Nicolas Davies, *Alternet,* "Armed Rebels and Middle-Eastern Power Plays: How the U.S. Is Helping to Kill Peace in Syria," http://www.alternet.org/world/armed-rebels-and-middle-eastern-power-plays-how-us-helping-kill-peace-syria

495   Julian Borger and Bastien Inzaurralde, "West 'ignored Russian offer in 2012 to have Syria's Assad step aside,'" https://www.theguardian.com/world/2015/sep/15/west-ignored-russian-offer-in-2012-to-have-syrias-assad-step-aside

496   Nick Schifrin, ABC News, "Was Teen Killed By CIA Drone a Militant — or Innocent Victim? Family says Tariq Khan, 16, was killed while running errand for his mother," December 30, 2011, https://abcnews.go.com/Blotter/tariq-khan-killed-cia-drone/story?id=15258659 Also: Farea Al-muslimi testimony at Drone Wars Senate Committee Hearing, https://www.youtube.com/watch?v=JtQ_mMKx3Ck

497   *The Mirror,* "Navy Seal Rob O'Neill who killed Osama bin Laden claims

US had no intention of capturing terrorist," http://www.mirror.co.uk/news/world-news/navy-seal-rob-oneill-who-4612012 Also: *ABC News*, "Osama Bin Laden Unarmed When Killed, White House Says," http://abcnews.go.com/Blotter/osama-bin-laden-unarmed-killed-white-house/story?id=13520152

498 *The Washington Post*, "Gaddafi accepts road map for peace proposed by African leaders," https://www.washingtonpost.com/world/african-leaders-arrive-in-libya-in-attempt-to-broker-cease-fire-gaddafi-hopes-for-sympathy/2011/04/10/AF0VH6ED_story.html

499 Richard Norton-Taylor, *The Guardian*, "Blair-Bush deal before Iraq war revealed in secret memo," February 3, 2006, https://www.theguardian.com/world/2006/feb/03/iraq.usa

500 Julian Borger in Washington, Brian Whitaker and Vikram Dodd, *The Guardian*, "Saddam's desperate offers to stave off war," https://www.theguardian.com/world/2003/nov/07/iraq.brianwhitaker

501 Julian Borger in Washington, Brian Whitaker and Vikram Dodd, *The Guardian*, "Saddam's desperate offers to stave off war," https://www.theguardian.com/world/2003/nov/07/iraq.brianwhitaker

502 Julian Borger in Washington, Brian Whitaker and Vikram Dodd, *The Guardian*, "Saddam's desperate offers to stave off war," https://www.theguardian.com/world/2003/nov/07/iraq.brianwhitaker

503 Memo of meeting: https://en.wikisource.org/wiki/Bush-Aznar_memo and news report: Jason Webb, *Reuters*, "Bush thought Saddam was prepared to flee: report," http://www.reuters.com/article/us-iraq-bush-spain-idUSL2683831120070926

504 Rory McCarthy, *The Guardian*, "New offer on Bin Laden," https://www.theguardian.com/world/2001/oct/17/afghanistan.terrorism11

505 Clyde Haberman, *New York Times*, "Pope Denounces the Gulf War as 'Darkness,'" http://www.nytimes.com/1991/04/01/world/pope-denounces-the-gulf-war-as-darkness.html

506 David Swanson, War Is A Lie: Second Edition (Charlottesville: Just World Books, 2016).

507 Richard Norton-Taylor, *The Guardian*, "Blair-Bush deal before Iraq war revealed in secret memo," February 3, 2006, https://www.theguardian.com/world/2006/feb/03/iraq.usa

508 Mark J. Allman & Tobias L. Winright, *After the Smoke Clears: The Just War*

Tradition and Post War Justice (Maryknoll, N.Y.: Orbis Books, 2010).

509   Mark J. Allman & Tobias L. Winright, *After the Smoke Clears: The Just War Tradition and Post War Justice* (Maryknoll, N.Y.: Orbis Books, 2010) p. 43.

510   Department of Justice White Paper, http://msnbcmedia.msn.com/i/msnbc/sections/news/020413_DOJ_White_Paper.pdf

511   2002 National Security Strategy, http://www.globalsecurity.org/military/library/policy/national/nss-020920.pdf

512   Erica Chenoweth and Maria J. Stephan, *Why Civil Resistance Works: The Strategic Logic of Nonviolent Conflict* (Columbia University Press, 2012).

513   David Swanson, World BEYOND War, "Health Professionals Tackle War," September 17, 2018, https://worldbeyondwar.org/health-professionals-tackle-war

514   Christopher Hawtree, *The Guardian*, "Harry Patch," July 25, 2009, https://www.theguardian.com/world/2009/jul/25/harry-patch-obituary

515   David Swanson, "Ever More Shocked, Never Yet Awed," March 18, 2013, https://davidswanson.org/iraq

516   UNICEF, "Patterns in conflict: Civilians are now the target," https://sites.unicef.org/graca/patterns.htm

517   Tom Vanden Brook, *USA Today*, "Suicide kills more U.S. troops than ISIL in Middle East," December 29, 2016, https://www.usatoday.com/story/news/nation/2016/12/29/suicide-kills-more-us-troops-than-isil-middle-east/95961038

518   Adil E. Shamoo, Foreign Policy in Focus, "Starvation and Cholera in Yemen: War is taking Yemen back to the dark ages, with U.S. assistance," December 5, 2017, https://fpif.org/starvation-cholera-yemen

519   Nicolas J S Davies, Consortium News, "How Many Millions Have Been Killed in America's Post-9/11 Wars? Part 3: Libya, Syria, Somalia and Yemen," April 25, 2018,   https://consortiumnews.com/2018/04/25/how-many-millions-have-been-killed-in-americas-post-9-11-wars-part-3-libya-syria-somalia-and-yemen

520   *The Ultimate Wish: Ending The Nuclear Age*, produced by Robert Richter and Kathleen Sullivan, https://theultimatewish.wordpress.com

521   Richard Engel, NBC News, "Former drone operator says he's haunted by his part in more than 1,600 deaths," June 6, 2013, http://investigations.nbcnews.com/_news/2013/06/06/18787450-former-drone-operator-says-hes-haunted-by-his-part-in-more-than-1600-deaths

522   David Swanson, "U.S. Wars and Hostile Actions: A List," https://davidswanson.org/warlist

523 Amanda Macias and Nate Rattner, CNBC, "Global arms trade is a nearly 200 billion business and the US drives nearly 80% of it," February 4, 2020, https://www.cnbc.com/2020/02/04/global-military-expenditure-and-arms-trade-report.html

524 David Vine, *The Nation*, "The United States Probably Has More Foreign Military Bases Than Any Other People, Nation, or Empire in History, And it's doing us more harm than good," September 14, 2015, https://www.thenation.com/article/archive/the-united-states-probably-has-more-foreign-military-bases-than-any-other-people-nation-or-empire-in-history

525 World BEYOND War, "Mapping Militarism 2020," https://worldbeyondwar.org/militarism-mapped

526 David Swanson, *20 Dictators Currently Supported by the U.S.* (Charlottesville: David Swanson, 2020).

527 Meredith Bennett-Smith, *Huffington Post*, "Womp! This Country Was Named The Greatest Threat To World Peace," January 23, 2014, https://www.huffpost.com/entry/greatest-threat-world-peace-country_n_4531824

528 Dorothy Manevich and Hanyu Chwe, Pew Research Center, "Globally, more people see U.S. power and influence as a major threat," August 1, 2017, https://www.pewresearch.org/fact-tank/2017/08/01/u-s-power-and-influence-increasingly-seen-as-threat-in-other-countries

529 Dorothy Manevich and Hanyu Chwe, Pew Research Center, "Globally, more people see U.S. power and influence as a major threat," August 1, 2017, https://www.pewresearch.org/fact-tank/2017/08/01/u-s-power-and-influence-increasingly-seen-as-threat-in-other-countries

530 Al Jazeera, "Retired US general: Drones cause more damage than good," July 16, 2015, https://www.aljazeera.com/news/2015/07/retired-general-drones-damage-good-150716105352708.html

531 Rob Paul Liberty Report, Youtube.com, "Why is Terrorism on the Rapid Rise?" May 12, 2015, https://www.youtube.com/watch?v=fF2beaBcdhc&feature=youtu.be

532 Jon Queally, Common Dreams, "Leaked Internal CIA Document Admits US Drone Program 'Counterproductive'," December 18, 2014, https://www.commondreams.org/news/2014/12/18/leaked-internal-cia-document-admits-us-drone-program-counterproductive

533 Dennis C. Blair, *New York Times*, "Drones Alone Are Not the Answer," August 14, 2011, https://www.nytimes.com/2011/08/15/opinion/drones-alone-are-not-the-answer.html

534 World BEYOND War, "Even The Warriors Say The Wars Make Us Less Safe," https://worldbeyondwar.org/lesssafe

535   Julian Borger, *The Guardian,* "Afghanistan war tactics are profoundly wrong, says former ambassador," May 25, 2011, https://www.theguardian.com/world/2011/may/25/afghanistan-tactics-profoundly-wrong-ambassador

536   The News Hour With Jim Lehrer, October 29, 2009, https://archive.org/details/WMPT_20091029_220000_The_NewsHour_With_Jim_Lehrer

537   Michael Hastings, *Rolling Stone,* "The Runaway General: The Profile That Brought Down McChrystal," June 22, 2010, https://www.rollingstone.com/politics/politics-news/the-runaway-general-the-profile-that-brought-down-mcchrystal-192609

538 Mujib Mashal, *New York Times,* "'Time for This War in Afghanistan to End,' Says Departing U.S. Commander," September 2, 2018, https://www.nytimes.com/2018/09/02/world/asia/afghan-commander-us-john-nicholson.html

539   Global Terrorism Index, 2014, http://visionofhumanity.org/app/uploads/2017/04/Global-Terrorism-Index-Report-2014.pdf

540 Peace Science Digest, "Military Support and an Increased Vulnerability to Terrorist Attacks," April 4, 2016, https://peacesciencedigest.org/military-support-and-an-increased-vulnerability-to-terrorist-attacks

541   Wikipedia, "2004 Spanish General Election," https://en.wikipedia.org/wiki/2004_Spanish_general_election

542 The Doomsday Clock, https://thebulletin.org/doomsday-clock

543   Robert Jervis, *The Nation,* "Eric Schlosser and the Illusion of Nuclear Weapons Safety: A new book explores the alarming threat of accidental nuclear detonations," October 15, 2013, https://www.thenation.com/article/archive/eric-schlosser-and-illusion-nuclear-weapons-safety

544   David Swanson, "Yet Another Mass Shooter Was a Military Veteran," February 27, 2020, https://davidswanson.org/yet-another-mass-shooter-was-a-military-veteran

545 Brown University, "Summary: Pentagon Fuel Use, Climate Change, and the Costs of War," June 12, 2019, https://watson.brown.edu/costsofwar/files/cow/imce/papers/2019/Summary_Pentagon Fuel Use%2C Climate Change%2C and the Costs of War (1).pdf

546 Overseas Base Realignment And Closure Coalition, "U.S. Military Bases Overseas: The Facts," https://www.overseasbases.net/fact-sheet.html

547 The Associated Press, "Some facts on military fuel consumption," 2008,

https://usatoday30.usatoday.com/news/washington/2008-04-02-2602932101_x.
htm

548   SAE Mobilus, "Logistics and Capability Implications of a Bradley Fighting Vehicle with a Fuel Cell Auxiliary Power Unit," March 8, 2004, https://saemobilus. sae.org/content/2004-01-1586

549   Bove, V., Gleditsch, K. S., & Sekeris, P. G. (2016). "Oil above Water": Economic Interdependence and Third-party Intervention. Journal of Conflict Resolution, 60(7), 1251–1277. https://doi.org/10.1177/0022002714567952 Cited by: Patrick Hiller, Peace Science Digest, "Fueling Conflict: The Link Between Oil and Foreign Military Intervention in Civil Wars," March 8, 2016, https://peacesciencedigest. org/fueling-conflict-the-link-between-oil-and-foreign-military-intervention-in-civil-wars-2

550   Emerson Urry, Enviro News, "Department of Defense, Third Largest Polluter of American Waterways," February 10, 2016, https://www.environews.tv/world-news/analysis-dept-of-defense-third-largest-polluter-of-waterways-in-america

551   Pat Elder, World BEYOND War, "Pentagon Reports 250 New Sites Are Contaminated with PFAS," March 27, 2020, https://worldbeyondwar.org/pentagon-reports-250-new-sites-are-contaminated-with-pfas

552   Rob Hotakainen, Lindsay Wise, Frank Matt, Samantha Ehlinger, McClatchy, "Irradiated: The hidden legacy of 70 years of atomic weaponry: At least 33,480 Americans dead," http://media.mcclatchydc.com/static/features/irradiated/#story

553   Christophe Schpoliansky, ABC News, "Did CIA Experiment LSD on French Town? Mystery illness hit French town in 1951, killing seven and making others crazy," March 22, 2010, https://abcnews.go.com/Health/International/book-claims-cia-lsd-experiment-made-french-town/story?id=10171002

554   Homeland Security Digital Library, "S. Prt. 103-97: Is Military Research Hazardous to Veterans' Health? Lessons Spanning Half a Century, A Staff Report Prepared for the Committee on Veterans' Affairs, United States Senate, December 1994," https://www.hsdl.org/?abstract&did=438835

555   Mickey Z., No Innocent Bystanders: Riding Shotgun In The Land Of Denial (CWG Press 2008).

556   Rob Nixon, "Of Land Mines and Cluster Bombs," Cultural Critique No. 67, Edward Said and After: Toward a New Humanism (Autumn, 2007), pp. 160-174, Published by: University of Minnesota Press, https://www.jstor.org/stable/4539824

557   Jennifer Leaning, "Environment and health: 5. Impact of war," CMAJ: Canadian Medical Association Journal, vol. 163, no. 9, 2000, pp. 1157-61.

558 Scott Horton, *Harper's Magazine*, "Madison on the Dangers of War," July 7, 2007, https://harpers.org/2007/07/madison-on-the-dangers-of-war

559 Robert Pollin and Heidi Garrett-Peltier, University of Massachusetts Amherst, "The U.S. Employment Effects of Military and Domestic Spending Priorities: 2011 Update," November 28, 2011, https://www.peri.umass.edu/publication/item/449-the-u-s-employment-effects-of-military-and-domestic-spending-priorities-2011-update

560 National Priorities Project, "The Militarized Budget 2020," https://www.nationalpriorities.org/analysis/2020/militarized-budget-2020

561 William Hartung and Mandy Smithberger, *TomDispatch*, "Tomgram: Hartung and Smithberger, A Dollar-by-Dollar Tour of the National Security State," May 7, 2019, https://www.tomdispatch.com/blog/176561

562 Global Peace Index, http://visionofhumanity.org/indexes/global-peace-index

563 SIPRI Military Expenditure Database, https://www.sipri.org/databases/milex

564 Chris Hellman, TomDispatch, "Tomgram: Chris Hellman, $1.2 Trillion for National Security," March 1, 2011, http://www.tomdispatch.com/blog/175361

565 Yonatan Neril, *Huffington Post*, "$13.6 Trillion Is The Cost Of Violence Last Year. What Is The Price Of Peace?," October 12, 2016, https://www.huffingtonpost.com/yonatan-neril/what-is-the-price-of-peace_b_12428828.html

566 World BEYOND War, "Statistic on Billboard Explained," https://worldbeyondwar.org/explained

567 UN News, "Improving water and sanitation access would cost $11.3 billion more a year - UN," April 27, 2004, https://news.un.org/en/story/2004/04/101652-improving-water-and-sanitation-access-would-cost-113-billion-more-year-un

568 TED, Youtube.com, "Poverty isn't a lack of character; it's a lack of cash | Rutger Bregman," June 13, 2017, https://www.youtube.com/watch?v=ydKcaIE6O1k

569 ICAN, "Nuclear Spending vs Healthcare," https://www.icanw.org/healthcare_costs

570 Atle Staalesen, *The Barents Observer*, "Preparing for the unknown, Norway bolsters its Armed Forces," April 17, 2020, https://thebarentsobserver.com/en/security/2020/04/preparing-unknown-norway-bolsters-national-defense

571 *The Times of Israel*, "US alerted Israel, NATO to disease outbreak in China in November — TV report: White House was reportedly not interested in the intel, but it was passed onto NATO, IDF; when it reached Israel's Health Ministry, 'nothing was done'," April 16, 2020, https://www.timesofisrael.com/us-alerted-israel-nato-to-disease-outbreak-in-china-in-november-report

CPSIA information can be obtained
at www.ICGtesting.com
Printed in the USA
LVHW031512070622
720660LV00008B/466